A Charge for Change

A Charge for Change

A Selection of Essays from the Annual
20th Biennial Conference of the
Rhetoric Society of America

Edited by
Elizabethada A. Wright and David Beard

Parlor Press
Anderson, South Carolina
www.parlorpress.com

Parlor Press LLC, Anderson, South Carolina, USA

© 2023 by The Rhetoric Society of America. Individual chapters are copyrighted by the respective authors and published under Creative Commons license, "Attribution-NonCommercial-NoDerivatives 4.0 International (CC BY-NC-ND 4.0)," subject to the standard conditions.

All rights reserved. Printed in the United States of America
S A N: 2 5 4 - 8 8 7 9

Library of Congress Cataloging-in-Publication Data on File

Cover design by Savannah Schmelzer
Interior design by David Blakesley.
Photo by Martin Sanchez on Unsplash. Used by permission.
RSA 2014 logo designed by Lori Klopp.
Printed on acid-free paper.

1 2 3 4 5

Parlor Press, LLC is an independent publisher of scholarly and trade titles in print and multimedia formats. This book is available in print and digital formats from Parlor Press on the World Wide Web at https://parlorpress.com or through online and brick-and-mortar bookstores. For submission information or to find out about Parlor Press publications, write to Parlor Press, 3015 Brackenberry Drive, Anderson, SC 29621, or email editor@parlorpress.com.

Contents

Acknowledgments   *ix*

Introduction: A Charge for Change   *xi*
Elizabethada A. Wright

Part I: Race and Colonialism   *1*

1 Entangled Remembrance: Indigenous Representation and Settler Colonialism at an Unlikely Memory Site   *3*
Amy J. Lueck

2 Linguistic Injustice and Citizenship in Ghana: Epistemological Decolonization and Stranger-Relationality as Rhetorical Arts of Resistance   *13*
Mohammed Sakip Iddrisu

3 Digital Archival Futures: Discoverability and Collaboration as Activism in a Post-Pandemic World   *25*
keondra bills freemyn

4 Description and Abstraction After Racial Violence: The Case of Jesse Washington   *30*
Wallace S. Golding

5 Slavery Was Never "Kindly Intentioned": Exposing the Entirely Hidden Role of a White Editor Who Blotted Malcolm X's Identity   *40*
Keith D. Miller

6 Constituting Truth and Reconciliation Ad Bellum Purificandum   *48*
M. Elizabeth Weiser

Part II: The Pandemic, and Other Kairotic Rhetorical Concerns   59

7 Mapping the Rhetorical and Statistical Landscape of COVID-19 and Neoliberalism's Biopolitics   61
Kathryn Lambrecht

8 "Do your own research!": Constructions of Ethos within the "Disinformation Dozen"   71
Aaron Hess

9 Temporalities of Change: Up-Tempo Discourse and Public Culture   81
Jeffrey St. Onge

10 *Conocimiento* in the Landscapes of Housing Insecurity   91
Jason Michálek

11 The Sheepdog Ethos: Armed Citizenship as Caring Labor   98
Daniel A. Cryer

12 Redefining the Climate Crisis as a "Security" Threat: The Biden Administration's Progress and Limitations in Addressing This Charge to Change   108
Heidi E. Hamilton

13 The 'War on Christmas' and Preventive War   119
Patricia Roberts-Miller

Part III: Eternal Issues of Rhetoric in Our Kairotic Moment   133

14 Sleuthing Toward Bethlehem: Hitler's Theory of Reading and Learning and the Enduring Appeals of Confirmation Bias   135
Ryan Skinnell

15 From Plato to Paulo Freire: Re-Exploring Ann Berthoff's Pedagogical Theory and Its Rhetorical/Philosophical Roots in Light of Contemporary Challenges   142
Andrew L. Sigerson

16 Ibn Sina on Style: A Dialogue between Aristotelian
  Rhetoric and Arabic Poetics   154
    Maha Baddar

17 Rhetorical Possibilities of Spectral Listening   167
    Leah Senatro

18 Festschrift in Honor of RSA Founder Janice Lauer
  Rice—What Janice Lauer Rice Taught Us about
  Rhetoric (and Life): A Tribute   175
  Richard Leo Enos, Janet M. Atwill, Jennifer L. Bay,
  Thomas J. Rickert, David Blakesley, and Richard E. Young

Contributors   183

Index   187

About the Editors   195

Acknowledgments

This book is a product of the Rhetoric Society of America (RSA)'s Twentieth Biennial Conference, held in Baltimore in May 2022 with the theme "A Charge for Change." For many conference participants, it was their first return to large group meetings, and (for the most part) we wore our masks proudly. For the conference to occur in such circumstances required the courage and determination of many people, including all the RSA members and its board. Most particularly, that the conference occurred is in large part due to the efforts of the RSA presidents from 2020 to 2022 (Kirt Wilson, Michelle Baliff, and Vanessa Beasley) and Executive Directors (Gerald Hauser and Leslie Dinauer) who kept the organization strong throughout the difficult period of the pandemic.

In putting together this collection, we reviewed an enormous number of very strong papers, having to make the difficult decision of selecting a small group that represented the variety of charges for change to which members of our field are called. We thank everyone who submitted to this collection. Reading all these papers, we have been impressed with the vitality of the field as well as its position in the world to actually make change. We hope this collection provides inspiration, as it recognized that it excludes more than it is able to include.

Reviewers provide unpaid labor that is often overlooked, but absolutely essential for the publication of work such as this. For this work, we would like to thank: Desire Baloubi, Charles Bazerman, Rebecca Dingo, William Edward Duffy, David Gold, Daniel Grano, Stephen Hartnett, Glenn Hutchinson, Robert Ivie, Mary Kahl, Steven Katz, John Logie, Jordan Loveridge, Arabella Lyon, Terese Monberg, Michael Pfau, Megan Renee Poole, Samantha Quade, Jeffrey R. Rice, Edward Schiappa, Gregory Schneider-Bateman, Craig Stroupe, Dave Tell, and Jamie White-Farnham among others. We also owe a debt to our Writing Studies intern, Savannah Schmelzer, for her insight and commentary.

This collection, then, is, first and foremost, a record of the work of the Rhetoric Society of America at a moment in time. All essays in *The Charge for Change* were subject to multiple levels of editorial review. After the RSA conference, a call for full manuscripts went out to all presenters. All manuscripts (except the articles celebrating Prof. Janice Lauer Rice) were sent for double-blind peer review (in which the name of the author was withheld from the reviewer as the reviewer responded to the essay, and the name of the reviewer was withheld from the author when the feedback was delivered).

Charging ourselves with change, David Beard and I attempted to work within the guidelines provided by *Anti-Racist Scholarly Reviewing Practices: A Heuristic for Editors, Reviewers, and Authors,* but we recognize that our work in that area is incomplete. Notably, we encouraged all scholars seeing their work included within this volume to consider those guidelines as they develop their work for publication in other venues. As editors of this volume, we look forward to the day that both editors and authors have internalized the recommendations within that document (for example, for inclusive citation)—a change toward which we hope this volume contributes.

For their encouragement putting this collection together, we thank our personal support teams (including Zomi Bloom, Scott Segee, George Segee-Wright, and James Segee-Wright) as well as those who taught us about the power of rhetoric (including S. Michael Halloran and Arthur Walzer). Liz especially wants to thank Martha Cheng and Suzanne Bordelon for their years of collaboration that has made so much work possible. We also convey our sincere appreciation to Parlor Press and David Blakesley, whose partnership makes this collection possible.

Finally, we want to express gratitude for those of you who continue to have faith in rhetoric, as we turn to constantly modified theories to make change, to charge us in varieties of ways. And rhetoric does make change.

Introduction: A Charge for Change

Elizabethada A. Wright

Fall 2022 was the first semester, for many of us, in which we once again taught students in face-to-face settings, getting back to "normal" as the pandemic morphed into an endemic. However, for many of us, the semester wasn't all that normal. The classroom felt different. Students were reluctant to talk, they seemed resistant to any critique, and they often came unprepared to class—if they came at all. The numbers of students who were failing because they just didn't come to class increased drastically, no matter how many times we reached out to them asking how we could help. Certainly, we had experienced these issues previously, but the numbers of students who seemed reluctant to be in the classroom appeared to have escalated dramatically.

One day, my class had a breakthrough. The students in class switched their discussion from analyzing a text to talking about why they appeared so uncommitted to class. The students told me that they were frustrated, especially with rhetoric. They'd heard it all.

They reminded me that they had grown up in a post-9/11 world, where terrorism and taking shoes off at the airport were normal. They had been through countless trainings in class about how to deal with a shooter, and every time there was another mass shooting, spokespeople from the left blamed guns and supporters of the Second Amendment defended their Constitutional rights. The students told about how the recession of 2008 had changed their families' lives economically when they were children, and when the country began to emerge from that crisis, we lived in a vast political divide in which we had "alternative truths," conspiracy theories, and challenges to our system of government. COVID-19 hit and George Floyd was murdered, and nothing seemed to make sense as the students tried to attend their classes on Zoom screens and do lab experiments in their living rooms or kitchens.

We have lived in a rhetorical situation like none other, and it was in this world that the Rhetoric Society of America met in Baltimore in May 2022 to discuss "The Charge for Change." For many of us, the RSA Conference was the first time we'd joined a large gathering in years, and we wore masks and vouched for our COVID-19 shots. As might be expected, many conference papers discussed the Kairos of 2022: the pandemic, the Black Lives Matter movement, climate change, the political divide, guns. However, unlike my students, we approached this moment with faith in the power of rhetoric to make change.

After listening to my students and grasping how they saw the world, I asked how this kairotic moment differs from that facing US students in the 1960s. Most men knew that upon leaving high school or college, they would travel to Vietnam. Children of the 1960s had practiced mostly futile "duck and cover" exercises in case missiles ventured over the United States or conflict between world powers might cause a nuclear war. People of color marched and protested to gain basic civil rights in a country that professed equality in theory but rarely illustrated it in practice. Young people, in not only the 1960s and not only in the United States but everywhere, have faced ugliness in the world. The moments differ, but the crises and pain of the moments' potential consequences are similar.

I understand the students' frustration of the current debates, and the huge divide that hinders dialogue. I understand the bitterness of hearing the same conversations repeatedly, with no seeming change. I understand the anger at people not understanding why black lives matter. I also understand that we have moved the world in the past because rhetoric has the power to make change. Martin Luther King and the many participants in the civil rights movement did not make change happen quickly or completely. Protestors of the Vietnam War did not end the war immediately, or completely satisfactorily. Negotiators within the Cold War did not make nuclear weapons disappear. It takes time, rhetorical knowledge and skill, and faith in what rhetoric can achieve. Rhetoric can bring change.

This collection, then, brings together eighteen examples of the conversations from this conference, and how these conversations illustrate the potential of rhetoric to affect change. The first group of articles focuses on the rhetoric of race and colonialism, a focus that is certainly not new but one that has been gaining rhetorical space in the second decade of this century. Amy Lueck's "Entangled Remembrance" begins at, of all places, the San Jose tourist attraction: the Winchester Mystery House. Considering the many contradictory narratives about this place, Lueck provides a model for better understanding complex remembrance so that rhetoricians, and the public, can better perceive and change systems of coloniality. Moving from California to Ghana, in "Linguistic Injustice and Citizenship in Ghana," Mohammed Sakip Iddrisu shows how systems of coloniality can be disrupted. Iddrisu illustrates how linguistic injustices can be interrupted by stranger-initiated efforts. Using Western theories of linguistic hegemony, Iddrisu demonstrates the existence of—and means to stop—colonial logics in Ghana. In "Digital Archival Futures," keondra bills freemyn more directly illustrates how hegemonic forces can be interrupted. freemyn discusses the methodology of Black Women Writers Project, an archival project with which freemyn was involved during the pandemic to ensure easy access of its information to researchers. freemyn discusses an archival methodology that combines traditional archival methods with new ones created from critical perspectives.

Wallace S. Golding also discusses methodology in "Description and Abstraction After Racial Violence." Using the example of discussions of Jesse Washington's 1916 lynching in Waco, Texas, Golding argues that the use of critical description as method can disrupt the racial abstraction that is necessary for systems of white supremacy. Keith Miller's "Slavery was Never 'Kindly Intentioned'" also attempts to undermine systems of white supremacy. Discussing Murray Fisher's role in the editing of *The Autobiography of Malcolm X*, Miller demonstrates how Fisher actively changed Malcolm X's text in significant ways, changes that Malcolm X was unable to correct because of his traveling schedule and assassination. With this argument, Miller also calls for researchers to continue this project to rectify incorrect understandings of Malcolm X caused by this editorial interference. M. Elizabeth Weiser's "Constituting Truth and Reconciliation Ad Bellum *Purificandum*" suggests that twenty-first century public history museums are already creating change by presenting difficult histories via epideictic, rather than forensic, visual displays. Such an approach counters the "knowledge is division" arguments heralded by the critics of Critical Race Theory. Weiser illustrates how this approach instead creates a "safe place for unsafe ideas."

The second group of articles in this collection considers how rhetoric has been impacted by issues very much of the moment: the pandemic, housing insecurity, climate change and national security, the "War on Christians," and the debate over the importance of gun rights. Kathryn Lambrecht's "Mapping the Rhetorical and Statistical Landscape of COVID-19 and Neoliberalism's Biopolitics" begins this section with an analysis of the language used within the public statements of COVID-19 risk assessment presented by three major US cities. Noting the differences among the various choices made, Lambrecht concludes that all three cities prioritized economics over individual safety within these statements, suggesting a change for future communications. Aaron Hess also analyzes communication of the pandemic in "'Do Your Own Research!'" except Hess examines how the plethora of information streaming to audiences during the pandemic engaged its audiences. Considering the various ways the creators of disinformation create ethos, Hess provides a framework for working against such erroneous information. Jeffrey St. Onge, in "Temporalities of Change," is similarly concerned with the vast amounts of information provided during the almost-world-wide quarantine, though St. Onge examines how the speed at which information spread impacts meaning and allows for increases of disinformation. St. Onge observes how information in the public sphere, public wisdom, and connotations are impacted when information increases its "tempo."

Jason Michálek examines the housing crisis that was part of the pandemic, but not unique to it. In "*Conocimiento* in the Landscapes of Housing Insecurity," Michálek offers a hopeful perspective, illustrating how digital community action can create means of care that would not be possible otherwise. Daniel Cryer explores a very different urgent issue: that of guns. In "The Sheepdog Ethos," Cryer considers the argument that individuals with guns are necessary for society in order to protect it: they are the sheepdogs who protect the sheep from the wolves. Using a lens regarding the ethics of care, Cryer challenges this conclusion by showing how the "sheepdog's" identity limits its abilities to care. Heidi E. Hamilton takes on the kairotic issues of both climate change and world security in "Redefining the Climate Crisis as a 'Security' Threat." Taking a feminist perspective, Hamilton critiques the Biden Administration's definition of the climate crisis as a security threat. Hamilton argues that while this definition might appear hopeful, it actually perpetuates a militarized mindset as it insufficiently considers how climate change impacts individuals. The gaping political divide is the subject of Patricia Roberts-Miller's "The 'War on Christmas' and Preventive War." Roberts-Miller analyzes political conservatives' arguments that their values, and Christmas, are under attack by liberals. Considering the conservatives' rhetoric of "being at war," Roberts-Miller contends that this argument is actually used to justify policies that seek to exterminate political liberals' values.

While the final grouping of articles is concerned with eternal issues of rhetoric, these articles come very much out of our twenty-first century moments. Focusing on confirmation bias in "Sleuthing Towards Bethlehem," Ryan Skinnell extends Roberts-Miller's analysis of the political divide as well as Hess's and St. Onge's discussions of communication during the pandemic, except Skinnell compares Adolph Hitler's theories of reading, that make false claims look legitimate, to current debates in which people maintain their beliefs despite recognitions of their own beliefs' illogic. Andrew L. Sigerson's "From Plato to Freire: Re-Exploring Ann Berthoff's Pedagogical Theory and its Rhetorical/Philosophical Roots in Light of Contemporary Challenges" does exactly what its sub-title promises. In so doing, it suggests rhetoricians re-examine and embrace Berthoff's theories for what they can contribute at this historical moment to help students, in first and third worlds, better read and write the world. In "Ibn Sina on Style," Maha Baddar discusses the rhetorical theory of an important rhetorician of the Arabic tradition: Ibn Sina. Exploring his theories of style and poetics, Baddar illustrates Sina's knowledge of and independence from Western rhetorical traditions.

In "Rhetorical Possibilities of Spectral Listening," Leah Senatro considers how digital texts can "re-member" the dead. Building on Galen's second-century CE medical text, Senatro conveys how multi-modal texts are able to recompose the decomposing body, to bring it to engagement with the living. Finally, in a tribute to Janice Lauer Rice, Richard Leo Enos, as well as Janet M. Atwill, Jennifer L. Bay, Thomas J. Rickert, David Blakesley, and Richard E. Young, do exactly what Senatro describes: they re-member the great rhetorician Lauer Rice, commenting on the many ways Lauer Rice shaped this discipline to be what it is today. They overview the change she felt charged to make—that hopefully rhetoricians can long continue.

As we publish this collection, after the US government has declared that the COVID-19 Health Emergency is over, many of the other concerns discussed within this volume cannot have such similar declarations: racism and colonialism still plague the world, climate change threatens everything, war is never-ending, and misinformation and confirmation bias poison public debate as does the dramatic political divide.

Yet we continue, charged to make change.

Part I: Race and Colonialism

1 Entangled Remembrance: Indigenous Representation and Settler Colonialism at an Unlikely Memory Site

Amy J. Lueck

Abstract

This chapter uses an unlikely site of public memory—the Winchester Mystery House, which is a famous "haunted house" historical house tour in San Jose, California—as a site to examine the settler memory and the possibilities for what I call *entangled remembrance*. From this perspective, the story of Sarah Winchester—which is most often told as a ghost story about the spiritualism, grief, and perhaps even insanity of a woman building a strange house—is revealed as, above all else, a story about Native dispossession and histories of gun violence, and also of land, gender, domesticity, and capitalism. This case provides a model for conceptualizing entangled remembrance practices at other sites of history, memory, and identity.

Entanglement One: Gender, Race, and Land

On the front page of the *San Francisco Chronicle* in 1895, a full-page spread farcically described "A New Man for the New Woman." The article vividly rendered the threat of emasculation as a result of woman's shifting gender roles in the nineteenth century, signified by the idea of the "new woman," which the article framed as presaging full gender role reversal by the year 2000.

Later in that same issue appeared an illustrated story, "Moquis on Alcatraz," reporting on the imprisonment of nineteen Hopi men of the southwest United States and Mexico, who were arrested for refusing to send their children to government schools. The image accompanying that article was a sketch of five Native men standing beside two large logs that they are said to have been sawing as part of their prison labor, "for what use no one deigns to explain."

On the same page was another illustrated article titled "The Strange Story of a San Jose House." Featuring a large sketch of the house and its elaborate grounds, this article was among the first to publicly discuss Sarah Winchester, heiress to the Winchester Repeating Arms Company fortune, in relation to the large Victorian mansion she was building in San Jose, and it sketched the contours of what would become a powerful, durable legend with precise efficiency in its subtitles alone, which read: "Mrs. Winchester Builds to Live. A Mansion Big Enough for an Army. The Widow of the Rifle Inventor Believes She Will Die When the Work Stops."

The article described a large and ever-expanding house, which Sarah Winchester designed, built, and remodeled numerous times over several decades around the turn of the century, along with other properties purchased and developed during the same time. The house was notable for its size and also the duration of its construction, which would eventually encompass some thirty-eight years of building and remodeling. This unusual building project gained notice of the neighbors first, whose suspicions were fueled by the fact that Winchester was a private woman. Nationally circulating what had once been local gossip and speculation about this house and the motives of its (single, if widowed, female) owner, the article was reprinted in several local papers and as far afield as New York, where it appeared with small changes in *The Sun*. It was the first of very, very many.

Projecting into the future with competing visions of traditional gender and family disrupted, spanning geographical divides in the movement of bodies and lives out of place, and unfolding narratives of action without purpose and space done wrong, the juxtaposition of these articles within the pages of one daily newspaper brings into focus the inextricability of gender, race, and place in the US, and highlights the imbrication of structures of power, discipline, and domination that animate and undergird these intersectional experiences. It reveals them as deeply entangled with one another.

But none of these entanglements are visible in the text of an individual article. Instead, the discrete focus of each story, along with the methodological difficulty of locating and linking such sources within databases that tag them as unrelated and the onerous task of deep reading required to unearth these contexts and connections in the present, remind us of the frequent tendency to discuss such stories as separate. Disentangled.

This was my own initial impulse when I began researching the Winchester Mystery House four years ago. Having begun this research as a feminist recovery of a woman trapped in a centuries-old legend of ghosts and madness, it took me nearly the entirety of that four years to see how my own analysis of this site could not just be about this woman, but instead was imbricated with the other stories of gender, sexuality, race, land, and, above all, settler colonialism. White supremacy and settler colonial culture require that we strive to unsee this web, this interconnected network of threads leading into the future—that we disentangle.

In this chapter, I follow indigenous and decolonial feminist scholars in arguing that our work for future justice and reconciliation lies instead in efforts to re-tangle these threads of gender, coloniality, and place (Arvin, Tuck, and Morrill; Montoya and Zuni-Cruz). To amplify relationality and responsibility in feminist rhetorical historiography and public memory work (Powell et al; Riley-Mukavetz). This is what I'm calling, within feminist historiography and public memory studies, entangled remembrance. Entangled remembrance looks for the threads of experience and narrative that intersect with the one you are following, purposefully reaching for those threads into the pre-colonial past, the settler colonial present, and the decolonial future. It entangles explicitly with ongoing systems of settler colonialism shaping memory and experience today, implicating ourselves and our own complex identities. Entangling.

In what follows, I use this unlikely site of public memory—the Winchester Mystery House, which is a classic "haunted house" historical house tour in San Jose, California—as a site to examine the work of disentanglement and possibilities for entangled remembrance. Though seemingly unrelated, each of the articles in the opening of this chapter is, through the pursuit of entanglement, revealed as expressing similar anxieties about the maintenance of heteropatriarchal settler ideals, which Kevin Bruyneel has demonstrated are grounded in defenses of the "heteronormative white settler domestic realm" (10). That is, the image of a male-led family unit with sole ownership over a piece of land, which is understood as commodity, has animated and justified ongoing settler colonial activities and remembrance practices into the present. From this perspective, the story of Sarah Winchester—which is most often told as a ghost story about the spiritualism, grief, and perhaps even insanity of a woman building a strange house—is revealed as, above all else, a settler story. A story about Native dispossession and histories of gun violence, and also of land, gender, domesticity, and capitalism. It is a story about ongoing settler colonial domination in San Francisco's Bay Area and beyond.

Approaching this argument through story, I emphasize the provisional nature of remembrance and representation in the ongoing story-so-far of this place (Massey; see also Riley-Mukavetz; King). In the brief vignettes that follow, we begin to understand the ways such sites draw on the discourse of history and intertwined ideologies of gender and coloniality for their effect, and we begin to explore the stakes of such practices for intersectional, counterhegemonic women's public remembrance practices. As I will show, the entanglements of race, gender, and land in this settler colonial story become even more pronounced as time passes, gradually merging in the white settler imaginary as the national guilt of "Indian Removal" is neatly projected onto the heiress of the Winchester rifle fortune. But the context of heteropatriarchal settler domesticity that animated this connection remains disavowed. Through tracing this process across several historical moments, I will demonstrate how insidious this paradigm has been, and reveal the necessity of entangled remembrance practices for everyday sites of history, memory, and identity.

Entanglement Two: A Haunted House Tour

Some forty years after the initial articles about her house appeared, Sarah Winchester died, and her house was purchased by a family involved in the amusement industry who opened it to the public the next year. In an article that appeared just five years after the house's opening as a tourist attraction, in the April 1928 issue of the *American Weekly* Sunday supplement, the stories of Winchester and her strange house had been expanded to run the length of five magazine pages.

By this time, the story had been elaborated to suggest that the victims of the Winchester "repeaters" haunted Sarah Winchester and her house, and that Winchester continued to build to appease their spirits. As the article asserted, "The worst haunters would be Indians" ("Mrs. Winchester's Extraordinary 'Spook Palace'").

In this version of the story, Winchester comes into focus as a distinctly (if still implicitly) gendered, classed, and raced figure: a would-be society woman desirous to keep away "the spooks of Indians, low grade white men, . . . and other undesirables," while striving not to "offend the respectable citizens of the spiritual world with whom she hoped to associate when her own time came." This contrast between "the nicer sort of spirits with whom she wished to take her rightful position as a wealthy society woman" and "the low and degraded spirits" is repeated and increasingly racialized throughout, culminating in a lengthy account of "ghosts of no-good Indians with whom she was especially afflicted" ("Mrs. Winchester's").

Figure 1. "Mrs. Winchester's Extraordinary 'Spook Palace,'" in *American Weekly*, April 1928.

The image in the article emphasized the racial contours of this narrative (see Figure 1). Through a pane of glass, it shows a Euro American man hammering a nail into the wall, while outside the glass five ghosts lurk, seemingly trying to get inside. The caption with this image explains that "As long as the sound of hammers was heard in her home the spiritualist medium assured [Sarah Winchester] that all would be well. And thus it was that all day long and all night long, even Sundays and holidays, carpenters were incessantly busy building additions, until year after year the house straggled over acres of ground in all directions" ("Mrs. Winchester's").

The idea of this man's continual building invokes the ongoing labor of upholding systems of white privilege against the interests of people of color ever knocking at the national door—a source of potential horror for white audiences, but also one pleasurably displaced onto the figure of Winchester, and imaginatively contained through this narrative.

More specifically, as historian Mary Jo Ignoffo has argued, the elaborate legends of Native ghosts and hauntings provided an outlet for Euro-American guilt about the violence of US settlement of the West, particularly the brutal forced migration of Native peoples that was increasingly uncomfortable for white Americans to remember from the vantage point of the more "civilized" days of the Assimilationist period. This national guilt, linked only obliquely to systems of capitalism, class inequality, and ongoing structures of settler colonial domination, was placed firmly on the shoulders of Winchester in the narratives of this house. She was the one who should feel guilty for the deaths of people killed by the guns that made her rich, these stories announced. Doing so absolved from responsibility the white audiences who would rather not explore their own role in ongoing racial subjugation and colonial domination. Coloniality was able to continue unabated.

Moving ahead in time from its original printing in 1928, this article was reprinted in full in the official souvenir booklet produced by the Winchester Mystery House in the 1970s. This was sometime after the house received recognition as a state historical site and was included as part of the city of San Jose's bicentennial celebrations in 1976. Indeed, the site's increasingly self-conscious status as a historical landmark reflecting civic culture, identity, and history for the local dominant class in this moment is part of what must have spurred them to include the reproduction of a lengthy article from the early twentieth century—to convey a sense of longevity and, thereby, authenticity to the popular stories of haunting that had been more strictly amusing. Meanwhile, Native-settler relations had emerged as a popular historical theme to explore, featured at other amusement sites like the nearby Frontierland. Such parks firmly established colonialism as an event, a thing of the past, and a commodity to consume for non-Native audiences. It was also around this time that students writing into the local "Pioneers" essay contest started to write Winchester back into the history of the area, to recover her from her legends and assert her place as a founder of San Jose. And all of this relied on the figure of the ghosted Native to function.

The image on the inside cover of that brochure makes that fact palpable in its representation of Native figures. Invoking what had by then become powerfully familiar imagery in the US, animating white settler claims to "discovery," or what historian Jean O'Brien calls moves of "firsting and lasting," the Native figures are little more than caricatures, each donning feathered headdresses and completely non-specific in tribal affiliation, land-based experience, family, or identity. Here, they take on a metaphoric status in the settler imaginary that is brought to its natural conclusion as an empty outline tracing shadow and light, but vacant of flesh and meaning, and shot through with bullet holes to boot: Native ghosts.

Historian Renee Bergland demonstrates the force of such characterization of American Indians as ghosts in the American literary and cultural imagination from its earliest beginnings. Through such discursive maneuvers, both living and deceased Native Americans are equally cast as insubstantial, fantastical figures, remarkable only for their mythic levels of alternately primal or degenerate nature, residing only in the realms of either the white imagination or the ancestral past. Notably, too, the understanding of colonialism inherent here, then, is as a *fait accompli*. Something done in the past, and which only Winchester need answer for (or be absolved from).

ENTANGLEMENT 3: ONGOING SETTLER COLONIAL CAPITALISM

Finally, a third entanglement. The context is the present day, when the house is about to celebrate its centennial anniversary as an attraction open to the public. The scaffolds of a new high-rise condominium development loom over the house, as the fever-pitch of corporatization and development in San Francisco's South Bay area continue to push thousands of residents, including low-income families, families of color, and Indigenous families, further from the area.

Featured in a Facebook post on Dec. 4, 2018, a photograph shows a close-up view of a bronze statue of a Plains Indian man, which is on the grounds of the Winchester Mystery House. The figure is identified in the caption as "Chief Little Fawn, a Native American who died defending his homeland," and as one of the site's best-known statues. In the post, the Winchester Mystery House staff write: "it is said that Mrs. Winchester erected this statue to placate the spirits of the hundreds of thousands of Indians who were killed by Winchester repeating rifles" (Winchester Mystery House). The statue's surroundings are not visible. Instead, the image takes the already anatopistic (or out of place) statue further out of time and place, with its own location and context just a faded blur in the background, telegraphing the haunting image of non-specific Native American suffering and removal in the Euro-American imaginary once again. In a way, the photo is aptly symbolic of the ways one story tends to come into focus only at the expense of seeing another layer. It is profoundly disentangled.

Notably, this figure (and such occasional posts like the one that featured it here) are now among the only mentions of Native Americans, fictional or otherwise, in the site's website and other public materials. It seems that in order to avoid racist appropriations of Native experience at this site, the alternative has been to avoid discussing race and colonialism altogether. To disentangle. Thus, the opportunity for a more complex treatment of Winchester's role in ongoing systems of coloniality, including the ongoing struggle for recognition and land rights of the local Muwekma Ohlone tribe on whose lands she built, is for the moment foreclosed. How can we see these layers simultaneously, and activate them in public historical discourses at such sites?

Conclusions

I have tried to illustrate through a brief tour of these historical and representational moments how the ideologies of gender, race, colonialism, and space that came out in those first newspaper articles—simply laid out side by side across the span of pages in a way that would have been easy enough to leave in isolation—are actually deeply entangled, and with high stakes for the politics of remembrance and visions of the future.

It would be—and has been—easy enough to allow these narrative threads, lines of analysis and inquiry, and discourses of public remembrance to remain separated, apparently disentangled. Too often, scholars and publics too simply accept or even actively pursue a *woman's* story, a *racial* story, a *colonial* story, or the like, without sufficiently striving for the intersectional complexity that links these each to the other. Marita Sturken links this effacement of complexity and multiplicity to the narrative process itself, arguing that "the desire for narrative closure thus forces upon historical events the limits of narrative form and enables forgetting" (8).

By contrast, entangled remembrance is a heuristic by which we might signal to ourselves and our audiences the need to recover and hold many simultaneous stories-so-far, and particularly the need to always keep the context of heteropatriarchal white settler domesticity in view as the context of those stories and their circulation (or obscurity).

Part of this attempt lies in a microhistorical approach—digging closely into smaller case studies and microhistories that enable the thick description necessary to capture these entanglements. Local sites of public memory are ripe for this kind of analysis. But it must go further, too. Entangled remembrance also entails locating *ourselves*—as either researchers or audiences—within that matrix, implicating ourselves in ongoing discourses and systems of white settler colonial domination as part of our research, storytelling, and remembrance practices. It entails seeing the threads entangling inextricably with our own lived experience, pulling on them, tightening the weave, and knowing that we can never actually sever the connection with any of these threads, but only perhaps reconfigure the pattern that emerges from them for the future.

My hope is that by following such threads across space-time and attending to their deep local entanglements, we can work towards entangled remembrance practices that better capture this complexity, and that draw on the insights of public memory scholarship in conjunction with indigenous and decolonial feminisms to implicate *ourselves* in those visions of history and futurity, recognizing and striving to unsettle the ongoing structures of settler coloniality that continue to haunt us all.

Works Cited

Arvin, Maile, Eve Tuck, and Angie Morrill. "Decolonizing Feminism: Challenging Connections between Settler Colonialism and Heteropatriarchy." *Feminist Formations*, vol. 25, No. 1, 2013, pp. 8–34.

"A New Man for the New Woman." *San Francisco Chronicle*, 24 Feb 1895.

Bergland, Renée L. *The National Uncanny: Indian Ghosts and American Subjects*. UP of New England, 2000.

Bruyneel, Kevin. *Settler Memory: The Disavowal of Indigeneity and the Politics of Race in the United States*. U of North Carolina P, 2021.

Ignoffo, Mary Jo. *Captive of the Labyrinth: Sarah L. Winchester, Heiress to the Rifle Fortune*. U of Missouri P, 2012.

King, Thomas. *The Truth about Stories*. Dead Dog Café Productions, Inc., 2003.

Massey, Doreen. *For Space*. Sage Publications, 2005.

Montoya, Margaret, and Christine Zuni-Cruz. "Narrative Braids: Performing Racial Literacy (Interviewed by Gene Grant)." *American Indian Law Journal*, vol. 33, 2008, pp. 153–99.

"Moquis on Alcatraz." *San Francisco Chronicle*, 24 Feb 1895.

O'Brien, Jean M. *Firsting and Lasting: Writing Indians Out of Existence in New England*. U of Minnesota P, 2010.

Powell, Malea, et al. "Our Story Begins Here: Constellating Cultural Rhetorics." *enculturation, 25*, 2014, https://enculturation.net/our-story-begins-here.

Riley-Mukavetz, Andrea. "Developing a Relational Scholarly Practice: Snakes, Dreams, and Grandmothers." *College Composition, and Communication,* vol. 71, no. 4, 2020, pp. 545–65.

Sturken, Marita. *Tangled Memories: The Vietnam War, the AIDS Epidemic, and the Politics of Remembering.* U of California P, 1997.

"The Strange Story of a San Jose House." *San Francisco Chronicle,* 24 Feb 1895.

"Mrs. Winchester's Extraordinary 'Spook Palace.'" *American Weekly,* 1 April 1928. Reprinted in *Winchester Mystery House, San Jose, California: Gardens and Historical Museum,* souvenir booklet, circa 1970. Item in possession of author.

Winchester Mystery House. "Chief Little Fawn." Facebook, Dec. 4, 2018.

2 Linguistic Injustice and Citizenship in Ghana: Epistemological Decolonization and Stranger-Relationality as Rhetorical Arts of Resistance

Mohammed Sakip Iddrisu

Abstract

In this study, I problematize a recent case in Ghana to theorize how residues of colonial logics of domination perpetuate and normalize linguistic injustices in public life. In my analysis, I attend to stranger-initiated trans local rhetorical efforts to decolonize and co-construct knowledge. Then I theorize how such efforts dismantle the colonial logic of linguistic hegemony in ways that democratize knowledge making and recognize, reaffirm, and legitimize the national belonging of speakers of minoritized languages in Ghana. Ultimately, I argue that stranger-initiated rhetorical efforts are viable in resisting linguistic injustice and contributing to making public life safe and inclusive for the most vulnerable among us.

Introduction

What constitutes linguistic justice, and how might everyday rhetors in public life make it manifest within multilingual contexts? In rhetoric and writing studies, recent studies have theorized the inadequacies of traditional language pedagogies in accounting for the emotional harm experienced by Black students in US educational settings and the ways in which Black students negotiate language use informed by their racial and linguistic identities (Baker-Bell). From a colonial perspective, Roche argues that the erasure of Tibetan minority languages is a form of language oppression and injustice fueled by the colonial projects of the People's Republic of China (487). An epistemic space that remains under-theorized in the literature relates to the manifestation of linguistic injustice and its implications on the realization of full citizenship for minorities in highly multilingual and postcolonial nation-states in Africa such as Ghana.

In Ghana, colonial logics and legacies have instituted ethnic and linguistic hierarchies and inequalities where some languages such as Twi—the dominant indigenous language in Ghana—and their speakers gain access to national and public resources and symbols. On the contrary, speakers of other minoritized languages such as Ewe experience material constraints and risks of having their citizenship challenged in their quest to access those resources. The struggles of everyday people, especially linguistic minorities, to access these resources thus create a charged rhetorical site for cross-linguistic conflicts that engender linguistic injustices against minorities, resulting in a denial of national belonging and Ghanaian citizenship.

The Need for Epistemological Decolonization via Stranger-Relationality

In this study, I analyze a recent case in Ghana to theorize how residues of colonial logics of domination perpetuate linguistic injustices in public life. The study features strangers deploying rhetorical prowess and invention to deconstruct, interrogate, and challenge those colonial legacies instigating the injustice. I argue that such exercise of rhetorical agency enacted by strangers *in situ*—both in real time and subsequently via social media—constitute feats of what African philosopher Mahmoud Mamdani calls epistemological decolonization in public life (79). Attending to epistemological decolonization is urgent in Ghana because of the legacies of British colonialism and their effects on the linguistic dynamics of Ghana post-independence. Although there are several nationally recognized indigenous languages in Ghana including Ewe, a minoritized indigenous language, Twi, another indigenous language, largely remains the lingua franca of many people from different ethnic groups. This sociolinguistic reality has culminated in Twi assuming a privileged linguistic orthodoxy as synonymous to Ghanaian citizenship by language proficiency.

I problematize this linguistic phenomenon and theorize how the case illustrates the linguistic premise and colonial logic underlying the contestation of the citizenship of non-Twi-speaking Ghanaians in public life. More importantly, I attend to stranger-initiated trans local rhetorical efforts to decolonize and co-construct knowledge that dismantles the colonial logic of linguistic hegemony in ways that democratize knowledge making and recognize, reaffirm, and legitimize the national belonging of non-Twi-speaking Ghanaians.

RACISM AND COLONIAL DIMENSIONS OF LINGUISTIC INJUSTICE

Linguistic Justice and Injustice

In theorizing linguistic justice and injustice, the primary concern for theorists is to understand how to politically manage and recognize different languages and language communities within a particular political context in ways that are just and fair (De Schutter and Robichaud). Based on an understanding that the linguistic politics of a nation-state extends from policy to pedagogy and vice versa, scholars have theorized linguistic justice from the political to the pedagogical. In *Linguistic Justice: Black Language, Literacy, Identity, and Pedagogy*, April Baker-Bell frames the concept as "an antiracist approach to language and literacy education" geared towards "dismantling anti-Black linguistic racism and white linguistic hegemony and supremacy in classrooms and in the world" (7). In this critically important work, Baker-Bell demonstrates that there are rife linguistic and racial injustices and practices in current classrooms that train Black students to associate "blackness" and Black language "with wrongness and whiteness with rightness" (24). In the multidialectal American context, the humiliation and shaming of Black people and their language perpetuate an injustice and linguistic discrimination by elevating and equating white mainstream English as the standardized dialect representative of language use in America, a survival reality that coerces Black people to adopt bidialectal identities as speakers of Black language/African American English and white mainstream English. For example, H. Samy Alim and Geneva Smitherman demonstrate that Barack Obama's exhibition of this rhetorical mastery—a combination of Black ways of discourse and articulation and White Mainstream English—was crucial to his political survival and success as America's first Black president.

Through her antiracist framework, Baker-Bell challenges the normative and pervasive assumption that proficiency in white mainstream English is central to dismantling white supremacy and to the survival and success of Black students in academic and non-academic environments, arguing that "we are witnessing Black people being mishandled, discriminated against, and murdered while using white mainstream English, and in some cases, before they even open their mouths" (7).

If linguistic minorities continue to experience linguistic injustice, in our charge for justice, the questions that arise and demand scholarly attention are: How is it that everyday people (including those who are strangers to one another) contribute to (trans local) public efforts of linguistic justice in highly multilingual societies? What can these efforts contribute to our scholarly understanding of the advocacy of linguistic justice when we consider these contestations over language use as vernacular feats of epistemological decolonization—particularly at the intersection of policy and lived experience?

Colonialism, Intercultural Knowledge-Building, and Epistemological Decolonization

Within the context of Ghana, considering these questions within the framework of epistemological decolonization is crucial to undo the socio-ethnic tensions and conflicts traceable to the "divide-and-rule" strategy of European colonialism (Morrock 129). These tensions foreground the potential that intercultural knowledge-building holds in projects of epistemological decolonization. The fields of community literacy and public rhetorics have been theorizing intercultural knowledge-building for some time now (Flower, Long, Clifton). In this piece, I am extending this line of scholarship to test the potential of intercultural knowledge-building among strangers to advance epistemological decolonization in public life. As a collaborative, public feat, intercultural knowledge-building has these interconnected features: "designing an intercultural forum" (Flower 247), "structuring a dialogue to use difference" (Flower 254), and "building new knowledge" (Flower 266).

Intercultural forums provide spaces for different actors to render problems of public concern where different, competing and/or complementary voices are heard. In this study, public actors' use of Facebook creates such affordances where they, through original posts, render and circulate a case of linguistic injustice and engender local, albeit virtual, vernacular publics of strangers (Hauser) to converge and engage in discourse around the problem. In such forums, posts and comments made by participants on Facebook also constitute texts and documentation that are a critical part of dialoguing and the knowledge-making process in intercultural knowledge-building (Flower 266). The discourse that ensues among the strangers is structured along the problem of language differences in a multilingual nation-state, and the strangers so constituted around the discourse participate in the dialogue cognizant of their own linguistic and ethnic differences and privileges. The essence of such deliberative dialogues is interdependence and relationality with strangers (Hauser 53–54) to deconstruct hegemonic discourses and build new knowledge or transform prior knowledge to resolve shared problems grounded in intercultural differences (Flower 254). This vernacular feat thus, as Flower observes, "puts knowledge building in the hands of ordinary people," a rhetorical feature that is fundamental to Mamdani's concept of epistemological decolonization (271).

According to Mamdani, epistemological decolonization attends to "categories with which we make, unmake and remake, and thereby apprehend, the world" (79). Decolonizing knowledge thus requires public actors, scholars, and intellectuals to be active participants and take critical stances in interrogating established categories of knowledge. Mamdani notes that the epistemological labor required to decolonize knowledge collapses the boundary between a scholar and a public intellectual in ways that call "each to take on the standpoint of the other" (79). In this study, the trans local epistemological decolonizing efforts of public intellectuals or *stranger-advocates*, whom I define as strangers who solidarize for change by invoking their rhetorical acuity to intervene and challenge hegemonic logics of injustice and advocate for justice, seek to dismantle the harmful ways of conceptualizing national-belonging predicated on proficiency in the language of an ethnic majority.

The Case

Below, the case includes a summary, a close analysis of the manifestation of linguistic injustice, the cultural and public rhetorical work of posting on Facebook, and the theoretical implications of the case.

Case Summary: "bcos you are Togolese"

On August 2, 2020, Kafui (a pseudonym), a Ghanaian citizen acting as a stranger-advocate, posted an incident on Facebook in which he unpacked the injustice faced by a young mother nursing her five-month-old baby. Kafui wrote:

> I became aware of a young woman who registered at my polling station here inside Regimanuel. She doesn't have a passport, but only NHI card & a previous Voter ID. Which are invalid. Thanks to your Supreme Court.
> After going through the whole registration process, an NPP agent at the centre asks her, if she speaks any Ghanaian language. She speaks only Ewe. Bcos, she is of course an Ewe who grew up in the Volta Region. Then she [the NPP agent] asked if she [the young woman] can speak twi. She said no.
> Then she [the NPP agent] says, I challenge you bcos you are a Togolese. (Dake)

As part of exercising her political right as a citizen of Ghana, the young mother had gone to register for a voter's ID at Regimanuel, a high-end estate in Accra, the cosmopolitan capital city of Ghana. After registering, she was confronted by a political party agent of the ruling party, the New Patriotic Party (NPP) who questioned her whether "she speaks any Ghanaian language." Although the young mother responded in the affirmative, noting that she spoke Ewe, a legally recognized indigenous Ghanaian language, the party agent further asked if she spoke Twi. When the young mother responded in the negative, the party agent asserted that "Then I challenge you [your citizenship] because you are a Togolese." As a non-Twi-speaking citizen with little education, the young mother could not speak much English as well and her voter ID "card was withheld." Caught in that precarious situation, the young mother was fortunate to have the intervention of the stranger-advocate, who posted the incident on Facebook, and three lawyers for "her to get her card and an apology" (Dake).

Making the Case: Manifestation of Linguistic Injustice in This Case

Linguistic injustice manifests in rhetorically and politically charged contexts where an individual experiences discrimination in social practices that not only contradict the linguistic heterogeneity of the nation-state, Ghana, but more importantly imposes a version of *de jure* statelessness on that individual. In the critical incident rendered above, the party agent acknowledges the linguistic pluralism of Ghana by asking if the young mother spoke "any Ghanaian language." However, when the young mother responds by alluding to her proficiency in "Ewe," a response that does not fit into the Twi hegemony that dictates the epistemic linguistic expectation of the party agent, she invokes a rhetoric of non-belonging that imposes "Togolese" citizenship on the young mother. A Togolese is a person who is a citizen of Togo, a country that is on the eastern border of Ghana and where Ewe is the de facto dominant language (Essizewa viii). Historically, members of the Ewe ethnic group vote largely for a political party called the National Democratic Congress (NDC), while members of the dominant Akan ethnic group whose language is Twi largely vote for the New Patriotic Party (NPP) (Adotey 24). Given these voting dynamics, it is not uncommon for non-Twi speaking Ewe citizens of Ghana to be accused of being Togolese and not Ghanaians as the NPP party agent did in the case rendered above. Thus, when the NPP party agent claims that the young woman is Togolese, the former is asserting that the latter is a citizen of Togo and is unqualified to register to vote in Ghana given that voting is a right reserved for only citizens of Ghana.

The follow-up question that introduces proficiency in Twi demonstrates the coloniality evident in the party agent's logic because it implies, erroneously, that to be Ghanaian is to be Twi-speaking, and to be non-Twi-speaking is to be a non-citizen of Ghana. Such discriminatory social practices reify legacies of British colonialism where English-speaking members of the colonized were elevated and granted access to resources and political participation by their mere proficiency in the language of the dominating political force. While the party agent invokes and superimposes Togolese citizenship on the young mother, in that material moment when the young mother's voter ID card was "withheld," she became de jure stateless in real time because she was not a Togolese and there was no way that the nation-state of Togo would have recognized her as a Togolese if she were deported.

Going Public: Creating a Public via Facebook

This incident was one incident witnessed by a bystander whom I refer to as a stranger-advocate. His decision to post on Facebook becomes a kind of *call-response*, an African-derived rhetorical strategy, in this case exercised in a virtual space (Daniel and Smitherman 33). This *call* (posting on Facebook) and the *response* (Facebook users sharing their own experiences and observations as shown below) has the rhetorical potential of generating a critical mass of other experiences to demonstrate that such injustices against linguistic minorities are commonplace. Indeed, there had been several media reports of such incidents happening elsewhere in the country. Consequently, his post does the public cultural rhetorical work of opening a virtual space for other minorities to render their own experiences, observations, and witnesses of linguistic injustice.

Beyond demonstrating the extent of the injustice across the nation-state, building such a critical mass of experiences from cross-linguistic and ethnic Facebook users is fundamental for establishing an ethos that this issue should be a matter of public concern and intervention. Without demonstrating the extent to which such injustice has become commonplace, and certainly intensified in an election year, in the lives of linguistic minorities, the public mobilization and intervention required to initiate, sustain, and produce alternative knowledge towards decolonization may be impeded. Below are exact responses/comments of three different Facebook users:

> Kakra (a pseudonym): Here in Ghana if you can't speak twi, you're not Ghanaian enough, such primitive ideology
>
> Edem (a pseudonym): Come to think of it. In Accra, and if you cannot speak twi but only ewe, you are classified a Togolese. In Accra, Ga ma shikpon. Where did we go wrong

Saha (a pseudonym): This is exactly what they have been doing to many dagaartis who have difficulty speaking twi in ashnati [correct spelling "Ashanti"] region. I am on the review committee and I can say the frustration is just so disturbing. Unfortunately, u have a committee chairman who is so biased that the burden of proof does not work . . . Nobody is more Ghanaian than another. (Dake)

Each of the Facebook users above coalesced, and through their comments, they actively participated in highlighting the prevalence of linguistic injustice against ethnic linguistic minorities in Ghana. Kakra criticizes this linguistic injustice by noting the extent to which a person's claim to being Ghanaian is predicated on the ability to speak Twi. Her framing of such colonial-inspired and monolingual view of being Ghanaian as a primitive ideology suggests a need to decolonize the illiteracy of national belonging in the Ghanaian society. Likewise, the second user, Edem, reinforces the sociolinguistic reality that in Accra, the capital city of Ghana, where the incident happened, people get classified as Togolese because they are proficient in only Ewe and not Twi. In his comment, when Edem writes "Ga ma shikpon" (referring to Accra as the land of the Indigenous Ga people who speak Ga as their language), he is asserting that even the Ga people do not insist on the use of Ga in public life on their ancestral land. By implication, in the rhetorical context of Accra, Twi, which is not the native language of the Ga people, should not be used as the litmus test of citizenship or national belonging. Saha, the third user, constructs an ethos for himself as a member of the committee that reviews challenges to people's eligibility to register. Then, he recounts an incident similar to the case I narrated above. According to him, Dagaartis, another minority ethnic group, face similar challenges like the young mother in the case because they can't speak Twi and NPP agents use that as grounds to call their citizenship into question. This is why he states that one cannot claim to be more Ghanaian than the other based on linguistic proficiency.

Twi is used as a linguistic hegemony to oppress linguistic minorities. These comments from the Facebook users indicate that the centrality of language proficiency as a determinant of national belonging calls for decolonizing language hegemony and the illiteracy that fuels the use of language to question citizenship in social practices in Ghana. To decolonize language domination, therefore, there needs to be a reimagination of a literacy of national belonging that recognizes that in any rhetorical and communicative encounter, linguistic heterogeneity is the norm and not the exception in Ghana. Reimagining literacy that is attentive to linguistic pluralism and national belonging as a decolonizing endeavor requires the trans local efforts of multi-tribal and Indigenous individuals, including those who are members of the linguistic majority, to recognize and dismantle the residue of the colonial logic perpetuating the injustice.

Decolonizing Epistemologies via Stranger-Relationality

That linguistic injustices fueled by legacies of colonial epistemologies will manifest themselves in public is predictable; what people witnessing linguistic injustices will do, far less so. This case demonstrates that public actors possess the rhetorical agency to resist such injustices by enacting epistemological decolonization through stranger-relationality—a way of dealing with strangers (Warner). Decolonizing knowledge production involves both unlearning knowledge systems and worldviews instituted by colonialism and dismantling the coloniality of logics that underscore ways of knowing in contemporary societies. In contemporary public life, the materiality of trans local epistemological decolonizing efforts towards linguistic justice can be rendered across *two main sites*: (1) responsive rhetorical interventions of calling others—including strangers—to dialogue across difference in real time (Clifton); (2) publicly, albeit virtually, protesting and deconstructing the colonial logic by extending and circulating public knowledge production of "*what went down*" (Long 31; emphasis in original) via social media posts.

As regards the first site, when public actors who may be strangers to one another rhetorically intervene in instances of linguistic injustice and initiate dialogue, irrespective of their linguistic, indigenous, ethnic, and political differences (geared towards offering alternative epistemologies to hegemonic knowledge systems), they actually set in motion efforts towards epistemological decolonization. According to Mamdani, the public intellectual engaged in epistemological decolonization needs to act responsively to unforeseeable situations in public including challenging policy-informed or state sanctioned social practices that are relics of colonialism. In addition to its responsiveness, the rhetorical and epistemological values of, literally, calling strangers to dialogue and challenge discriminatory knowledge systems create two useful possibilities in public life. First, they make possible strangers' capability to solidarize and democratize knowledge production in public in ways that protect vulnerable individuals. Second, they offer "epistemological situatedness," which is crucial for producing contextually dependent knowledge frameworks relevant to people's lived experiences (Diversi and Moreira 33).

What rhetorical and epistemological value is there in a rhetor's efforts to call strangers to dialogue across difference in real time in unforeseeable situations? The epistemological situatedness such calls afford is a fundamental element of public intellectuals' effort to decolonize knowledge (Mamdani).

In such contexts where policy does not reflect social reality, as is the case of the linguistic situation in Ghana, context-dependent knowledge of everyday public rhetors becomes a viable rhetorical tool for epistemological decolonization because such actors have knowledge of the *now* and *real*.

As the case shows, linguistic injustice is embedded in specific social rhetorical contexts. Mamdani, like other decolonization scholars, argues that on the ground, lived experiences constitute one of the hopes of the public intellectual and rhetor engaged in epistemological decolonization. According to him, "the public intellectual hoped to work closer to the ground, to be as close to the ground as possible so as to work with local communities" (79). Working with local communities then affords the public rhetor the ability to not only witness and render critical incidents of linguistic injustice but also the capability to build relations with others, understand the intricacies of stranger relations and interethnic tensions, and invite others to dialogue across difference and intervene in situations of injustice against vulnerable community members. Further, such situated knowledge enables the public rhetor to offer insights into the nuances of people's lived experiences of injustices in ways that policy cannot sufficiently account for.

Regarding the second site, social media constitutes a public platform where public rhetors can circulate the happenings of a critical incident of injustice and harness the potentiality of strangers to do the work of epistemological decolonization. Such work begins with rendering "what went down" post facto and gathering strangers, through social media tags for example, to protest an injustice and deconstruct the logic that perpetuates such an injustice. Social media, in this case Facebook, functions as a virtual place of protest where the stranger-advocate publicizes the linguistic injustice and further initiates a trans local epistemological effort towards decolonization. In this case, the stranger-advocate invites the public to the epistemic dialogue by first asking "WHO & WHERE are the (wo)men of conscience in #GhanaToday?" (Dake).

Before rendering the critical incident I summarized at the beginning of this section, the stranger-advocate tags several people, including known and unknown cross-ethnic personalities in the Ghanaian civil society and media spectrum, to participate in the effort. Further, such personalities and regular Facebook users did react and comment on the injustice with many of them simultaneously demonstrating how widespread the Twi hegemony is as a criterion for national belonging and professing alternative knowledge that reflect the reality of Ghana as a linguistically heterogeneous nation-state. Essentially, the stranger-advocate's use of social media not only demonstrates social media as a rhetorically responsive tool to protest injustice, but more importantly as an epistemic forum to publicly deconstruct and co-construct knowledge with strangers towards achieving linguistic justice.

Conclusion

Throughout this paper, I have argued that epistemological decolorization enacted through trans local stranger-relationality in physical and virtual contexts constitutes a viable rhetorical and democratizing knowledge-making framework with the capacity to deconstruct and decolonize hegemonic knowledge systems and practices that perpetuate linguistic injustice in postcolonial and multilingual contexts such as Ghana. The attainment of linguistic justice through epistemological decolonization has material implications for linguistic minorities as it makes possible their experience and enjoyment of full Ghanaian citizenship without the risk of having their national belonging questioned. As the interventions of the stranger-advocates show, the trans local rhetorical efforts required to do the epistemological work of decolonizing linguistic hegemony are grounded in the situated knowledge and rhetorical practices of everyday people who are committed to mobilizing and solidarizing to make public life safe and inclusive for the most vulnerable populations among us. Indeed, within a global context where logics of domination abound, and where our identities as majorities and minorities shift across different spaces, we, as rhetorical scholars in the public domain, need to take cues from the stranger-advocates in this study. We need to exercise rhetorical abilities through our situated knowledge to respond to cases of injustice in public life in real time by taking up exigencies of strangers as they encounter threats of injustice in their quest to access public goods as rightful citizens, or even noncitizens.

Works Cited

Adotey, Edem. "'Operation Eagle Eye': Border Citizenship and Cross-border Voting in Ghana's Fourth Republic." *Journal of Borderlands Studies*, vol. 38, no.1, 2023, pp. 21–38.

Alim, H. Samy, and Geneva Smitherman. *Articulate while Black: Barack Obama, Language, and Race in the US*. Oxford UP, 2012.

Baker-Bell, April. *Linguistic Justice: Black Language, Literacy, Identity, and Pedagogy*. Routledge, 2020.

Clifton, Jennifer. *Argument as Dialogue across Difference: Engaging Youth in Public Literacies*. Routledge, 2016.

Dake, Mawuli. "Pardon my Rant." *Facebook*, 2 Aug. 2020, https://www.facebook.com/mawuli.dake/posts/10156988854347282. Accessed 6 May 2022.

Daniel, Jack L., and Geneva Smitherman. "How I Got Over: Communication Dynamics in the Black Community." *Quarterly Journal of Speech*, vol. 62, no.1, 1976, pp. 26–39.

De Schutter, Helder, and David Robichaud. "Van Parijsian Linguistic Justice–Context, Analysis and Critiques." *Critical Review of International Social and Political Philosophy*, vol. 18, no.2, 2017, pp. 87–112.

Diversi, Marcelo, and Claudio Moreira. *Betweener Talk: Decolonizing Knowledge Production, Pedagogy, and Praxis*. Routledge, 2016.

Essizewa, Komlan Essowe. *Sociolinguistic Aspects of Kabiye-Ewe Bilingualism in Togo*. 2007. Dissertation. New York U.

Flower, Linda. "Intercultural Knowledge Building: The Literate Action of a Community Think Tank." *Writing Selves and Society: Research from Activity Perspectives*, Edited by David Russell and Charles Bazerman, WAC Clearinghouse, 2002, pp. 239–279.

Hauser, Gerard A. *Vernacular Voices: The Rhetoric of Publics and Public Spheres*. U of South Carolina P 1999.

Long, Elenore. *A Responsive Rhetorical Art: Artistic Methods for Contemporary Public Life*. U of Pittsburgh P, 2018.

Mamdani, Mahmood. "Between the Public Intellectual and the Scholar: Decolonization and Some Post-independence Initiatives in African Higher Education." *Inter-Asia Cultural Studies*, vol. 17, no.1, 2016, pp. 68–83.

Morrock, Richard. "Heritage of Strife: The Effects of Colonialist "divide and rule" Strategy upon the Colonized Peoples." *Science & Society*, 1973, pp. 129–51.

Roche, Gerald. "Articulating Language Oppression: Colonialism, Coloniality and the Erasure of Tibet's Minority Languages." *Patterns of Prejudice*, vol. 53, no. 5, 2019, pp. 487–514.

Warner, Michael. "Publics and Counterpublics." *Public Culture*, vol. 14, no. 1, 2002, pp. 49–90.

3 Digital Archival Futures: Discoverability and Collaboration as Activism in a Post-Pandemic World

keondra bills freemyn

ABSTRACT

Archival repositories continue to increase their acquisition of electronic records and creation of digital reproductions allowing greater offsite access to historical records. The increase in availability of digitized records provides greater opportunities for engaging broader and more global audiences. Reflecting on the practices of care and commitment to accessibility archivists enacted during the COVID-19 pandemic provides a glimmer of possibility into a reimagined future that prioritizes inclusion towards an expansive historical record. Digital archives are integral in achieving this vision, though their existence alone is not enough. Improving discoverability of digital archival records, expanding traditional notions of audience, and centering collaboration as a means of accountability and mutual respect are key in ensuring inclusive archival practice in a post-pandemic world.

The creation of new ideas and ways of expressing them is often, directly, and indirectly influenced by the historical record. The interpretation and construction of the historical record relies heavily on archival materials, positioning archivists and archival practice as not only necessary but imperative to the functioning and development of ideas in society. Despite its vital contribution to the creation of new ideas and reinterpretation of existing ideas, archival practice does not exist only in support of other disciplines. Archivists determine what is valued, what is saved, and what objects remain available for future generations to interpret for the historical record.

In recent years, the archival profession has begun reckoning with its legacy of inequity, as more and more practitioners look toward reparative models that are more inclusive (Hughes-Watkins 4). Thinking through our role as archivists and how we support the development and use of rhetoric that is used to effectuate change at a societal level, there is great opportunity for merging our praxis with the political. Not political in the sense of partisanship, but in the ways that reflect our values as information professionals to meet the needs of our constituencies and combat misinformation and exclusion.

Despite the current process of reckoning within the archival profession, dominant values of extraction and exclusion persist, marking any actions against the status quo as subversive. Therefore, what might otherwise be seen as professional duty is often marked as activism. Despite this reality, the commitment to telling the broadest range of stories and preserving the necessary histories to achieve that goal has more in common with activism than it does not. Just as archives can be a place of violence and erasure, they have the potential to be a site of activism and expansion. I argue that digital archival practice is central to this goal, with increased accessibility, improved discoverability, and an investment in collaboration as necessary components to realize progress, particularly in the post-pandemic reality.

Like contemporary grassroots activism, digital platforms are useful in creating and sharing information to broad audiences. Tools and approaches like linked open data and encoded archival description allow for repositories of all sizes to share information widely, simplifying the archival discovery process for researchers. Capturing relationships between archival data across repositories not only simplifies the discovery process, but it also more fully reflects the reality of our lives.

In the early stages of defining the scope and direction of the digital archival and humanities initiative, Black Women Writers Project (BWWP), I was struck by the concept of constellations. Beginning with a reflection on my personal archival process and intimate connections, I noticed that my personal archives did not simply tell the story of a singular life—they were a record of my peers and community members. Through my experience as a poet and non-fiction writer, I have collected numerous unpublished manuscripts by fellow writers, fliers and other ephemera from poetry readings and book releases, and an endless number of digital photos that reflect the intimacies of creative work and those whose love and friendship have kept me afloat. Digital records are not only integral to proper contextualization of my own creative work but also serve as portals into the lives and works of others.

These constellations are not happenstance. They are a result of intentional community-building and a commitment to bearing witness to lives beyond my own. Current digital archival tools cannot capture the dynamism of these constellations yet are a foundational resource for researchers to begin visualizing connections where they could once only infer. Digital archival tools allow for the development of new and more expansive narratives and greater visibility and insight into the intimate structures of lives across the historical record.

I hesitate to position digital archives as the sole solution to long-standing challenges related to archival discovery and use, particularly as it relates to records of marginalized communities. Dorothy Berry emphasizes, "digitization as panacea assumes both that complicated and sometimes idiosyncratic catalogs and findings contain all the information that users need for digital discovery, and furthermore that the institutional digital access points, often behind university logins and paywalls, are somehow less intimidating and prohibitive" (113). The digitization of records and creation of more robust metadata undoubtedly improve availability and discoverability of information, though the burden of interpretation remains on the researcher.

Launched during the COVID-19 pandemic and driven by a desire to ensure information could be easily findable for all types of researchers, BWWP takes a user-focused approach and aggregates information in an intuitive way. One way BWWP manages this is by sharing archival images collected from hundreds of digital collections on social media. Using Instagram as the primary platform, the Black Women Writers Archive page provides biographical information as well as extended captions that include the location of the writer's primary archives and image identifiers to promote discovery of digital collections. The use of hashtags allows for an enhanced layer of information accessibility not otherwise available at the repository level. Instagram users can view posts related to the subject of the post with one click. Not only does this allow interested users to identify information relevant to their interests, but it also contextualizes the image among other posts featuring the writer's books, clips of interviews and performances, and other archival footage. BWWP leverages the virality and accessibility of social media posts to communicate the contributions of Black women and gender-expansive writers to the literary canon. The literary work and thought production of Black women and gender-expansive writers has positively impacted the lives of many people who may never enter a traditional reading room at an institutional archive. Our approach to promoting archival discovery subverts conventional notions of the public, research, and researchers, and relinquishes expectations around how and when archives should be accessed and to whom that access is given.

Digital discovery tools make the existence and geographical distribution of records apparent but still require researchers to muddle through large amounts of information. The push for digital access to collections has likely improved experiences for many researchers. However, a multifaceted approach is necessary to fully realize activism in the archives. Many of the archives highlighted by BWWP are not yet completely accessible digitally. Copyright restrictions, lack of financial resources for digitization, and embargoed materials are some of the challenges that deter full access. Apart from a few notable hubs like Emory University's Rose Library, Harvard's Schlesinger Library, Spelman College Archives, and New York Public Library's Schomburg Center for Research in Black Culture, the papers and archives of Black women writers are geographically dispersed.

The organization and classification of archival records still relies heavily on practices that privilege traditional organizational structures over ease of wayfinding and contextualization. Archival concepts designed to preserve the arrangement of records in their original order, inadvertently create arbitrary delineations in information that cannot be overcome solely by increasing the availability of digital finding aids and searchable metadata. Traditional archival arrangement practices aim to create a uniform approach and exact order to archival records, yet they also hinder culturally specific concepts of creation and community. Archivists need to continue to think more critically about the traditional structures of archival practice and how our commitment to these structures potentially deters engagement.

The success of efforts to reevaluate our practices will be contingent upon our ability to collaborate. In my role as coordinator of Project STAND (Student Activism Now Documented), I am intimately aware of how seriously our members take this charge. Project STAND is a radical grassroots archival consortium of over eighty institutions and individual members that "aims to foster ethical documentation of contemporary and past social justice movements in under-documented student populations" (Mission). Project STAND was founded in 2017, though the demand for guidance on the ethical collection of activism-related records increased in 2020 as institutions looked to document student uprisings in response to the deaths of Ahmaud Arbery, Breonna Taylor, and George Floyd. Project STAND members share with each other their experiences with contemporaneous collecting, engaging student activists, and confronting issues of surveillance and safety in the archives. Together, members have developed guides such as the Archiving Student Activism Toolkit and the SAVE Methodology to spark conversations between archivists and students throughout the collecting process. Additionally, Project STAND hosts information about its members' student activism-related collections on its website, improving discoverability of relevant records. Project STAND does not have any physical holdings, leveraging the Internet as a virtual convening space and repository for its own organizational records. Project STAND prides itself on being a space for information exchange, but it is also an example of successful collaboration and a community of practice that reimagines the possibilities of effective interorganizational networks. An independent initiative, Project STAND serves as a model for engagement outside of institutions, fostering an environment where members can learn from each other and contribute to a community that values the contributions of all to the collection and preservation of historical documentation.

The COVID-19 health crisis continues to move from pandemic to endemic, leaving a trail of devastation and possibility in its wake. In this new era, Archival institutions are charged with finding sustainable ways of maintaining accessibility and engagement with communities beyond physical reading rooms. The existence of a true post-pandemic world may be in question, but opportunities for engaging new pathways to archival discoverability and encouraging collaboration remain ripe. We can collectively hope to arrive on the other side of the pandemic with a stronger commitment to acknowledging and preserving a greater range of archival records. The way forward relies greatly on the extent to which we reflect on our missteps and identify options for expanding our capacity for empathy and grace. The possibility of creating just archival futures is only limited by the borders of our collective imagination. Our belief that our profession and our world can be transformed relies heavily on how we harness the untapped potential of digital archives and how we choose to wield that power in service or against the new world that awaits.

Works Cited

Berry, Dorothy. "Take Me into the Library and Show Me Myself: Toward Authentic Accessibility in Digital Libraries." *Transactions of the American Philosophical Society*, vol. 110, no. 3, 2022, pp. 111–26. *JSTOR*, www.jstor.org/stable/45420503.

Hughes-Watkins, Lae'l. "Moving Toward a Reparative Archive: A Roadmap for a Holistic Approach to Disrupting Homogenous Histories in Academic Repositories and Creating Inclusive Spaces for Marginalized Voices." *Journal of Contemporary Archival Studies*, vol. 5, no. 1, 2018. *EliScholar*, Yale U, www.elischolar.library.yale.edu/jcas/vol5/iss1/6.

"Mission." *Project STAND*, 2021, www.standarchives.com/misson/ [sic].

4 Description and Abstraction After Racial Violence: The Case of Jesse Washington

Wallace S. Golding

Abstract

This essay argues that rhetoricians should take seriously the potential of critical description as method. Drawing from conversations on absence and racial abstraction, I show that critical description should be understood as a process of de-scripting, or the peeling back of those social scripts that enable some modes of being and foreclose others. To demonstrate how this method is useful in practice, I turn to the case of Jesse Washington, a 1916 lynching victim whose story was told in the pages of *The Crisis*, the NAACP's official magazine. In its report, the publication critically describes the circumstances of Washington's alleged crime and death such that readers would be forced to recognize his lynching as part of a pattern of violence that worked to legitimize white supremacy by abstracting the humanity of Black people. I conclude with a brief discussion of the limits and lessons of critical description as a method.

Description is a central component of rhetoric and rhetorical criticism. It is part and parcel of different rhetorical terms (e.g., *phantasia, ekphrasis, enargeia*), and theorists have both praised its rhetorical force and maligned its specificity (Hauser 24–25). With a need for knowledge of the particular, description became an important method for speakers hoping to make their words matter in the world. Rhetors describe events, places, and things to make them matter to an audience. Rhetorical critics describe the twists and turns of discourse and, as rhetors themselves, use description to make their own meta-rhetoric matter. Yet, description is not touted as a reasonable *critical* method for rhetorical criticism. Following Raymie McKerrow's assertion that what is absent is equally as important as what is present, the question of how description can be used critically becomes clear (107–08). How are we to describe what is absent?

McKerrow's claim describes absences resulting from power differences. The less powerful appear to appear less, even if we know this is not truly the case. Some have discussed how rhetorical critics might manage this specifically in the context of archival absence. Davis Houck, for example, has pointed out that his work requires a considerable amount of relationship-building with activists or former activists who may have the texts he needs or at least know someone who does (113–14). One person's rhetorical junk is another's rhetorical treasure. Those artifacts do not exist in an archive as such, but rather often in informal collections of papers housed in garages, attics, and everywhere in between. Equally common are the cases where the scale of an informal archive might inhibit the focused rhetorical criticism we desire. Digital humanists have noted that metadata is valuable in describing the rhetorical past, too. Historical rhetorical resources like newspapers provide records of speeches, valuable even as we may not have the address itself in our hands (VanHaitsma 26–27). Lest we forget archives are themselves ideological, Cara Finnegan reminds us that the rhetorical negotiations of classifying artifacts impacts how we describe what we find ("What Is This a Picture Of?" 119–20).

Rhetorical critics also face the issue of describing what readers cannot see. Visual rhetorical scholars are particularly skilled at this, and describing an artifact's visual grammar is fundamental to their method. Describing an image's content, organization, color, and light are all imperative to arguing about visual artifacts (Finnegan, "Studying Visual Modes" 254). Visual rhetorical critics face the challenge of convincing their audience to see—literally and figuratively—a visual artifact *as they want them to*. Such a process is necessarily descriptive. Those processes of describing and seeing are embedded within larger ideological networks (Jack; Kaszynski). This self-reinforcing pedagogy of sight, as Jordynn Jack calls it, "instructs readers *how* to view images in accordance with an ideological or epistemic program" (192). Critics studying non-visual artifacts also need to describe their objects of study, and they also face the challenge of asking audiences to see (or read) a text as they want. Applying Jack's argument to rhetoric in its general sense, then, proves important for all rhetorical critics: If all rhetorical critics describe, how are we to describe in a way that does not reinforce the ideas we are arguing against?

Implicitly responding to this question, Dave Tell has argued "if description has occasionally registered as a non-critical or apolitical methodology, this just means that the method has never been descriptive enough" (256). Critical description must, to borrow from Patricia Davis and colleagues, "escape the ahistorical collapse into whiteness." We must not rely on the white ahistorical subject for our descriptive materials, but rather scrutinize the materials from which we ourselves are doing the describing (351). Put differently, the descriptive, the personal, the biographical even "is not about navel gazing," as Christina Sharpe says, but rather about trying to look at historical and social processes and different identity formations as a window onto social and historical processes. It is meant to "tell a story capable of engaging and countering the violence of abstraction" (Sharpe 8).

It is in this spirit, and in the spirit of Tell's claim, that I argue we must envision critical description as a method that moves beyond the descriptivist approach criticized by Achille Mbembe as a "series of anecdotes and negative statements" (26). Critical description is not describing for description's sake. To demonstrate how we might accomplish this, I argue first that we must understand critical description as a process of de-scripting, or a peeling back of social scripts that enable some modes of being and foreclose others.[1] Put differently, we must understand critical description as fundamentally opposed to abstraction, the recursive process around which white supremacy coheres (Dyer 1–2; Nakayama and Krizek 296–97). I then turn to a story grounded in that tug-of-war between description and abstraction, that of Jesse Washington, who was brutally lynched by a white supremacist mob in Waco, Texas, in May 1916. More specifically, I turn to how *The Crisis* responded to the event to demonstrate how critical description provided the publication with the tools necessary to counter the racial abstraction that legitimized white supremacist practices and enabled the coherence of whiteness. I conclude with some brief thoughts on the limits and lessons of critical description as a method.

Critical Description and Abstraction

I understand critical description as a process of unveiling the scripts on which white supremacist logics rely. Racial abstraction, or the depiction of Blackness (or non-whiteness more generally) as a thing for consumption rather than as an epistemological or ontological position, recurs through time and space

---

1. I am grateful to Jenny Rice for helping me articulate the idea of "de-scripting" after my presentation at RSA in 2022 and to and to Brandon Erby, Juliette Lapeyrouse-Cherry, Dave Tell, and Kristin Wagel for their feedback on earlier versions of this project.

and delegitimizes modes of being different than those endorsed by whiteness. Racial abstraction obscures the logics of white supremacy by promoting whiteness as default and white-defined histories as truth. Critical description, when used appropriately, can function as an opposing force to this social script. There are several assumptions on which I rely to think through the usefulness and importance of critical description.

First, white supremacy relies on racial abstraction for it to cohere. A white supremacist regime—indeed, this white supremacist regime in which we all live and die—needs racial abstraction for it to make sense. Under this regime, whiteness becomes the default epistemological and ontological position. Following Afropessimists, this means that Blackness is a presumption of social death or deathliness, an imposed condition wherein "violence without sanctuary is the *sine qua non* of Blackness" (Wilderson 161; Marriott). By obscuring the humanity of non-white individuals, racial abstraction provides the rhetorical space necessary for whiteness to make sense. Put differently, abstraction is fundamental to "the problem of whiteness, to the structures that delimit Black possibility, that at once predict and preordain premature Black death" (Raiford).

Second, by virtue of its ties to whiteness, abstraction is a dominant social script. It dictates how some can identify (or not), live (or not), and move through the world (or not). It opens rhetorical possibilities for some and closes them for others. It structures day-to-day life insofar that it determines the ways in which we interact with one another—in the classroom, on the street, and everywhere else. Racial abstraction is realized through its inherence in the systems and structures we all operate within and as such negatively conditions the lives of those whose identities those systems must marginalize to maintain its legitimacy (Walcott 93). Because whiteness relies on racial abstraction to make sense, it must also rely on abstraction as a powerful social script that maintains its coherence, or else risk its collapse.

Finally, the third assumption proceeds logically from the first two. If whiteness relies on racial abstraction for it to cohere and abstraction operates as a dominant social script, then it needs a rhetorical counterforce: critical description. When used judiciously, critical description has the rhetorical force to disrupt abstraction. If abstraction and whiteness seek to make Black life, Black experiences, Black rhetoric *not* matter, then critical description seeks to make those things *matter in the world*. This is particularly the case if we understand it as a process of its component linguistic parts, de-scripting, a peeling back of the social scripts that dictate how we each individually interact with and in the world around us, those that enable some modes of being and foreclose others. White supremacist scripts fall apart under the scrutiny of critical description, and critical description is indeed a project of describing the social scripts that condition Black being in the world.

The role of critical description, then, is not to describe for description's sake. It is rather both to reveal those scripts that thrive when obscured through racial abstraction and to attempt to speak against them. Consequently, the project of critical description is to take seriously alternative modes of being, modes that often fundamentally contest the abstraction around which whiteness coheres. It is a practice or method that asks rhetorical critics to witness and account for alternative histories and narratives. Through such a method, rhetorical critics can better understand and critique not only the white supremacist rhetorics and logics underwriting how we move through the world, but also more deliberately amplify those epistemologies and ontologies that contest those rhetorics and logics.

The Case of Jesse Washington

The case of Jesse Washington, a seventeen-year-old Black man from Waco, Texas, is particularly illustrative of critical description's rhetorical force. In 1916, Washington worked as a farmhand for Lucy Fryer, a white woman, in nearby Robinson. When she was found bludgeoned to death near a shed, Washington was named a suspect immediately. He was eventually made to confess after hours of interrogation, and he told police where they could find the murder weapon, a blacksmith's hammer he said he had placed under some brush outside the shed (Dray 216).

A trial was held for Washington on May 15, 1916, seven days after Fryer's murder. Judge Richard Irby Monroe allowed 1,500 spectators into a courtroom designed for five hundred, and he did little to quell the heckling directed at Washington from the crowd. The trial was a sham. The judge rushed through the proceedings, and the jury took all of four minutes to return their verdict: guilty (SoRelle 520–24; "The Waco Horror" 3–4). After the jury announced the verdict, the mob attacked Washington, taking him into their custody and rushing him out a back door down an alleyway to the city hall. As he was rushed along, mob members kicked and stabbed him and threw bricks and rocks at his nearly naked body. The crowd grew quickly to 15,000 as others wandered over to witness the imminent lynching. Washington was tied up, burned, and hanged from a tree outside city hall (Dray 217–18; SoRelle 527–28; "The Waco Horror" 4–6).

The lynching itself was gruesome but did not depart from the era's norms for punishing Black flesh. Nor did reports of the lynching depart from what was typical of the era. The mainstream national press largely overlooked the event, and most national newspapers published some version of the same four-hundred-word report. By this time, though, the NAACP's research and publications arm was burgeoning. The organization sent a white suffragist, Elizabeth Freeman, to investigate the lynching, which resulted in a July 1916 report titled "The Waco Horror." The report circulated widely—more than 43,000 copies were distributed to its subscribers and to public officials—and readers of the report encountered eight pages of reporting with eleven photographs scattered throughout.

The report's pages overflow with specificity and detail. They describe the context and act of Washington's lynching through testimony from public officials, firsthand accounts of the event, and court documents. This detail was put to a specific persuasive end: to critically describe the circumstances of Washington's alleged crime and death such that readers would be forced to recognize the murder of Washington not only as disproportionately cruel, but also as indicative of a white desire for Black death, a pattern of violence that worked by abstracting the humanity of Black people.

For example, when the publication described how onlookers reacted to and participated in the lynching, they wrote: "Onlookers were hanging from the windows of the City Hall and every other building that commanded a sight of the [event], and as [Washington's] body commenced to burn, shouts of delight went up from the thousands of throats" ("The Waco Horror" 6). The sheer detail of the account, the way it asks readers to see for themselves the effects of white supremacist violence, begins to unveil the underlying logics of anti-Blackness, the social scripts that enabled Washington's murder. Combined with explications about the lynching "industry," the description above and many others like it contest the status quo. Not only does it suggest the deck is stacked against Black people in the South and nationally, but also that this is *intentional*, that it is characteristic of a system that profits off Black death. The industrial metaphor tells us as much and more. The lynching industry section is only two paragraphs in length but begins by arguing "this is an account of one lynching. It is horrible, but it is matched in horror by scores of others" ("The Waco Horror" 8). Washington was but one of the thousands victimized by an industry that characterized the logics of white supremacy undergirding civil society.

This claim was supported by other vivid details found in the report's eight pages. When describing the lynching itself, the publication went to great lengths to capture the brutality of what had occurred: "While a fire was being prepared of boxes, the naked boy was stabbed, and the chain put over the tree. He tried to get away but could not. He reached up to grab the chain and they cut off his fingers" ("The Waco Horror" 4). Importantly, these details and others did not appear in other publications. *The Crisis* reprinted them not to relish in the racial trauma of lynching, but rather to highlight the disproportionate response of whites. The punishment—gory, traumatizing, and racist—did not fit the crime.

Similar critical descriptive work can be found throughout the report, but it is not necessary to reproduce those details here. Voyeurism is not the goal of this essay, but rather to understand how *The Crisis* deployed its own critical description to contest racial abstraction. Perhaps this is the first lesson of critical description, which will be addressed in more detail in the conclusion. It is imperative that scholarly accounts of critical description are careful not to reproduce or "affirm the spectacle" of abstraction (Wolters 400–02). The lynching of Washington, like the white supremacist practice itself, abstracted his humanity. He was no longer a "boy" or "young man" in the eyes of lynchers, but rather was made abstract, a thing for consumption and punishment for its alleged transgression of white societal norms.

The violence as it is captured in the case of Jesse Washington left *The Crisis* with little rhetorical recourse. The publication had few options if it was to reinscribe Washington, and all those Black men he represented synecdochally, as a person or as people. We should not discount the rhetorical force of critical description in this moment. A Northern publication, and a Black Northern publication at that, called into question a white Southern identity organized around anti-Black violence by revealing its underlying scripts and refuting them. It of course sought recognition of lynching as a national crime, but it did so by describing events as they unfolded in Waco and across the South, arguing "the civilization of America is at stake. The sincerity of Christianity is challenged" ("The Waco Horror" 8).

Conclusion, or the Limits and Lessons of Critical Description

In the case of Jesse Washington, *The Crisis*'s use of critical description challenged the dominant racial scripts of the era, namely those that relied on racial abstraction to define Black people, particularly Black men, as savage threats to the sanctity of white society. It was only under that definition that whiteness and its attendant racist practices could cohere. Abstraction made rhetorical space for whiteness. *The Crisis*, however, recognized the necessity of describing Jesse Washington and others as human, of peeling back those scripts that white supremacy, as the primary organizational paradigm of American life, had imposed upon them. Through critical description, the publication de-scripted.

While critical description has the potential to operate as a challenge to the hegemony of white supremacist racial abstraction, there is an ethical concern critics must also consider, particularly those who, like me, identify as cis-het white men. The common question of whether it is ethical to tell stories that do not belong to you applies here, but even more potent is the question of how much description is too much description, even as it is put to a critical end. This is an impossible question to answer, and we should not pretend that critical description as a method is not without its limits. Recall, though, that critical description is not merely describing for description's sake. It must "escape the ahistorical collapse into whiteness" (Davis et al. 351). Put differently, critical description must strive to not reproduce "the spectacular nature of Black suffering and, conversely, the dissimulation of suffering through spectacle" (Hartman 22).

This need permits three questions, which may appear obvious given the state of rhetorical criticism today. Critics engaging in or identifying critical description would do well to foreground the following:

1. How is a particular artifact or text limited or precluded by the prevailing social scripts or ideological conditions of its context?
2. How might critics go about understanding the rhetorical implications of this artifact apart from those logics? That is, does this artifact adhere to different epistemological or ontological scripts?
3. How must criticism adjust to take seriously and amplify the alternative histories, modes of being, and/or narratives of this artifact?

These questions are not meant to be an all-inclusive list of considerations for critical description, but rather as a starting point for further conversation and critique.

There are two major assertions this essay hopes will inspire important and productive conversations around critical description as method. First, description is and always has been an incisive critical method for those denied access to more "rational" discursive avenues. It can operate as a counterforce to racial abstraction, and it is useful in asserting counter memories, counter histories, and the right to live. Second, as it appeared in the case of Jesse Washington, critical description gave *The Crisis* the tools necessary to make sense of Washington's lynching and insist upon his humanity. It de-scripted and allowed the publication to question the legitimacy of white Southern society's organizing paradigms. It contested the coherence of whiteness as Wacoans, as Southerners, as Americans knew it, and it did so by being intentional in identifying and peeling back the dominant social scripts of the region and nation, those that required racial abstraction for white society and its norms to make sense.

Works Cited

Davis, Patricia, et al. "Decolonizing Regions." *Rhetoric & Public Address*, vol. 24, no. 1/2, 2021, pp. 349–64.

Dray, Phillip. *At the Hands of Persons Unknown: The Lynching of Black America*. Random House, 2002.

Dyer, Richard. *White*. Routledge, 1997.

Finnegan, Cara A. "Studying Visual Modes of Public Address: Lewis Hine's Progressive-Era Child Labor Rhetoric." *The Rhetoric of Handbook and Public Address*, edited by Shawn J. Parry-Giles and J. Michael Hogan, Blackwell Publishing, 2010, pp. 250–70.

—. "What Is This a Picture Of?: Some Thoughts on Images and Archives." *Rhetoric and Public Affairs*, vol. 9, no. 1, 2006, pp. 116–23.

Hartman, Saidiya. *Scenes of Subjection: Terror, Slavery, and Self-Making in Nineteenth-Century America*. Oxford UP, 1997.

Hauser, Gerard A. "Empiricism, Description, and the New Rhetoric." *Philosophy and Rhetoric*, vol. 5, no. 1, 1972, pp. 24–44.

Houck, Davis W. "Textual Recovery, Textual Discovery: Returning to Our Past, Imagining Our Future." *The Handbook of Rhetoric and Public Address*, edited by Shawn J. Parry-Giles and J. Michael Hogan, Blackwell Publishing, 2010, pp. 111–32.

Jack, Jordynn. "A Pedagogy of Sight: Microscopic Vision in Robert Hooke's *Micrographia*." *Quarterly Journal of Speech*, vol. 95, no. 2, 2009, pp. 192–209.

Kaszynski, Elizabeth. "'Look, a [Picture]!' Visuality, Race, and What We Do Not See." *Quarterly Journal of Speech* 102, no. 1, 2016, pp. 62–78.

Marriott, David. "Judging Fanon." *Rhizomes*, vol. 29, 2016, www.rhizomes.net/issue29/marriott.html, Accessed 3 April 2022.

Mbembe, Achille. *Out of the Dark Night: Essays on Decolonization*. Columbia UP, 2021.

McKerrow, Raymie E. "Critical Rhetoric: Theory and Praxis." *Communication Monographs*, vol. 56, no. 2, 1989, pp. 91–111.

Nakayama, Thomas K., and Robert L. Krizek. "Whiteness: A Strategic Rhetoric." *Quarterly Journal of Speech*, vol. 81, no. 3, 1995, pp. 291–309.

Raiford, Leigh. "*Burning All Illusion*: Abstraction, Black Life, and the Unmaking of White Supremacy." *Art Journal*, vol. 79, no. 4, 2020, http://artjournal.collegeart.org/?p=15113, Accessed 3 April 2022

Sharpe, Christina. *In the Wake: On Blackness and Being*. Duke UP, 2016.

SoRelle, James M. "The 'Waco Horror': The Lynching of Jesse Washington." *Southwestern Historical Quarterly*, vol. 86, no. 4, 1983, 517–36.

Tell, Dave. *Remembering Emmett Till*. U of Chicago P, 2019.

VanHaitsma, Pamela. "Between Archival Absence and Information Abundance: Reconstructing Sallie Holley's Abolitionist Rhetoric Through Digital Surrogates and Metadata." *Quarterly Journal of Speech*, vol. 106, no. 1, 2020, pp. 25–47.

"The Waco Horror." *The Crisis*, July 1916, 1–8.

Walcott, Ronaldo. "The Problem of the Human: Black Ontologies and 'the Coloniality of Our Being.'" *Postcoloniality—Decoloniality—Black Critique: Joints and Fissures*, edited by Sabine Broeck and Carsten Junker, Campus Verlag, 2014, pp. 93–105.

Wilderson III, Frank B. *Afropessimism*. Liveright, 2020.

Wolters, Wendy. "Without Sanctuary: Bearing Witness, Bearing Whiteness." *JAC*, vol. 24, no. 2, 2004, pp. 399–425.

5 Slavery Was Never "Kindly Intentioned": Exposing the Entirely Hidden Role of a White Editor Who Blotted Malcolm X's Identity

Keith D. Miller

Abstract

Long hidden from researchers, a chapter draft for *The Autobiography of Malcolm X* features Malcolm X's handwritten condemnation of a judge for enacting "Nothing but legal, modern slavery!" Appending three words, a previously well-concealed white editor created the phrase, "Nothing but legal, modern slavery—however kindly intended." Passing through all editorial filters, this totally illogical, utterly repugnant statement surfaced in the final text of *Autobiography*, demonstrating that Malcolm X lost control over this part of the book. The conclusion narrates a late-in-life epiphany that spurred him to drop Black Nationalism and embrace Gandhian nonviolence and integration. Thorough, painstaking examination of chapter drafts, editorial correspondence, and literally hundreds of his own handwritten pages would resolve the question of the authorship. Until such an investigation occurs, no one can know whether the final chapters reveal his later identity or mangle it, as an editor did in the telltale sentence in Chapter 1.

Attributed to Malcolm X and his collaborator, Alex Haley, *The Autobiography of Malcolm X* became a blockbuster best-seller, reshaped perceptions of the fierce Black radical, and impacted millions of Americans' conceptions of race. The book is generally regarded as his premier rhetorical expression and lasting philosophical legacy. As Robert Terrill accurately stated in 2010, the now-classic work lies "at the center for all studies of Malcolm X" ("Introduction" 3).

Yet the authorship of *The Autobiography of Malcolm X* has never been clarified. Pointing to Malcolm X as the writer, the first edition failed to list Haley's name on the cover.[2] Following the title of the book, several scholars name Malcolm X as the author.[3] Rodnell Collins, Malcolm Jarvis, and others who knew Malcolm X seem to assume that he generated *Autobiography*, with unspecified assistance from Haley.

Decorated researchers, however, provide nuanced accounts. In a Pulitzer Prize-winning biography of 2011, Manning Marable discusses "Malcolm's autobiography" but also declares that Haley "coauthored" the volume."[4] In a biography that received a National Book Award in 2020 and a Pulitzer Prize in 2021, Les Payne and Tamara Payne repeatedly assert that Malcolm X "wrote" portions of the book while simultaneously designating Haley as the "co-writer" and "coauthor."[5] Like other scholars, Marable and Payne and Payne don't attempt to distinguish specific contributions by Malcolm X or Haley, largely because early drafts of the book's chapters were unavailable for study until 2018. Lacking access to these drafts, researchers haven't even begun to examine—or even wonder about—the editors' possible impact on the text.

Here I maintain that a never-before-cited editor converted one of Malcolm X's wholly logical sentences into an extremely illogical one that never spilled from the Black militant's mouth, pen, or typewriter, yet survived several layers of editorial filters to surface in the final text of *The Autobiography of Malcolm X*. I contend that, by itself, the presence of that dubious sentence problematizes the assumption that the work serves as Malcolm X's most crucial rhetorical and philosophical bequest. Further, that single, absurd sentence spotlights the need to determine who controlled the book, including its final chapters, which present a huge self-transformation during his pilgrimage to Mecca. I conclude by advocating archival research as a necessary method for unmasking the identity of well-hidden white editors masquerading as African American writers.

The book began when, after Haley interviewed Malcolm X for *Playboy* magazine in early 1963, the two men signed a contract with Doubleday, a hugely successful trade press. At that time the militant orator served as the top national spokesperson for the Nation of Islam (NOI), a Black separat-

---

2. For a photo of the cover of the first edition, see Abernethy 88.

3. See, e.g. Tyner 1; DeCaro 158; Dyson 55, 134.

4. Marable, *Malcolm X* 7, 9, 23, 28, 51.

5. For Malcolm X "wrote," see Payne and Payne 71, 72, 94, 130, 139, 153, 161, 169, 170, 173, 181, 206, 212, 282. For Haley as "co-writer" and "coauthor," see Payne and Payne 131, 150, 225, 384.

ist organization espousing the doctrine that all whites were literally devils. Obviously, the entirely white team of Doubleday editors who worked on the book, including its highly regarded editor-in-chief, Kenneth McCormick, did not view themselves as Satanic. For that reason, for months after the contract was signed, Malcolm X and the editors gazed at each other across a deep philosophical chasm. In addition, far from sympathizing with Malcolm X's Black Nationalism, Haley regarded the NOI as a hate-fueled organization comparable to the Nazis in Germany (Haley and Balk).

When Malcolm X visited Haley's apartment in Greenwich Village and related his life story, Haley took notes and later assembled a plot. After initially drafting several chapters of the narrative, the as-told-to collaborator handed these typed early drafts to someone who is never acknowledged in *The Autobiography of Malcolm X* and whose participation in the book-building process has never previously been noticed. Murray Fisher, a white, racially moderate editor at *Playboy*, handwrote his views on the drafts.[6]

Hidden for more than fifty years before finally landing at the Schomburg Center, these drafts feature Fisher's large, block, capital letters that form words in the left margin imploring Malcolm X to reconfigure passages. For example, in the Draft of Chapter Two, Fisher emphatically disapproved of the dissident's Black Nationalist interpretation of his boyhood: "AFTER PAGES OF SMOOTH-FLOWING NARRATIVE, THIS IS A JARRING AND SHRILL NOTE OF ROTE-RECITED SPEECHIFYING." Fisher also entreated: "UNDILUTED, THIS SOUNDS LIKE A MUSLIM LITANY, NOT A SPONTANEOUS BELIEVABLE STATEMENT IN AN OTHERWISE NONPONTIFICAL AUTOBIOGRAPHY."

The outspoken editor even tried to persuade Malcolm X to reject the core NOI doctrine of racial separation. In this early, typed draft of Chapter Two, the narrator describes his own failed attempts to assimilate into whiteness, then contends that racial integration will never work because African Americans could never become white. Fisher remonstrated: "NOT AS LONG

---

6. Draft of Chapter 2. Haley handwrote emendations on some chapter drafts, using his readily identifiable, small, cursive script, almost always in green ink and never in the left margins—a sharp contrast to the large, block, capital letters in the left margins that rebuke Malcolm X. In his "Acknowledgements" page for *Roots*, Haley credits Fisher for helping draft portions of that book; Haley's biographer, Norrell, finds Fisher "an overbearing and interfering man who exceeded the bounds of an editor" (135) while working on *Roots*—a description that fits the editor who chastised Malcolm X. Fisher states that he helped edit *Autobiography* (x). The person who scolds Malcolm X in the left margin refers knowingly to working with Haley and the militant on the *Playboy* interview. The only sensible conclusion is that Fisher wrote the lines that I ascribe to him.

AS YOU CALL INTEGRATION TRYING TO BE WHITE RATHER THAN JUST GETTING ALONG WITH THEM. IN THE LIGHT OF RECENT INSIGHTS, IS THIS STILL THE WAY YOU FEEL?"

After Fisher finished his pleading, Malcolm X received the draft. Although the Pan-Africanist chose not to handwrite any response to Fisher's exhortations, he *did* pick up a red pen and, using his fairly small, readily identifiable, cursive script, handwrote his own emendations on some early chapter drafts.[7]

In Haley's typed draft of Chapter One, the narrator recalls the abrupt, gruesome death of his father, Earl Little, when he—Malcolm—was six years old. As the chapter continues, the narrator explains the horrific impact of that catastrophe on the now-impoverished family and white officials' decision to dispatch his widowed mother, Louise Little, into a psychiatric hospital. The narrator then spotlights one person's power over his family: "A Judge McClellan in Lansing . . . had authority over me and all of my brothers and sisters. We were 'state children,' court wards; he had the full say-so over us." Reading these typed sentences, Malcolm X reached for his red pen and handwrote an extra line (which I italicize below) to express the utter disgust and loathing that he and his siblings felt toward Judge McClellan (Russell): "A Judge McClellan in Lansing . . . had authority over me and all of my brothers and sisters. We were 'state children,' court wards; he had the full say-so over us, *a white man in charge of a black man's children! Nothing but legal, modern slavery!*" After the dissenter added the line that excoriated the judge, Fisher returned to the manuscript, read Malcolm X's new, handwritten phrase, then appended three words, which I italicize and underline: "A Judge McClellan in Lansing had authority over me and all of my brothers and sisters. We were 'state children,' court wards; he had the full say-so over us, *a white man in charge of a black man's children! Nothing but legal modern slavery, <u>however kindly intended</u>*. By appending the phrase "*<u>however kindly intended</u>*," Fisher created a self-contradictory statement that simultaneously damns and compliments the judge. Even more absurdly, this sentence transformed Malcolm X's unequivocal denunciation into the totally illogical and egregiously false claim that a form of slavery was "kindly intended."

As amended, first by Malcolm X, then by Fisher, this revised passage slipped through all editorial filters—of two publishing houses—before surfacing in the final text as "A Judge McClellan had authority over me and all of my brothers and sisters. We were 'state children,' court wards; he had the

---

7. Malcolm X consistently used the same cursive script in many manuscripts archived at the Schomburg Center.

full say-so over us. A white man in charge of a black man's children! Nothing but legal, modern slavery, however kindly intentioned" (*Autobiography* 21).

On hundreds of occasions, the Black Nationalist condemned slavery in the strongest possible terms. For that reason, no one even remotely familiar with him could possibly believe that he would *ever* utter or write such a preposterous sentence. By creating this extremely peculiar and disturbing statement, Fisher functioned as a never-acknowledged co-author of Chapter One, a co-author who blotted the rhetoric and the identity of Malcolm X.

Consider the order of the emendations on the draft of Chapter One: first, Fisher; second, Malcolm X; third, Fisher. Surprisingly, Malcolm X never handwrote any comments *after* Fisher created the hugely incongruous sentence—a clear indication that the militant never scrutinized the draft after Fisher's second intervention. Nor did Malcolm X ever veto the disturbing statement at any later time. *His failure to do so demonstrates that he lost control over at least this part of the book.*

To examine the final eighteen months of the life of the Pan-Africanist— the time in which *The Autobiography of Malcolm X* was being composed—is to uncover one likely reason: he regularly hopscotched the nation to deliver addresses and spent almost six months crisscrossing the Middle East and Africa. Instead of laboring on the book, he produced a travel diary. Had he wanted to, he could have easily generated an outstanding autobiography without any collaborator at all. Instead, he preferred to reach far-flung audiences in person while relying on his stellar strengths from the podium.

Consider the initial publication date of *The Autobiography of Malcolm X*—eight months after Malcolm X's assassination. Given his itinerant life, devotion to oral performance, and all-too-sudden death, it seems extremely likely that he never painstakingly examined *any* later draft of Chapter One and, therefore, never had the opportunity to veto the bizarre sentence.

A serious question arises: did he carefully scrutinize and endorse later drafts of *other* chapters? During years of repeatedly combing through Malcolm X-related and Haley-related archives at Schomburg Center, Library of Congress, Columbia University, New York University, University of Tennessee, and Syracuse University, I never encountered any *later* drafts of any chapters bearing the radical's own emendations. Nor, after years of poring over Malcolm X-related scholarship, have I ever read any account that mentions or cites such drafts.

The absence of such manuscripts underscores the importance of re-evaluating the final two chapters of the volume, which spotlight the dissenter's pilgrimage to Mecca in 1964. According to the concluding segments, he experienced an epiphany while meeting pilgrims of every ethnicity, including whites, and recognized their sincere devotion to Sunni Islam and utter lack of racism—an experience that, the chapters indicate, persuaded him to abandon racial separatism and Pan-Africanism in favor of Gandhian nonviolence and racial equality. But did he actually compose—or, at the very least, endorse—these chapters? Or did someone else create them without his knowledge, just as someone else mangled and muffled his invective against the judge?

In addition to the preposterous sentence, his overloaded travel schedule, and the absence of documentation demonstrating his scrutiny of later chapter drafts, other evidence suggests that he may have not have carefully examined or approved the final two chapters. Two days *after* the assassination, a Doubleday employee telegrammed editor-in-chief McCormick to ask whether the book was finished (Lusty). In reply McCormick declared that Haley had not yet submitted the closing chapters.

When McCormick donated his voluminous editorial correspondence to the Library of Congress in 1992, he wrote an "Introductory Note" to the file of each of his authors, including one for Haley, but none for Malcolm X. In his note for Haley, the veteran editor oddly deems *The Autobiography of Malcolm X* to be Haley's "biography" of Malcolm X. Containing an extensive, lengthy correspondence between himself (and other Doubleday editors) and Haley, the file surprisingly lacks any letters between the Black radical and anyone at Doubleday and even lacks any suggestion that anyone at Doubleday ever talked to Malcolm X about the content of *The Autobiography of Malcolm X.*

Inasmuch as McCormick apparently communicated exclusively with Haley, the editor-in-chief's telegram indicates that he—McCormick—did not know whether Malcolm X served as the source of the last two chapters, which, two days after the assassination, McCormick had yet to receive.

Those chapters convinced millions of readers that Malcolm X and Martin Luther King Jr. merged philosophically; many historians, including the highly regarded Peniel Joseph in 2020, have reiterated that claim. If Malcolm X did carefully examine and approve those chapters, then he did drop his Black Nationalist and Pan-Africanist philosophy and did become a Gandhian and an integrationist, thereby converging ideologically with King, Fannie Lou Hamer, and other mainstream civil rights leaders, just as Joseph and others maintain.

On the other hand, recalling conversations with Malcolm X shortly before the assassination (and months after the pilgrimage), Jan Carew records the firebrand declaring that he was "carrying on the work" of his parents, who were disciples of Marcus Garvey, the leading Black Nationalist and Pan-Africanist of their era (89). Further, Malcolm X's own disciple, Herman Ferguson, who closely associated with the Black dissenter during months after Mecca, declares that his exemplar never disavowed Black Nationalism.

A final answer to the question of who wrote *The Autobiography of Malcolm X* would result from a painstaking examination of all drafts of the book (archived at the Schomburg Center and at Syracuse University); all related editorial correspondence (housed at the Library of Congress, Syracuse University, and the University of Tennessee); all the speeches, interviews, and articles that he generated after the pilgrimage (stored at the above archives, Columbia University, and elsewhere); and all interviews with family members and close associates.

Inasmuch as Malcolm X would neither write nor endorse a sentence claiming that some form of slavery was "kindly intentioned," researchers must determine the actual authorship of the renowned volume by exhaustively investigating treasure chests of primary sources held in far-flung repositories. By revealing the authorship, such a probe would inform the nation whether Malcolm X actually shed his earlier stance and converged philosophically with King or whether his identity was blotted in the final two chapters, just as it was blotted in the telltale sentence of Chapter One.

During the 1980s, Jean Fagan Yellin spent years conducting intensive archival research related to *Incidents in the Life of a Slave Girl* (1861), a narrative that was pervasively deemed a novel generated by Lydia Maria Child, a well-known white writer. Fortified by her thorough understanding of germane manuscripts, Yellin demonstrated conclusively that Harriet Jacobs, a formerly enslaved African American, wrote that book as her autobiographical testament, with Child as her editor. Without Yellin's praiseworthy archival research, Jacobs' voice and identity would have remained buried and unknown.

Rhetorical scholars should join Yellin in treating archival research as an indispensable methodology. As Valerie Palmer-Mehta explains, ". . . archival resilience creates a record of marginalized lives . . . despite a hostile, disconfirming culture" (292). Malcolm X's editors presented him with such a culture. As a result, not even the most laureled researchers can accurately determine who created most of *The Autobiography of Malcolm X*. But a thorough exploration of hundreds of salient, archived manuscripts would resolve the question of authorship and thereby illuminate the radical's final months.

Until that happens, any effort to discern Malcolm X's identity after Mecca will prove fruitless. And anyone who announces that identity will be whistling in the wind.

Works Cited

Abernethy, Graeme. *The Iconography of Malcolm X*. U of Kansas P, 2013.

Carew, Jan. *Ghosts in Our Blood*. Lawrence Hill, 1994.
Collins, Rodnell (with Peter Bailey). *Seventh Child*. Kensington, 1998.
Draft of Chapter One of *The Autobiography of Malcolm X*. Malcolm X Manuscripts. Schomburg Center. MG 951, Box 1.
Draft of Chapter Two of *The Autobiography of Malcolm X*. Malcolm X Manuscripts. Schomburg Center. MG 951, Box 1.
DeCaro, Louis. *Malcolm and the Cross*. New York UP, 1998.
Dyson, Michael Eric. *Making Malcolm*. Oxford UP, 1996.
Ferguson, Herman. "Herman Ferguson Interview." Manning Marable. In *The Portable Malcolm X*. Ed. Manning Marable and Garrett Felber. Penguin. 437–465.
Fisher, Murray. "Introduction." *Alex Haley: The Playboy Interviews*. Ballantine. 1993.
Haley, Alex. "Acknowledgements." *Roots*. Doubleday, 1976.
Haley, Alex and Alfred Balk. "Black Merchants of Hate." *Saturday Evening Post*, January 26, 1963. alexhaley.com/2018/08/06/black-merchants-of-hate.
Jacobs, Harriet. *Incidents in the Life of a Slave Girl*. 1861. Ed. Jean Fagan Yellin. Harvard UP, 1987.
Jarvis, Malcolm (with Paul Nichols). *The Other Malcolm—"Shorty" Jarvis*. Ed. Cornel West. McFarland, 2001.
Joseph, Peniel. *The Sword and the Shield*. Basic, 2020.
Lusty, Bob. Telegram to Kenneth McCormick. 23 February 1965. Box 44, Folder 9. Alex Haley File. McCormick Collection, Library of Congress. Washington, D.C. Accessed 14 July 2021.
Malcolm X. *The Autobiography of Malcolm X: As Told to Alex Haley*. Grove, 1965.
Marable, Manning. *Malcolm X*. Viking, 2011.
McCormick, Kenneth. "Introductory Note" 1992. Box 44, Folder 9. Alex Haley File.
McCormick Collection, Library of Congress, Washington, D.C. Accessed 14 July 2021.
McCormick, Kenneth. Telegram to Bob Lusty. 23 February 1965. Box 44, Folder 9. Alex Haley File. McCormick Collection, Library of Congress, Washington, D.C. Accessed 14 July 2021.
Norrell, Robert. *Alex Haley and the Books That Changed America*. St. Martin's, 2015.
Palmer-Mehta, Valerie. "'It's the Truth about Women—That We Get Lost': Andrea Dworkin, Public Memory, and Archival Resilience." *Quarterly Journal of Speech*, vol. 108, no. 3, June 28, 2022. 292–316. DOI: 10.1080/00335630.2022.2038839.
Payne, Les and Tamara Payne. *The Dead Are Arising*. Liveright, 2020.
Russell, Jessica. *The Life of Louise Norton Little*. Amazon Digital Services, 2021.
Terrill, Robert. "Introduction." *The Cambridge Companion to Malcolm X*. Ed. Robert Terrill. Cambridge UP, 2010. 1–9.
Tyner, James. *The Geography of Malcolm X*. Routledge, 2005.
X, Malcolm. *The Diary of Malcolm X*. Ed. Herb Boyd and Ilyasah Al-Shabazz. Third World, 2014.

6 Constituting Truth and Reconciliation *Ad Bellum Purificandum*

M. Elizabeth Weiser

Abstract

In 1939, Kenneth Burke famously cautioned against a situation like one we face today, in which the idea of internal division becomes so anathema that enforced silence becomes a popular alternative. Despite today's push to ban divisive concepts in classrooms, the educational efforts of American public history museums are experiencing a surprising upsurge. New museums are countering the myth that silence promotes unity. By refusing to engage in either antithetical or placating discourses, they chart a path that centers subaltern experiences while celebrating a shared future. I consider the implications of their truth and reconciliation rhetoric by comparing the approaches taken in three museums on the aftermath of the Civil War. Two of them are purifying war through an epideictic approach to historical and present-day narratives, and I point toward the constitutive rhetoric that they are using to reshape identification with the re-visioned national narrative.

Introduction: A New National Story

Visitors entering the central hall of the National Museum of American History (NMAH) in Washington, DC expect an encomium to American heritage, and the museum therefore greets them with the giant golden flag sculpture that marks the Star-Spangled Banner exhibit. Recently, though, two newer displays complicated that monumental introduction. In the middle of the hall was a battered purple roadside marker—the bullet-ridden sign that marked the place where young Emmett Till's mutilated body was pulled from the Tallahatchie River in 1955. Signage around the artifact tied the repeatedly damaged sign to ongoing racism and anti-Black violence nationwide, and to the protestors today: "Centering Black life and protest, Black activists are not just fighting for change: they are imagining the world anew—a world where the joy of Black children like Till cannot be stomped out" (*Reckoning*). To the right of the marker, another display showcased the Wampanoag nation (the group that met the Pilgrims) and explained why each Thanksgiving they call for a Day of Mourning to highlight injustices still borne by Indigenous peoples. In case the NMAH's larger message was unclear, a column between these three displays tells visitors, "The stories of our past are more complicated than they may seem. Here we celebrate and mourn, explore and question."

The master narrative of American history has changed considerably in the past few years, and this change is not confined to the NMAH or its parent Smithsonian Institution, the world's largest complex of museums. In fact, much of this change is driven by smaller museums located in conservative cities and towns—places like Delta, Utah; Montgomery, Alabama; Tulsa, Oklahoma; or Matewan, West Virginia. These smaller, newer museums of conscience (Sevcenko 20), largely founded, staffed, or directed by people from marginalized communities, are dedicated to highlighting overlooked subaltern voices and bringing to light narratives of traumatic pasts that continue to impact an unjust present. That they are speaking with little public outcry and much public success is astonishing in today's polarized political atmosphere. By mid-2022, thirty-six state legislatures had either debated or passed laws banning "divisive concepts" in classrooms (Pendharker 8). Open discussion in public education of such issues as gender and sexuality, colonialism, or, especially, systemic racism, they say, needs to end. For these protestors and their legal and political promoters, it is knowledge of injustice, not injustice itself, that is causing our current deep polarization, and therefore silence must be its solution.

While we focus on the battles over public debate in the classroom, however, that other arena for education—the public history museum—is successfully presenting a picture of the national collective identity that counters this *knowledge is division* argument and promotes both diverse voices and an unsparing look at the traumatic moments of our collective identity. The new Legacy Museum in Montgomery, Alabama, a museum dedicated to exposing the historical connections between the mass lynching of Black people and current rates of mass incarceration, was named Alabama's Attraction of the Year in 2022 ("EJI's New"). The new Greenwood Rising Center in Tulsa,

Oklahoma, a museum commemorating a race massacre, finished seventh in a nationwide newspaper poll of best new attractions of 2021 ("Greenwood Rising"). The National Museum of African American History and Culture (NMAAHC), opened in Washington, DC, in 2016, receives about two million visitors each year, making it one of the most popular of the Smithsonian sites ("Visitor Stats"). Its founding director, Lonnie Bunch III, is now Secretary of the Smithsonian Institution and a major force in the global ethical stance of the modern museum. Museum professionals worldwide long ago decided that their institutions are not temples of knowledge but instead public forums (Cameron), and they are not neutral; they are, as the museum commonplace goes, safe places for unsafe ideas.

Truth and Reconciliation

The newly opened museums I am studying, scattered across the American hinterland, focus on truth—raising the voices of previously silenced communities—and on reconciliation—healing divisions as they place their story squarely into the mainstream of American history, asking what that past means for the collective present. I want to further examine these two terms, *truth* and *reconciliation,* whose ramifications we may not always consider as we seek to promote justice in a polarized nation. As we examine the idea of a *charge for change,* I call on its sense of "the spark that happens when two differently charged atoms [here, *truth-telling* and *reconciling*] draw near one another or when two people or groups meet, attracting through recognition and solidarity or repulsing in opposition and resistance" ("RSA Conference").

I doubt we have much difficulty with the idea that *truth* means telling the taboo stories, raising up the silenced voices. Like heritage museums everywhere, the approach taken by these new museums to truth-telling is epideictic rather than forensic—that is, they praise and condemn values rather than root out perpetrators. Instead of a retributive stance, they are purposely avoiding an antithetical Us vs. Them narrative in which They attacked Us and heroic Us fought Them off. The antithetical is a common narrative around the world, from the Oklahoma City and National 9/11 museums in the US to multiple national memory museums around the former Soviet sphere, to South American museums commemorating victims of Dirty Wars. It is a natural response: Perpetrators often position their victimized groups as Outsiders who must be eliminated from the community; later, when museums open to commemorate that atrocity, they re-position the perpetrators as the new Outsiders to be condemned as the community re-forms. As I've written elsewhere (Weiser 162–71), this is such a compelling narrative that in situations where the perpetrators come from within the community itself, they are often *linguistically* labeled Outsiders. Thus, museums in Berlin talk about Nazis, the Kigali Genocide Memorial talks about genocidaires, and museums in the US may say Confederates when they discuss the Civil War. No visitor today is a Nazi or a genocidaire or a Confederate—those are now safely historical Outsider groups: Them, not Us. Thus, the formerly oppressed group is welcomed in, but their warning that injustice is systemic and ongoing, not just the actions of some historical bad actors, is undermined by the story that all that injustice isn't who we are now.

How, then, do museums that want to break the silence over systemic injustices address these without an Us vs. Them narrative? How do they discuss injustice when it is not only committed by past-peoples who are not us but ongoing in their community? That can be divisive, making the visitor feel like Them—and none of us wants to be Them. Psychologically, we resist. Sociologically, we deny; we silence. Educationally we demand that schools don't teach it to our children. Culturally, we don't walk into that museum, if we open that museum at all—and so the truth-telling rhetoric will fail to reach its audience.

Reconciliation can also be problematic if we view reconciliation as merely papering over past injustices, silencing the traumatized. Such a stance is often demanded of subaltern victims, a problem nicely encapsulated in a recent article by Andre Johnson and Earle Fisher on the forgiveness offered by members of Mother Emanuel A.M.E. church toward white supremacist mass murderer Dylann Roof. They write: "The wider public not only expects a rhetoric of forgiveness when racial ghosts of the past (and present) manifest in ways that cause black pain but also [that] those grief-stricken black families must offer the forgiveness in non-threatening and expeditious ways that ease public consciences" (5). In other words, gestures toward truth and reconciliation become *I hurt you, now forgive me* or be seen an angry Black or Brown woman or man, along with its corollary, *why can't we all just forget and move on?*

Reconciliatory, Reconciliation, and Decolonizing Rhetorics

This is not the rhetoric of truth and reconciliation that I see being exhibited in the new museums tackling injustices. There visitors are not condemned, but they are also not coddled by forgetful silence and too-easy forgiveness. Let me demonstrate the difference in approaches with a quick comparison of the two major Civil War museums in the US: the National Civil War Museum in Harrisburg, Pennsylvania, opened in 2000, and the American Civil War Museum in Richmond, Virginia, repurposed and reopened in 2019. The older Pennsylvania museum demonstrates throughout its exhibits an attempt to reconcile with white Southerners by obscuring the truth, glossing over the atrocities underlying the war and its aftermath. It includes African Americans as sidebars to the purported national story, and therefore its version of national reconciliation can only marginalize both their suffering and their resistance. For instance, here is the museum's signage on the Lost Cause and the ongoing battle over accurate memory (*Lincoln: War & Remembrance*):

> Americans remember the Civil War in many ways. Sons and daughters of Union veterans remember the honors of their service. . . . Southerners, to this day, gaze across their landscape that was once scorched earth or a battlefield scarred by warring armies. They are the only Americans to have suffered through enforced martial law and the presence of occupation troops in their major cities.
>
> Immediately after the war, former Confederate leaders organized veterans' organizations, built monuments, and wrote partisan histories of the 'Lost Cause' . . . [W]riters of local color described a genteel, romantic way of life in which slaveowners were kind, slaves were loyal happy 'servants,' and plantations were exemplars of refinement, cultivation, and 'southern hospitality.' . . . They helped to fix a mythic image of the 'Old South' firmly in American memory and to gain a place for the South in our national heritage.

To be clear, the sign does call this *partisan* history—but they nowhere explicitly call it false, or morally indefensible, history. I would call this approach *reconciliatory*, not reconciling. Its focus on appeasement leads to exactly what Johnson and Fisher argue against—the requirement that Black America forgive and forget. Indeed, nearby signage goes on to quote out of context the pioneering Black priest Alexander Crummel to argue that "constant recollection of [slavery] would impede racial progress; instead . . . duty lies in the future." Lifelong abolitionist Crummel's audience, the first independent Black Episcopal congregation in immediate post-war Washington, DC, would have had quite a different sense of his meaning than the twenty-first century white tourist reading his one line in the museum.

Compare the NCWM's *reconciliatory* approach to the *reconciliation* approach exhibited in the newer American Civil War Museum (ACWM) in Richmond, Virginia, which aims to revise the Southern narrative of the war. This museum is a historic merger of the Museum of the Confederacy (opened 1896 to lionize the South) and the more inclusive American Civil War Center, bringing together the plethora of artifacts from the Confederacy Museum with the Center's diverse narratives and "goal of serving less as a site of reverence and more as a site of conscience and understanding," according to its former director, Christy Coleman (Oliver 2018). Its opening signage directly counters the myths of states' rights that dominate traditional white apologias for the Civil War: The nation in 1860, it says, was torn asunder by a clear binary: "Preserve the Union [or] Preserve Slavery." Unlike the older Pennsylvania museum, the Virginia museum purposely includes people of all races in its conception of Southerners, and because of this engagement with Black and Brown voices, its view is less romanticized and obscurantist. For instance, about the mythic image of the Old South it says (*A People's Contest*):

> In the Lost Cause, ex-Confederates created a history and ideology to vindicate themselves and justify their continued rule. Ex-Confederates claimed that secession had been lawful and their armies had demonstrated unsurpassed skill and courage. They also asserted that slavery had been good for black people and Reconstruction a cruel attempt at racial equality. The Lost Cause expressed itself in novels, historical works, museums, school textbooks, monuments, and art.

The Lost Cause, that is, was a created vindication of hegemony, not a mythic image—thus the museum does *not* call on African Americans to forgive and forget. Instead, it notes that defense of the Lost Cause moved "from a war of blood to a war of memory" (*A People's Contest*)—a war that the museum clearly sees itself still fighting as it strives, in this city that was the capitol of the Confederacy, to re-narrate history. That is the cultural battle for a more just reconciliation.

But there is also a decolonial battle, in which museums go beyond having the dominant story engage with marginalized voices, as the ACWM still must do as a museum *about* the war, to having those voices determine what story even needs telling. Such a determination was visible in a special exhibition, *Make Good the Promise,* in the National Museum of African American History and Culture in Washington, DC, in 2021–2022. It was an exhibition not on the Civil War itself but on Reconstruction, the period directly afterwards—the time during which four million people were suddenly able, as the exhibition put it, "to define themselves as free and equal citizens" (*Make Good*). The Lost Cause narrative paints Reconstruction as a failed experiment in Black emancipation and Northern rapaciousness. The NMAAHC exhibition re-narrated and re-documented Reconstruction as "a revolutionary political, social, and economic movement that reshaped the nation in profound and lasting ways" (*Make Good*). Black Americans made immediate material, political, educational gains that forced the nation to ask difficult, complex questions about what it meant to be a democratic land of opportunity. The nation—the white nation, focused on reconciliatory gestures to appease Southern whites—failed to answer well. The systemic nature of those failures as well as the endurance of its successes—from the rise of Jim Crow to the establishment of universal public education—meant that their legacy did not end with the death of nineteenth-century perpetrators who can be comfortably tucked into the historical-Other category. As the exhibition makes clear in its final displays of modern figures like Trayvon Martin and Stacey Abrams, those systems that killed the promise of Reconstruction are what all Americans must continue to struggle against today (*Make Good*).

Toward the Purification of War

This kind of truth-telling, which radically reframes what visitors thought they knew while linking its legacy to the present, does not call on good Us to blame bad Them, comfortable in the knowledge that we aren't like that now. As Eric Doxtader, who has spent a career studying South Africa's truth and reconciliation process, notes, reconciliation is not meant to be comfortable. Agonistic disagreement is a key trait of real reconciliation, he writes, as it involves "deliberative controversy about the form and substance of collective life" (278). That is, being willing to argue together is beneficial to communal life, as it necessarily springs from recognition that some possibility for shared agency is required, even as the co-participants disagree over what that collective life looks like.

This version of reconciliation does not respond to divisive concepts by refusing to discuss the concepts. It is instead closer to Kenneth Burke's democratic answer to totalitarianism in "The Rhetoric of Hitler's 'Battle'"—the celebration of agonistic debate. Burke writes, "For the parliament, at its best, is a 'babel' of voices. There is the wrangle of men representing interests lying awkwardly on the bias across one another, sometimes opposing, sometimes vaguely divergent" (7). Hitler named the "wrangle of the parliament" a serious problem of internal division, and he proposed to replace it "by the giving of *one* voice to the whole people, this to be the 'inner voice' of Hitler" (12). Burke saw Hitler's dismissal of the parliament as a cautionary tale for America, not unlike today's cautionary tales of the one voice of a Vladimir Putin or Donald Trump. Burke recognized in 1939 something we also see: the babel isn't pretty, and "people so dislike the idea of internal division that . . . their dislike can easily be turned against the man or group who would so much as *name* it, let alone proposing to act upon it" (11). Those echoes persist in today's divisive concepts legislation, but the wrangling parliament, for Burke, was the place of ultimate good, the antidote to war. Arguing together is *ad bellum purificandum*, the purification of war that moves it from physical destruction to the higher plane of debate—and from there, he hoped, through rhetoric to more effective debate. That is the kind of truth and reconciliation needed for restorative justice. As Bryan Stevenson, founding director of the Legacy Museum, tells visitors, "It is hard to confront these painful truths. But the powerful thing is when we have the courage to learn the truth, we open up doors that permit justice, that permit reckoning, that permit healing" ("Visit").

For this healing in the public sphere to be effective, however, the arguers need to be *open* to the possibilities for a shared future, as Doxtader points out. This is where public history museums, with their inspirational rhetoric of confronting the truth together, play a particularly important role. Somehow, these sites are successfully introducing so-called divisive concepts of systemic injustice into communities that are often quite conservative. It is true that theirs is a voluntary audience—people choose to walk into a museum on a race massacre or miners' wars. But why are people willing to have their unexamined beliefs challenged? Why are they willing to stand shoulder to shoulder and experience this challenge with strangers whose ancestors might have oppressed them, or been oppressed by them? Why are they willing to listen to views that had long been denied a voice? I would argue that the selection, arrangement, and narration in a museum work in combination to *constitute* the necessary open-minded audience. As Michael McGee writes, the rhetor "dangles a dramatic vision" before the audience that responds to it (239). Maurice Charland adds that that audience is narratologically constituted: "In telling the story of a *peuple,* a [collective] *peuple* comes to be" (140). In a museum, once I choose to voluntarily enter and learn something about interment or removal or lynching, I am confronted by sensory and narrative data drawing me into the dramatic story, in the presumption that I will be the kind of person who *wants* to know more. There is an illusion of freedom in this constitutive rhetoric, Charland notes, as rhetors speak of the people as a freely chosen entity while declaring that they are bound to fulfill a historical destiny (140–41). I become bound by the spatial arrangement of the museum itself to walk through, considering fresh ideas with the rest of the people who are all around me, doing the same, all of us constituted by the rhetoric of museums. I think of Chelsea Milbourne and Sarah Hallenbeck's idea of material chronotopes that orient users in space-time through the particulars of their material-rhetorical arrangements, which in this case are the sights/sounds/stories of moving through a museum exhibition. Charland notes that such rhetoric is action-oriented (143); Carolyn Miller argues that the action it produces is constrained by certain conditions and made possible by others (qtd. in Milbourne and Hallenbeck 405).

In other words, we open our minds to new ideas in a museum because that is how we embody what the time and place of the museum visitor experience demands of us. In these museums of conscience, which often end with a question to the visitor ("How would you reconstruct America?" in the NMAAHC exhibition), we are then reconstituted through epideictic education into a people less afraid of divisive concepts, and we are charged to act, carrying that new identity out of the material setting and back into a world that—if the argument is successful—we continue to reconstitute into a more reconciling nation, *ad bellum purificandum*.

Works Cited

Burke, Kenneth. "The Rhetoric of Hitler's 'Battle.'" *Southern Review*, vol. 5, 1939, pp. 1–21.

Cameron, Duncan. "The Museum, a Temple or the Forum." *Curator*, vol. 14, no. 1, March 1971, pp. 11–24. doi.org/10.1111/j.2151–6952.1971.tb00416.x.

Charland, Maurice. "Constitutive Rhetoric: The Case of the Peuple Québécois." *Quarterly Journal of Speech*, vol. 73, no. 2, 1987, pp. 133–50.

Doxtader, Eric. "Reconciliation – A Rhetorical Concept/ion." *Quarterly Journal of Speech*, vol. 89, no. 4, 2003, pp. 267–92.

Johnson, Andre E., & Fisher, Earle J. "'But, I Forgive You?' Mother Emanuel, Black Pain and the Rhetoric of Forgiveness." *Journal of Communication and Religion*, vol. 42, no. 1, 2019, pp. 5–19.

"EJI's New Legacy Museum Named Alabama Tourism's 2022 Attraction of the Year." *Equal Justice Initiative*, 12 Jan. 2022, eji.org/news/ejis-new-legacy-museum-named-alabama-tourisms-2022-attraction-of-the-year/.

"Greenwood Rising Is No. 7 on USA Today's Best New Attractions List." *Greenwood Rising*, 5 Jan. 2022, greenwoodrising.org/news-1/greenwood-rising-nominated-for-usa-todays-best-new-attraction-in-the-country.

McGee, Michael C. "In Search of 'The People': A Rhetorical Alternative." *The Quarterly Journal of Speech*, vol. 61, 1975, pp. 235–49.

Lincoln: War & Remembrance. Permanent exhibition, National Civil War Museum, Harrisburg, PA.

Make Good the Promises: Reconstruction and Its Legacies. 1 June 2021–21 Aug. 2022, National Museum of African American History and Culture, Washington, DC.

McGee, Michael C. "In Search of 'The People': A Rhetorical Alternative." *The Quarterly Journal of Speech*, vol. 61, 1975, pp. 235–49.

Milbourne, Chelsea Redeker, and Sarah Hallenbeck. "Gender, Material Chronotopes, and the Emergence of the Eighteenth-Century Microscope." *Rhetoric Society Quarterly*, vol. 43, no. 5, 2013, pp. 401–24.

Oliver, Ned. "In the Former Confederate Capital, There's No Longer a Museum of the Confederacy." *Virginia Mercury*, 2 Oct. 2018, www.virginiamercury.com/2018/10/02/in-the-former-capital-of-the-confederacy-theres-no-longer-a-museum-of-the-confederacy/. Accessed 5 Jan. 2023.

Pendharkar, Eesha. "Efforts to Ban Critical Race Theory Now Restrict Teaching for a Third of America's Kids." *Education Week*, vol. 41, no. 21, Feb. 2022, p. 8.

A People's Contest: Struggles for Nation and Freedom in Civil War America. Permanent exhibition. American Civil War Museum, Richmond, VA.
Reckoning with Remembrance: History, Injustice, and the Murder of Emmett Till. 3 Sept.–2 Nov. 2021, National Museum of American History, Washington, DC.
"RSA Conference." *Rhetoric Society of America*, rhetoricsociety.org/aws/RSA/pt/sp/conference. Accessed 31 August 2022.
Sevcenko, Liv. "Sites of Conscience: New Approaches to Conflicted Memory." *Museum International*, vol. 62, no. 1–2, 2010, pp. 20–25.
Stevenson, Bryan. "Visit the Legacy Museum." *YouTube,* uploaded by Equal Justice Initiative, 3 March 2022, youtu.be/GEXTR5rOpDI. Accessed 3 Jan. 2023.
"Visitor Stats." *Smithsonian*, Smithsonian Institution, July 2022, si.edu/newsdesk/about/stats. Accessed 5 Sept. 2022.
Weiser, M. Elizabeth. *Museum Rhetoric: Building Civic Identity in National Spaces.* Pennsylvania State UP, 2017.

Part II: The Pandemic, and Other Kairotic Rhetorical Concerns

7 Mapping the Rhetorical and Statistical Landscape of COVID-19 and Neoliberalism's Biopolitics

Kathryn Lambrecht

Abstract

The COVID-19 pandemic generated a vast amount of language related to risk, much of which reflected a focus on statistics, the impact of the pandemic on the economy, and the need for the government to find ways to return to normalcy. The goal of this research is to investigate the differences in risk language associated with the CDC and public health departments in the three largest US cities by population. The results show that, at multiple levels, pandemic communication focused on statistics and economic recovery, reflecting a neoliberal ideology that privileged the health of the State over the risk posed to individuals and communities. To avoid these trends in the future, risk communicators should ensure that individual safety is prioritized, outlined in clear terms, and valued above neoliberal logics guided primarily by economic considerations.

Since the early months of 2020, we have been living through a rare historical moment in which everyone—not just in our families, not just in our communities, or in the United States—but nearly everyone in the world has had to participate in risk assessment regarding a shared public health crisis. Immediate risks may not have happened on the same timeline, the consequences were not linear, and the impacts were certainly uneven, but all were impacted, nonetheless. We experienced the collective global heartbreak and exhaustion of the COVID-19 pandemic, and in many ways, we still are. As rhetoricians, we have occasion unlike we have perhaps ever had before—certainly not on this scale, not in our lifetimes—to study the way that humans communicate, organize, synthesize, and act on the rhetorics of risk, public health, and medical data. In the United States, the layers of inequity that the pandemic has laid bare—including in socioeconomic status, education, race, gender—and the neoliberal networks of ideology that sustain and entrench them, will give our field much to discuss and unpack in the years to come. In this paper, I will focus on a selection of the language that sustains those networks of ideology, specifically from the Centers for Disease Control and Prevention (CDC) and the public health departments of the three most populated cities in the US. I will argue that subject-framing, statistics, and risk assessments associated with pandemic communication reflect a deeply problematic trend of neoliberal and biopolitical discourses that prioritize individual risks that rely on capitalist logics at the cost of community safety and health.

Although individuals were given different information depending on their local environments, a framing of COVID-19 risks delivered via public health agencies in the first eighteen months of the pandemic relied on rhetorics of risk that divided populations into *healthy* versus *not healthy*—*at risk* versus *not at risk*—in ways that masked the inequities upon which these overly simplistic categories were built, and the neoliberal practices that guide them. According to Rob Asen, "Neoliberalism operates with the assumption that the market treats all actors equally; differences of race, gender, ethnicity, class, sexual orientation play no role in the behavior of market actors and their successes and failures. Incorporated into a neoliberal model of publicity, this assumption makes inequality invisible" (330–31). Because this is the assumption upon which much risk communication in the pandemic was built, the language framing the COVID-19 pandemic encouraged some individuals to assess their risk as low, allowing them to move on with their lives, secure in the idea that they would likely be fine—it was really only the elderly and the "vulnerable" who needed to worry.

Too often, what constituted vulnerability was left up to the imagination, or when vulnerability was defined, it entered the public imaginary as a condition largely linked to individual choices or conditions. This framing of subjectivity that characterized those healthy, productive members of the State as safe and deserving of "returning to normalcy" started early on in the pandemic, largely due to communications from the CDC. Building on an earlier project that discussed the role that the CDC played, this paper will layer the rhetorical strategies associated with individual cities—specifically Los

Angeles, Chicago, and New York—onto the national COVID-19 conversations about risk, revealing layers upon layers of statistics, the mathematical language of biopolitics.

CDC Communication

While the circulation of risk communication swamped citizens from many places during the acute phase of the COVID-19 pandemic, in the early days the CDC constituted the hub of communication regarding how seriously individuals should take the emerging virus. In a previous study published in the *Journal of Business and Technical Communication* special issue on "Communicating in Times of Crisis," I made the argument that communication from the CDC in the early months of the pandemic—January through April of 2020—started by framing risk subjects as belonging to a very general and abstract "public" and quickly shifted to a very specific subset of the population, making it easy to turn the page on vulnerability (Lambrecht 94). Although it was not a focus at the time of publication, in the context of neoliberalism and biopolitics this study reflects two important realities about pandemic communication: 1) the subject-framing practices early on from a national source constructed vulnerability in a very particular way that shaped the subsequent risk communication regarding the virus, and 2) these practices likely helped frame the communications that came out of public health departments.

I started my analysis of CDC pandemic communications by finding every instance of the word "risk" in the corpus of CDC documents that I collected (there were 147 such instances). I then analyzed the subjects that were attached to constructions of the term "risk" to determine who or what was at risk, and how that evolved over the first few months of the pandemic. In the month of January, nearly half of the time (47 percent), the subject of COVID-19 risk assessment was "the public" an abstract conception of individuals to stand in for a richly complex and situated public of people trying to make decisions about how to protect themselves and their families (Lambrecht 94). The phrase that the CDC repeated again and again was that the risk to the public was generally low. Unfortunately, we now know this wasn't the case. By February subjects changed from the "public" 47 percent of the time to only 14 percent of the time, and were replaced by "travelers/those who had returned from cruise ship" travel 44 percent of the time. By March, subjects that were associated with COVID-19 risk shifted again to those who were older/vulnerable nearly one third of the time. The problem with this was that the rapid escalation from a vague to specific rendering of subjects who were considered vulnerable allowed many individuals to turn the page on the true risks of COVID-19. In January, our "immediate risk" was low, in February, all was well so long as we hadn't been on a cruise, and by March, we needed only worry if we were vulnerable due to age, disease, or our own poor choices. All the while, the virus continued to circulate in our communities.

Though we were dealing with a new pathogen in a context rarely experienced, these communication trends are animated by neoliberal logics that, despite the best intentions of people who are trying to keep others safe, still prioritized the health of our economic system, the prosperity of our nation constituted by wealth and business as usual over proceeding with caution in light of a dangerous new illness. An example of this is reflected in every statement made by a politician who reflects back on this time with the sentiment that they didn't want to cause panic. From a biopolitical point of view, this is another way of saying that they didn't want to disrupt the economy and destabilize the system. This is not to say that there was not a monumental effort to keep people safe in ways that have shifted the way that our economy looks, perhaps indefinitely. It is to say, however, that vulnerability to the pathogen early on in the pandemic was likely influenced by the need to protect the system first, and individuals second. While there was a confluence of factors that shaped the pandemic, this rhetorical choice came at a high cost, and played a role in creating the conditions that led to a tremendous loss to human life. Recognizing that cost now might lead to a re-balancing of priorities when the next "unknowns" to our health emerge.

Public Health Department Communication

While CDC communication represents one part of an early chapter of COVID-19 risk communication in the pandemic, we can also trace how this framing filtered into communication for months to come when we consider state-level health departments. Building on the CDC study, I collected a corpus of public health communications from January 2020 through June 2021 (eighteen months of data) from the three largest cities by population. These cities are 1) regionally diverse (one west coast, one mid-west, one east coast), and 2) linked to health organizations, funded by governments, and serving local populations. The total corpus had 220,175 words, and focused only on posts that explicitly mentioned COVID-19:

- In the case of Los Angeles, I collected press releases from the County of Los Angeles Public Health. There were 128 posts in this time, totaling 113,800 words

- In the case of Chicago, I collected news releases from the Chicago Department of Public Health. There were ninety-three posts, totaling 80,478 words.
- In New York, I collected news releases from NYC Health—or the New York City Department of Health and Mental Hygiene. There were thirty-eight posts, totaling 25,897 words.

Although this paper takes the position that an overreliance on statistics masks underlying social and economic issues, the size and scope of each corpus is important to get a sense of how distributed the amount of communication was across contexts. In the same amount of time, there were a fifth of the posts in one city compared to the rest, and the numbers range from 25,000 to over 100,000. This is not an even sample, even if it is bounded by the same time constraints, and this speaks to how varied communication from health departments was in our first year and a half of pandemic life. Also, this sample shows that individuals in large part had to figure out much on their own when it came to how to respond to the pandemic. A vast amount of numbers, visualizations, and scenarios were shared with public audiences, but the interpretation of these numbers was largely left to individuals seeking to use this data to make choices amidst extreme uncertainty.

In order to understand how communication varied from city to city, I created rhetorical profiles based on the corpora I collected from each city to compare similarities and differences across environments. I did this by combining each sub-corpora into a larger reference corpus, and then used Wordsmith tools to produce a keyword list for each city. The keyword list shows which key terms used consistently are unique to each city. For example, the terms "health" "COVID" "people" and "department" were used across all cities, so none of those terms appear on the individual keyword lists of each city. However, in Chicago "lightfoot" "guidelines" and "progress" appear as keywords because they are used often in Chicago, but not in the other cities in the reference corpus (this makes sense because Chicago's mayor was Lori Lightfoot during the pandemic). In doing this, I was able to see what terms were unique in the communications of each public health department as compared to the others. From there, I did a close reading of the content of the news releases to get a more accurate picture of what was going on in each city, to check the keyword analysis against how they bore out rhetorically. I found that while each city mirrored the subject-framing of the CDC towards individuals and away from communities, each had its own unique way of communicating in the pandemic. Guided by Foucault's notion that population statistics are a tool of governmentality that exert biopolitical control, I will share a few of the most salient details about each city to illustrate how pandemic communication erased differentiation, masking inequities in the system and protecting the economic interests of the city over the population.

Los Angeles

Across the United States, communication about COVID-19 was often about monitoring and statistics—much of what public health departments did involved collecting and sharing health data to guide public decision-making. For Los Angeles, this process was largely guided by reporting new deaths and new cases by county. Over one hundred posts in the first eighteen months end with a long list of counties reporting the new cases and deaths, along with the statistical information linked to identity regarding those deaths. In the keyword list of LA—terms that were used uniquely more by LA than anywhere else—the three most used terms were 1) deaths 2) ages and 3) died. "Protocols" and "passed" rounded out the top five terms, though "passed" in this case could refer to either death or passing tests of certain kinds associated with pandemic monitoring. In tracking the deaths and cases related to COVID-19, individuals were constantly updated in terms of changes within their counties, though it is unclear how those numbers directly translate to assessing risk, beyond a numerical estimate of changes day to day.

There are several arguments one could make about why LA County chose to communicate with the public in this way. Certainly, it gave weight to the gravity of the pandemic and the seriousness of COVID-19. There is a utility in being able to track deaths and new cases in one's own county to aid decision-making about how much spread there is currently and how this might impact one's own personal risk. However, this strategy prioritized numbers in such a way that erased the actual people that they represented. The longer the strategy of daily death reports was used, the more distanced the reality that each number represented a human, a story, and a context became. It is hard to pinpoint the day, week, or month of the pandemic that numbers stopped carrying weight—after the first case reported in a county was published? The tenth? The hundredth? In reading through the public health documents, the differentiation of cases and the humans involved gradually falls off. In the US, community members likely knew a lot about the first person in our state or city to contract COVID-19, much about the first person who died, but almost nothing about individuals as the numbers climbed. The stories associated with the numbers, and the economic realities that made some individuals more vulnerable than others, fell by the wayside in exchange for the raw data. Stories gradually became statistics, and the impact of tracking became less and less meaningful.

Chicago

In the case of Chicago, keywords highlight that the public health department focused on messaging related to the government and what it was doing to minimize impact on the community or design policy around pandemic circumstances. Rather than focus mostly on statistics, the Chicago public health department shared news about what policy makers were doing to create COVID-19 protocols (the name of the governor of Chicago along with names of organizations related to governmental organizations were among keywords in Chicago, for example). A common trend that emerged from Chicago public health department communication involved tracking how the city was managing COVID-19 so that we could have a 'return to normalcy.' Among the keywords used in Chicago were Mayor Lightfoot, guidelines, progress, commissioner, and bars/restaurants. Metrics that relied on achieving certain, often numerical, benchmarks were frequently associated with the guidelines highlighted in the press releases from City of Chicago Public Health, communicating when "normalcy" had been achieved based on what was deemed an acceptable level of risk rather than on the felt sense of risk that individuals in the community were encountering in their daily lives.

While Chicago's strategy shifts significantly from the statistical focus of LA, there remains at the heart of Chicago risk communication a deeply embedded focus on the economy and its wellness. The pandemic communication about risk in Chicago is framed around the needs of the city and the need to resume normal activities. While one could argue (and many have) that a return to normalcy is linked to a healthy and prosperous city, an overemphasis on resuming activities can lead to erasure of vulnerability, pitting the health of individuals against the economic values that urge a return to the activities that sustain capitalism. One of the rhetorical impacts of this strategy was that it positions the city and the behavior of its residents as having the opportunity to win a war against the virus. With enough vigilance on the part of individuals, those living in Chicago were sent the message that they could get their normal lives back (at least in certain cases), the process of which would be mediated through the state. This strategy of health policy based on wins and losses linked to economic activity obfuscates what happens to those whose vulnerabilities are not accounted for in what it means to win the war against a virus articulated through a neoliberal lens focused on economic health.

New York

Although the strategy in LA was stark in its focus on sharing the daily numbers in broken-record fashion, other public health departments made data available, but without including it in their news releases about the COVID-19 pandemic. In the case of New York, keywords shifted to a rhetorical strategy focused on sharing the picture of health overall in the city, which included referencing multiple public health concerns (HIV, methadone, and the flu) and how these medical issues interacted with the pandemic. While this strategy arguably relies equally on statistics in that each of these concerns is linked to community monitoring via numbers, the discussion and inclusion of statistics is framed differently in the risk communications collected from New York. Of the three cities, New York paid the most attention to context, making many posts about the overlapping conditions and positionalities that contributed to a risk assessment designed to take into account more than one factor. Among the keywords for New York were "flu" "children" "HIV" "methadone" and "care." While these results do not alone suggest a revolutionary new approach to risk communication during the pandemic, it is an interesting contrast to terms like "death" and "died" that were highlighted in LA.

If LA had a strong focus on statistics, New York perhaps took an approach that broadened what is meant to be vulnerable, where to get resources, and how to care for one's family, at least from the set of risk communication examples collected in this case. The communications from New York seemed to focus energy on how to think through the pandemic as one health factor in a larger set of considerations. This broader approach could create more room for public action that connects individuals to a larger community—one trying to protect itself from a multiplicity of linked health concerns, representing many versions of what health could look like. This strategy that focuses on community could get closer to communicating the idea that "there is no singular, universal public good, but multiple articulations of a public good" (Asen 331). While there are still plenty of cautions about risk and individual concerns, communications from the New York City Department of Health and Mental Hygiene were less focused on statistics, and more distributed across different versions of what maintaining health looks like for the community overall. In this case, COVID-19 was treated as one puzzle piece in a larger picture of what constituted risk.

Conclusion

The communication of risk during the outbreak of a new virus, particularly one that caused the level of loss in its wake that COVID-19 did, is a complicated, messy, and constantly shifting task. There is no perfect way to communicate risk to keep everyone safe; rather, our goal should be to communicate in a way that prioritizes our humanity as much as possible.

At a time when we most needed to stay connected to each other, neoliberal frameworks linked to numerical estimates of risk rather than the narratives and experiences of our communities likely served to distance us. Relying on statistical language to communicate something that can never be as neatly captured as a number will always mean that the least tidy parts of who we are—those that highlight vulnerability and inequality—will be lost and subsumed under a capitalist ideal of the healthy community member contributing to a normal, functioning economy. An overreliance on numbers trades off with the more relatable narratives of how individuals and communities make decisions that strive to account for all, rather than some. Between the CDC and the health departments discussed here, the central strategy for communicating COVID-19 largely focused on numbers—of tests, of deaths, of positive cases, of metrics for returning to who we were before the pandemic. In its own way, each city represented an example of how neoliberalism filters through the way that public health departments frame health risks, each with varying degrees of commitment to prioritizing the health of people who were trying to make choices about their daily lives.

The way that each of the local health departments framed what constituted vulnerability, health, and risk shifted significantly, often calling attention to how the health of cities situated in economic terms outweighed the health of individuals, particularly those most vulnerable. Our discomfort with uncertainty meant that we erred on the side of everything being okay when it was not. Our systems of normalcy grounded in economic ways of knowing meant that we let statistics guide how we conducted ourselves, at the expense of the lived realities of our community and those who were suffering the most. The CDC and city health departments commonly referenced metrics—linked to bodies, economic interests, and personal behaviors—that could establish when publics might consider themselves removed from the vulnerability of COVID-19, but often glossed over vulnerability in those calculations. In preparing for the next pandemic, we might instead consider shifting to a framework of communication that focuses on how communities can build towards a goal of protecting each other, rather than prioritizing protecting the economy.

While statistics and benchmarks guided much of what we determined about our behavior, much less common were clear guidelines of what to do and how to assess risk, about how individuals could and should think about their larger communities in assessing risk levels, and about how the systems that we have built contribute to risk levels. Focusing on statistics largely resulted in one of two outcomes: the numbers became so overwhelming that they lost their meaning, or they became so arbitrary that they did not capture true vulnerability. Unfortunately, these examples show that the statistics won't save us—creating a safer community is a much more systemic issue than any of these communication strategies highlight. Going forward, coming to terms with what we prioritize in languages surrounding risk can help us work towards a deeper understanding of how our policies, practices, and economic focus shape the reality of health and safety for our communities in the future.

Works Cited

Asen, Robert. "Neoliberalism, the Public Sphere, and a Public Good." *Quarterly Journal of Speech*, vol. 103, no. 4, 2017, pp. 329–49.

City of Chicago Public Health. Public Health: News Releases, January 2020–June 2021, https://www.chicago.gov/city/en/depts/cdph/provdrs/health_protection_and_response/news.html.

County of Los Angeles Public Health. Press releases, January 2020–June 2021, http://publichealth.lacounty.gov/phcommon/public/media/mediapubyrsearch.cfm?unit=media&ou=ph&prog=media&resultyear=2020&row=25&start=676.

Foucault, Michel. *The Birth of Biopolitics: Lectures at the College de France 1978–1979*, edited by Michel Senellart, Palgrave Macmillan, 2008.

Lambrecht, Kathryn. "Tracking the Differentiation of Risk: The Impact of Subject Framing in CDC Communication Regarding COVID-19." *Journal of Business and Technical Communication*, vol. 35, no. 1, 2021, pp. 94–100.

New York City Department of Health and Mental Hygiene. NYC Health News: Press Releases, January 2020–June 2021, https://www1.nyc.gov/site/doh/about/press/pr2021/press-releases-2021.page.

Scott, Mike. *WordSmith Tools* (7.0), 2017, http://lexically.net/wordsmith/version4/index.html.

8 "Do your own research!": Constructions of Ethos within the "Disinformation Dozen"

Aaron Hess

Abstract

It has been well-documented that the COVID-19 pandemic has also been a pandemic of misinformation, disinformation, and outright lies (Grimes; Tagliabue et al.). Conspiracy theories, confusing health advice from the Centers for Disease Control and Prevention (CDC), and social media platforms guided by sensational politics have all led to various positions on the pandemic, ranging from speculative opinions to pseudoscience to profit-seeking deception. Much could be said about the overall contours of this rhetorical situation (Offerdal et al.), including elements of how social media contributes to the spread, profit guides its production, and confirmation bias leads the public to believe such disinformation. While all are worthy considerations, in this essay, I look to the ways that disinformation presents itself as credible in the face of debunking and fact-checking by medical professionals, and scientists attesting to the efficacy and safety of masks and vaccines. Ethos claims are frequent and necessary for those who contend the direct opposite of such overwhelming evidence, argument, and expert opinion. As such, looking to the particular case of the Disinformation Dozen, I argue that ethos is maintained in disinformation through traditional appeals to expertise, a positioning of virtuous character in the face of censorship, and the use of vernacular authenticity.

The Disinformation Dozen

In the thick of the COVID-19 pandemic, the Center for Countering Digital Hate (CCDH) reported that twelve sources accounted for up to sixty-five percent of the content deemed as mis- or disinformation regarding COVID-19 vaccines and related health interventions (6). Typically, these sources are spread through social media and target the COVID-19 vaccines. In their analysis, the CCDH traced and examined content over a period of about six weeks that came from a prominent group of anti-vaccine individuals, including Joseph Mercola, Robert F. Kennedy Jr, and Ben Tapper. The content takes many forms, including memes, tweets, videos, and other materials, and often invokes concerns for children, minority groups, and the medically vulnerable. Moreover, the claims are often offered through a lens of personal empowerment or presented in the face of some larger maleficent entity, such as Big Pharma, the CDC, World Health Organization (WHO), or head of the National Institute of Allergy and Infectious Diseases, Dr. Anthony Fauci. In these cases, the positioning of the anti-vaccination claims in contrast with larger, governmental entities aims to bolster the everydayness or even persevering hero mythos of the movement, a detail I will examine in more depth below.

Rather than going through and disputing each and every claim made by the Disinformation Dozen, the CCDH catalogs the extent of their spread of disinformation and contend that their true motivation is profit-seeking, as argued in an additional report, "Pandemic Profiteers." In some cases, leading anti-vaccination voices profited through government programs, such as the Paycheck Protection Program (PPP) forgivable loans that were dispersed early in the pandemic to support businesses in paying for employees while shuttered due to larger quarantine orders. Although questionable for such voices to take governmental funding, the more substantial form of income comes through the engagement with followers on social media, which the CCDH estimates could be worth up to $1.1 billion ("Pandemic Profiteers" 5). The specific figures regarding how much money is made from social media engagement are fuzzy at best; however, the promotion of such material via social media likely sustains their overall businesses. It is the messages themselves that are valuable and potentially profitable for the Disinformation Dozen, which warrants a closer examination of the means by which they credibly engage their audience.

Ethos

The artistic proof of ethos has been under considerable investigation before and during the pandemic. Troubled by the so-called "Post-Truth" era (d'Ancona) and the relative decline in the public support of and understanding of science (Nguyen and Catalan), the credibility of health experts, scientists, and governmental officials has been thoroughly questioned by the public. Certainly, in an era that democratizes information via social media (Dib et al.), thereby giving everyone an equal voice to make claims about the pandemic, the voices of prominent critics and anti-vaccination crusaders have been elevated through "likes, subscribes, and comments below." The COVID-19 pandemic provided fertile ground for disputes over masking, vaccines, and health advice on how to avoid the virus.

Tracing back to its ancient Aristotelian roots, ethos has been thoroughly theorized in many, many contexts (Baumlin; Halloran; McCroskey and Young), but is typically understood as being comprised of competence/expertise, a trustworthy character, and goodwill toward the audience. This understanding certainly guides my approach; however, given the reliance on social media by the Disinformation Dozen, ethos must be adapted to be understood in more contemporary contexts. Since the advent of digital and online communication, ethos has been theorized anew in order to attend to the specific cues that are found online. For example, early on, Warnick challenged traditional rhetorical criticism and its reliance on a stable author and text with finite bounds ("Rhetorical criticism"). Instead, she contended that critics examining websites, bulletin boards, and other early digital texts might need to look beyond logocentric approaches to the text and evaluate elements such as website style, speed of loading, and other contextual cues. Later, Warnick positions ethos in online contexts as "field dependent" and offers a model that adapts to the changing nature of digital technology (*Rhetoric Online*). Through the model, ethos is read through technological elements, external source links, and other extratextual sources.

Warnick's extratextual articulation of ethos expands ethos beyond a mere credible character. Etymologically, ethos is certainly derived from the ancient Greek notion of character, but also the concept of habit (Hyde, xiii). This connection underscores the relationship between ethos as something pertaining to the personhood of a speaker, but is measured within the larger context of social customs of a cultural place and time. Indeed, Reynolds directly connects the notion of ethos with location, as "space, place, or haunt" that is understood "as a social act and as a product of a community's character" (327). In previous eras, the character of the community might have been defined through local customs and culture. In our contemporary networked moment, an analysis of ethos should include the larger media ecosystems that provide individual users with larger digital, algorithmic, and filtered contexts for understanding all kinds of discourse. Beyond websites, ethos has been usefully extended to understand more recent platforms and their networked connections (Wilson). Similarly, I examine ethos as it spans from the primary sources in the Disinformation Dozen, but also beyond them as central *characters* within a larger ethotic drama that spans across comment sections, related media content, and links to additional sources.

Approach

Through a participatory approach (Middleton et al.) over a period of six months, I followed members of the Disinformation Dozen and their affiliated organizations and people. Following other participatory methods in digital contexts (Hess and Flores), I engaged their sites as a user would, reading articles, following links to other individuals, and reading through Twitter feeds or other digital spaces. The immersive approach was guided by curiosity, often letting links found in comments sections take me to new contexts. This led me to sources well beyond the original Disinformation Dozen, such as the Front Line COVID-19 Critical Care Alliance (FLCCC), which is affiliated with many members of the original twelve, but spans beyond into other networks, sources, and individuals. This rabbit-hole approach was particularly valuable in this context, given that users likely do not merely visit one member of the Dozen's website to learn of health outcomes, but follow multiple social media accounts, links to other sites found in comment sections, and other sites that come into view during their digital travels. This balance between systematized and immersive approaches gave both structure and texture to my read of the (dis)information found within these websites. Throughout my observations, I collected screenshots, took field notes, and collected sample texts from various sources.

Analysis

In what follows, I outline the various ethos strategies found within the Disinformation Dozen. My analysis oscillates between a vertical and horizontal read of the texts. Reading vertically, I analyze the specific ethos claims offered by the Dozen, looking to pointed efforts by the members of the Dozen to articulate ethos as tied to the speaker. Expertise, displays of goodwill, and trustworthiness can be found peppered throughout the texts. Reading horizontally, I look to the ways that disinformation is cultured through the larger digital context. Ethos is not necessarily understood through specific claims made by the Dozen, but is instead fostered through comments from audiences and other popularity metrics such as view counts or likes, algorithmic curations of additional content, and links to additional sources beyond the Dozen. A horizontal read of this content recognizes that ethos is built not only by the specific claims, but in the larger "digital habitus" that surrounds the Dozen. The central texts from the Dozen are indirectly supported by additional websites and sources, leading to larger groundswell of support for their claims.

Competency and Scientific Rigor

Ethos has long been understood as competency or expertise regarding a topic area, built through the practical wisdom of doing a profession (Halloran). In the case of the Disinformation Dozen and its affiliated materials, competency is frequently espoused although it varies between the particular member of the Dozen. For example, Joseph Mercola—named as the number one purveyor of disinformation—displays a remarkably straightforward claim to ethos. On his website under the "About" section, his medical background and credentials are on full display. Similarly, Dr. Sherri Tenpenny posts a full curriculum vitae on her website, including medical training. Certainly, in both cases, questions could be raised about the recency of their credentials and lack of primary research into the topics at hand. Still, claims about competency and expertise follow a traditional route. When responding to Biden's announcement about the Disinformation Dozen, Erin Elizabeth posted a video in which she claimed: "Most in the group are medical experts, medical doctors, surgeons, some of them double board certified."

In contrast, Ty and Charlene Bollinger lack medical or scientific training. Instead, their "About" section of the website relies on stories of relatives who have suffered through cancer and how they embarked on a mission to discover alternative treatments. During this mission, they claim to have found shocking information about the US health system, discovered advanced cancer treatments that could have saved their relatives' lives, and position themselves as fighting against totalitarian dictatorships. Given their lack of traditional markers of ethos as expertise, they rely on a virtuous approach, finding connections with other people who have struggled with medical related issues and are fighting the good fight against larger entities of power, a positioning that I explore below in the deplatforming debates. In an attached video, Ty Bollinger is shown breaking down in tears discussing his children and how they never had a chance to meet their grandfather. Here, the appeal to common ground and pathos is much stronger than any claim to expertise.

Finally, ethos is stylistically displayed in the advice given by the Dozen or linked organizations. The FLCCC, known for pushing alternative and unproven treatment for COVID-19 such as Ivermectin, offers its own set of treatments guidelines, known as I-Mask+. These guidelines stylistically follow other types of advice in medical pamphlets, such as offering Ivermectin dosing guidelines through tables with supporting evidence of efficacy, and the guidelines appear quite credible. When juxtaposed with other similar and established guidelines such as those from the CDC or WHO, they are polished, informative, and detailed. Stylistically, they support an ethos of expertise. Similarly, during my digital travels, I found links to Pierre Kory's Substack account, in which he blends fear appeals with demonic images of Bill Gates with syringes for teeth with statistical analysis of Ivermectin trials, allegedly supporting the drug's efficacy. Again, this display of statistical analysis is likely beyond the expertise of lay readers, and supports an overall ethos of expertise.

Censorship and Deplatforming as Ethos

The censoring and deplatforming of conspiracy theorists and disinformation agents has been met with considerable controversy. Armitage argues that regulation of social media companies for allowing vaccine misinformation—effectively censoring and deplatforming anti-vaxx voices—will cause more harm than good (e29). Allowing mis- and disinformation to exist makes their arguments easier to track and shine a light on the more conspiracy-laden beliefs. Although compelling, the reverse has often been the case. Twitter, Facebook, and YouTube have taken steps to remove offending accounts. Before Elon Musk's purchase of the social network, Twitter had arguably taken the greatest steps to remove disinformation and dangerous speech, famously removing former US President Donald Trump from the platform in 2021 after the January 6 insurrection.

In the face of deplatforming, members of the Dozen and their audiences believe that the move to independent databases or to alternative social media sites is a sign of credibility. Many members of the Dozen have turned away from mainstream news outlets and social media sites, looking for alternative sites that allow for questionable claims about the pandemic and other issues. For example, in January 2022, Joseph Mercola moved over 15,000 articles from his own website into Substack, an online publishing platform whose owners outwardly state that they will not engage in censorship or even much regulation of content (McKenzie et al.). In my digital travels for this project, I found that Substack, along with a few other notable sites such as Odysee for video and BitChute for news sharing, had become a central hub for anti-vaccine articles, comments, and videos. A common thread in many of these sources is how the mainstream media—traditional and social media—do not want messages out there that contradict the so-called pro-vaccine agenda. Declarations such as these are common and they articulate a sense of ethos through their mere presence on sites such as Substack. For example, in the comments section below Mercola's Substack announcement, several users decried the tyranny of morally bankrupt mainstream media and social media companies. Commenting users call his move to Substack—which costs $50 per year for users to access his materials—an act of bravery and tenaciousness. In his initial announcement, Mercola mentions that President Biden singled him (and other members of the Disinformation Dozen) out for their anti-vaccine views. In response, commenters take pride in Mercola as being 100 percent on target and as drawing more hatred from "their" side. In these instances, being deplatformed adds to Mercola's credibility as a virtuous anti-tyranny crusader.

Vernacular Ethos and Spectacle

Unsurprisingly, many of the posts found within the Disinformation Dozen rely on a sense of vernacular ethos that is common to social media displays. As I have argued elsewhere, video sharing sites such as YouTube or similar sites found within anti-vaccine groups such as Odysee or BitChute, rely on a sense of the everydayness of users (Hess 118). This often appears in the form of individual testimonials or Zoom video type discussions between individuals who discuss the benefits of alternative treatments for COVID-19 such as Ivermectin or the supposed side effects from mRNA vaccines. For example, the aforementioned FLCCC created a series of videos titled "MyStory" that features dozens of testimonials. In the videos, ordinary people narrate their experiences with COVID-19, their struggles to locate Ivermectin as treatment, and heap praise upon the FLCCC for fighting the good fight against censorship. These personal anecdotes position FLCCC in contrast with many of the larger studies that may embrace more generalizable methods to make their claims. The evidence for their claims is often found in their everydayness. They are people "just like you" struggling to discern a course of action with COVID-19 and weigh all the information out there. It is that struggle that gives credence to their arguments. Indeed, the internal logic of many of them may not hold up under much scrutiny. For example, one testimonial was of an unvaccinated person who suffered from a COVID-19 infection for weeks while taking Ivermectin. She eventually recovered from her infection, but the link between her Ivermectin use and recovery is weak, perhaps even circumstantial at best.

While anecdotal evidence is offered in the form of testimonials, other online sources push a far more spectacular logic that is tied to ethos. On the FLCCC Twitter page, the group promoted an independent documentary called "I Am Not Misinformation" via the video sharing site Odysee. The Canadian film, produced by Dan Peruzzo, follows a handful of people who claim to have suffered from side effects from the COVID-19 vaccines as well as health professionals. The video uses a combination of first-person testimonials, much like the MyStory videos referenced above, but combines them with stories of government tyranny, medical experimentation, and the death of democracy. One snippet from the film features an older woman comparing COVID-19 vaccination campaigns to Nazi Germany. These more spectacular moments in the videos push the narrative to extremes, and pit the overall FLCCC and its affiliated videos within a larger epic of good versus evil. In another example of sensational testimonials, Joseph Mercola's website featured a compilation video on May 18, 2022 that supposedly showcases a woman suffering through the side effects of the AstraZeneca vaccine. She is featured with a large rash all over her body and draws from Instagram reels and other social media posts to highlight the vernacular ethos of the claim. In further digging, I discovered that the woman, Rocyie Wong, does indeed suffer from an extreme form of psoriasis, but it is unrelated to her receiving the vaccine. Still, the logic of the disinformation is to tie the raw authenticity of her personal testimony with spectacular visuals of her body, all overlaid with false vaccine claims. Offered in contrast from positions of authority, these videos are credible in their everydayness, and without careful digging, are difficult to unpack on an individual basis.

Conclusion

In this analysis, I have shown how anti-vaccine proponents and those in the Disinformation Dozen strive to present a credible character for their claims. Through traditional ethos markers, the use of alternative platforms, and an everyday ethos, the anti-vaccine advocates present a credible character that is difficult to dispute on an individual basis and better understood through a distributed context. Indeed, ethos is not primarily read through the central character, but through dispersion into the digital context. Comments found underneath postings, myriad videos purportedly displaying vaccine side effects, and the platforms expressed commitments against censorship all support an ethos that surrounds the primary rhetor of each member of the dozen. Combating mis- and disinformation, in this context, proves difficult when the supporting apparatus of credibility is structured horizontally rather than vertically. Rhetorical research should continue to explore the ways that ethos is established in digital contexts such as these and with crisis-oriented topics, such as the COVID-19 pandemic.

Works Cited

Armitage, R. "Online 'Anti-Vax' Campaigns and COVID-19: Censorship Is Not the Solution." *Public Health* vol. 190, 2021, pp. e29–e30.

Baumlin, James S. "From Postmodernism to Posthumanism: Theorizing Ethos in an Age of Pandemic." *Humanities* vol. 9, no. 2, 2020, 46, doi.org/10.3390/h9020046.

Broniatowski, David A., et al. "Twitter and Facebook Posts about COVID-19 Are Less Likely to Spread Misinformation Compared to Other Health Topics." *PloS one*, vol. 17, no. 1, 2022, e0261768. doi.org/10.1371/journal.pone.0261768.

Center for Countering Digital Hate. "Pandemic Profiteers: The Business of Anti-Vaxx." 2021. https://counterhate.com/wp-content/uploads/2022/05/210601-Pandemic-Profiteers-Report.pdf.

—. "The Disinformation Dozen: Why Platforms Must Act on Twelve Leading Online Anti-Vaxxers." 2021. https://counterhate.com/wp-content/uploads/2022/05/210324-The-Disinformation-Dozen.pdf.

d'Ancona, Matthew. *Post-Truth: The New War on Truth and How to Fight Back*. Random House, 2017.

Dib, Fadia, et al. "Online Mis/disinformation and Vaccine Hesitancy in the Era of COVID-19: Why We Need an eHealth Literacy Revolution." *Human Vaccines and Immunotherapeutics*, vol. 18, no. 1, 2022, pp. 1–3. doi.org/10.1080/21645515.2021.1874218.

Grimes, David R. "Medical Disinformation and the Unviable Nature of COVID-19 Conspiracy Theories. *PLoS One*, vol. 16, no. 3, 2021, e0245900. doi.org/10.1371/journal.pone.0245900.

Halloran, S. Michael. "Aristotle's Concept of Ethos, or If Not His Somebody Else's." *Rhetoric Review* vol. 1, no.1, 1982, pp. 58–63.

Hess, Aaron, and Carlos Flores. "Simply More than Swiping Left: A Critical Analysis of Toxic Masculine Performances on Tinder Nightmares." *New Media & Society*, vol. 20, no. 3 2018, pp. 1085–102.

Hess, Aaron. "Democracy through the Polarized Lens of the Camcorder: Argumentation and Vernacular Spectacle on YouTube in the 2008 Election." *Argumentation and Advocacy*, vol. 47, no. 2, 2010, pp. 106–22.

Hyde, Michael J., editor. *The Ethos of Rhetoric*. U of South Carolina P, 2004

McCroskey, James C., and Thomas J. Young. "Ethos and Credibility: The Construct and Its Measurement after Three Decades." *Communication Studies*, vol. 32, no. 1, 1981, pp. 24–34.

McKenzie, Hamish, et al. "Society Has a Trust Problem. More Censorship Will Only Make It Worse." *Substack*, 26 Jan 2022, on.substack.com/p/society-has-a-trust-problem-more. Accessed 11 Oct 2022.

Middleton, Michael, et al. *Participatory Critical Rhetoric: Theoretical and Methodological Foundations for Studying Rhetoric In Situ*. Lexington Books, 2015

Nguyen, An, and Daniel Catalan-Matamoros. "Digital Mis/disinformation and Public Engagement with Health and Science controversies: Fresh Perspectives from COVID-19." *Media and Communication*, vol. 8, no. 2, 2020, pp. 323–28.

Offerdal, Truls Strand, et al. "Public Ethos in the Pandemic Rhetorical Situation: Strategies for Building Trust in Authorities' Risk Communication." *Journal of International Crisis and Risk Communication Research*, vol. 4, no. 2, 2021, pp. 247–70.

Tagliabue, Fabio, et al. "The "Pandemic" of Disinformation in COVID-19." *SN Comprehensive Clinical Medicine*, vol. 2, 2020, pp. 1287–89.

Warnick, Barbara. "Online Ethos: Source Credibility in an "Authorless" Environment." *American Behavioral Scientist*, vol. 48, no. 2, 2004, pp. 256–65.

—. *Rhetoric Online: Persuasion and Politics on the World Wide Web*. Peter Lang, 2007.

Wilson, Noah. "Algorithmic Dwelling: Ethos as Deformance in Online Spaces." *Rhetoric Review*, vol. 39, no. 2, 2020, pp. 216–29.

9 Temporalities of Change: Up-Tempo Discourse and Public Culture

Jeffrey St. Onge

Abstract

This essay investigates the relationship between speed and communication. I examine discourses surrounding the COVID-19 pandemic to explore the ways in which the increased tempo of information exchange requires a re-examination of three important features of rhetorical scholarship: the public sphere, conventional wisdom, and connotation. I ultimately argue that a better understanding of the increased speed of communication will aid both scholars of rhetoric and advocates in understanding and creating arguments in contemporary public culture.

In 2016, shortly after the US presidential election, I purchased a pin off a street vendor in Detroit that says "This is not normal." I thought it was a useful item to have around, so I attached it to the wall of my office. Two years later, when the pandemic hit, I glanced at the pin and thought "well, still true!" I often wondered: what is normal? COVID-19 seems to have moved into a more manageable endemic phase, but big questions persist: Did normal ever exist on any large scale? Will it ever return? What will it look like? What *should* be normal in US culture? Maybe this—whatever it may be—*is* normal. Where "normal" traditionally implies stability, normality in the present is better understood as a state of perpetual change: of ideas, of discourse, and of everyday life.

In this essay, I introduce a concept called up-tempo discourse, which seeks to provide a framework to better understand the shapes and flows of public culture in terms of stability and change. One thing that has been clear in the early twenty-first century, and even more so since the COVID-19 pandemic, is that American culture has *sped up* considerably. Information travels faster than ever, and it does so within a complex milieu of personal habits, changing media technologies, capitalist profit models, journalistic strategies, politics, and actions from prominent figures in the public sphere. In other words, a confluence of events, shifting norms, and changing contexts of public and private discussion have radically altered the experience of everyday life. Social media in particular has brought numerous challenges specific to questions of citizenship and public culture, including information overload, echo chambers, shortened attention spans, screen time issues for children and adults, and a cultural environment polluted more than ever by misinformation, disinformation, and propaganda (Pazzanese).

While these issues are frequently discussed, debated, and researched, one aspect that is often left out of conversations about rhetoric is the increased speed of communication at all levels. New media technologies have the effect of radically increasing the rate of communication and the quantity of material that can be communicated, thus impacting the nature and scope of rhetoric itself. Speed changes how we understand and process information. The mixture of fact and opinion is less clear, and something like an agreed-upon public record seems like a relic of a bygone era.

My goal in identifying and outlining the nature of up-tempo discourse is to draw attention to both the quickened nature of communication in the present and the need for scholars of rhetoric to address speed as a defining feature of contemporary communication. I examine social media and the pandemic as a way to illustrate the concept, but my hope is that this case study brings clarity to the role of speed in communication more generally. In other words, while I use this space to highlight problems, up-tempo discourse is not inherently problematic. Instead, the concept will ideally open numerous lines of thought and invention for scholars and practitioners of rhetoric.

Speed and the Pandemic

The pandemic slowed everyday life to a crawl. In March 2020, state governments began issuing stay at home orders, shutting down schools, and requiring businesses to close or drastically reduce services. Those who could work from home had to figure out quickly how to do so; those whose jobs could not be done remotely simply had to sit and wait, or, in many cases, brave exposure to the virus. At first, it seemed like a potentially short time, but as information was gathered and news trickled in it became clear that the pandemic would be indefinite. If there was one common thread that united everyone, it was wanting to know more. People increasingly turned to screens (particularly social media) for information, for work, for leisure, and for connection (Wagner et al. sec. 4).

While everyday life passed slowly, the information environment sped up. It is estimated that a staggering 2.5 quintillion bytes of data is created and shared every day, and the research is clear that false information moves faster than the truth (Menczer and Hills 55). According to a 2018 study from MIT, news stories deemed to be true (with 95–98 percent agreement among fact-checkers) spread more slowly than false stories, and they reached fewer people. As Vousoughi et al. write, "When we analyzed the diffusion dynamics of true and false rumors, we found that falsehood diffused significantly farther, faster, deeper, and more broadly than the truth in all categories of information" (1147). The authors argue that false news is novel and activates emotional responses, and is thus more likely to be quickly shared on social media (Vousoughi et al. 1151).

An example from the early days of the pandemic effectively demonstrates the rapid spread of misinformation. Dr. Vladimir Zelenko, an upstate New York physician, claimed success using the drug Hydroxychloroquine to treat patients and posted boastful videos on Facebook and YouTube. As described by the *New York Times*:

> What happened next is a modern pandemic parable that illustrates how the coronavirus is colliding with our fragile information ecosystem: a jumble of facts, falsehoods and viral rumors patched together from Twitter threads and shards of online news, amplified by armchair experts and professional partisans and pumped through the warp-speed accelerator of social media. (Roose and Rosenberg)

In other words, the pandemic created perfect conditions to see how speed impacts information exchange, often with problematic results. An article in *ABCNews* effectively captured the danger of these conditions:

> We've never had a global story like this where people are going through the same experiences in different countries. . . . We're seeing a lot of misinformation jumping from South Africa to London to New York. We haven't recognized the power of misinformation until now. A lot of it has been about political speech, but now this information could actually be harmful to people. . . . You hear people say, "I was told not to wear a mask, and now I'm being told to wear a mask." When you have a new virus, the data that you have is so young that the doctors haven't had a chance to do the research. (Gallagher)

Speed aids misinformation, and though this is not a new problem, the pandemic exacerbated it. As public health scholar Kasisomayajula Viswanath notes, "Social media platforms are one of the most significant abettors to the spread of misinformation and disinformation, and their algorithms have compounded the problem" (Sweeney sec. 3). The actions of those in charge accelerated the dangerous nature of the information environment: "What has made misinformation and disinformation about COVID-19 so bad is that it was picked up and spread by political figures, including President Donald Trump. That greatly amplified it and it brought misinformation and disinformation into the mainstream" (Sweeney sec. 1). Speed is thus not only an inevitable result of widespread engagement with new media and the society it has helped to shape, but also a political strategy used by right wing leaders (Virilio 63). It allows for the muddying of waters and the creation of a chaotic public sphere that supports an agenda of government through division (Ivie 63–64). Because of recent successes with this strategic approach, it is likely to be a regular feature of politics moving forward.

Given that public culture has sped up in numerous ways, it is important to explore its rhetorical dimensions. The speed of society has increased rapidly, thus necessitating a consideration of stability in the contexts of public discourse and the public sphere. "Debate" and "deliberation" seem to occur always and in all domains, but in a quickened context where people share only weak meanings or understanding of terms, ideas, and events which are already insta-filtered through sociological and ideological prisms. In what follows, I will examine the nature of speed as it relates to two other concepts central to the rhetorical tradition: connotation and conventional wisdom.

Rhetorical Dimensions: Connotation and Conventional Wisdom

Connotation is one of the most fundamental concepts outlining the relationship between communication and meaning. It concerns the flexible way in which people understand words; while denotation describes an objective, dictionary definition, connotation describes the myriad associations and suggestions of a term. For instance, "flag" denotes, according to the *Merriam-Webster* dictionary, "A usually rectangular piece of fabric of distinctive design that is used as a symbol (as of a nation), as a signaling device, or as a decoration." While different dictionaries have slight variation on this definition, they are essentially the same, reflecting an objective, agreed-upon meaning of the term. The word "flag" connotes many different things, though. Someone hearing the term might think of the American flag, a Pride flag, a relative in the military, an aversion to patriotism, or any number of associations. This is of course part of the challenge and opportunity of human communication. We have multiplicities of meanings and options for creative description. We can create arguments that harness connotative understandings of things to suggest, frame, or shape meaning for an audience (e.g., an automobile advertisement showing a flag to suggest patriotism or liberty for buying the product). Connotations also give clues to a message's ideological underpinnings (e.g., a politician wearing a rainbow flag patch suggests a socially liberal perspective) and is thus a useful starting point in rhetorical analysis.

For a word like *flag*, most people can easily rectify both denotative and connotative sets of meanings. Most know what a flag is and can also understand that it triggers different meanings for different people. Importantly, different connotative meanings relate to the original meaning, and the standard definition has long existed in uncontested form. As such, society can debate issues relating to flags (e.g., an anti-flag burning amendment to the Constitution) with knowledge that the word means different things to different people.

In the contemporary social matrix of mass communication, though, meaning has become destabilized such that a grounded debate is difficult or impossible. The word "vaccine," for instance, might mean a medical invention designed to fight disease, or it might mean Big Pharma or some other evil, anti-nature conspiracy. If we expand the meaning of connotation to include people, ideas, or events, we can see this happening more and more: "Anthony Fauci" is not an expert, but rather an empty signifier to support any political or medical cause; elections are not a democratic process but rather a simmering conspiracy; a school shooting is not an event with shared emotional meaning but rather an immediate entry into larger conversations about guns. These examples illustrate the ways that connotation and denotation can collapse into one another to the point of deeply destabilizing large-scale shared understanding. This has always occurred to a degree, but not with the scope, scale, and impact that it does in the present.

On a societal level, arguments travel quickly, and the ways people exist within social media echo chambers ensure that words, events, people, and the like are quickly supplied with loaded meanings already imbued with ideology (and, often, misinformation and propaganda). Basic argument theory demonstrates the challenge here: if people do not agree on facts, then it is simply not possible to discuss values or policy. If there is widespread disagreement about whether a pandemic even exists, for example, it is not possible to debate what is valued in addressing it (i.e., the economy vs. human lives) or how to then address it in terms of public policy.

The work of Paul Virilio is instructive here: his 1977 book *Speed and Politics* places speed as a key explainer of contemporary life. As he argues in the more recent *Administration of Fear*, "People are required to transfer their power of decision to automatic responses that can function at the immobile speed of instantaneity. The acceleration of reality is a significant mutation in history" (33). As Karotzogianni and Ronison argue in an analysis of Virilio's work:

> The political impact of speed is mediated by the sociology, or micropolitics, of affect. For Virilio, the main effects of the present situation are fear, terror, panic, and insecurity. These are not simply individual feelings, or neuroses, but sociological effects which are, in a sense, proportionate and rational responses to the real situation. Uncontrolled acceleration and resultant instantaneity generate widespread fear. (163)

Anna Gibbs describes the spread of emotion as affect contagions: "Contagious epidemics [of emotion] now potentially occur on a global scale and, thanks to electronic media, with incredible rapidity" (186). Feelings—rage, anxiety, despair, etc.—spread more readily than stable ideas and information. In social networks and in many mainstream news outlets and sites of political discussion, perpetual hysteria is the norm; a democracy of emotion favors extreme polarization and antagonism. The current system is ripe for exploitation by political actors seeking to incite panic and hatred through the rapid transmission of information via myriad media outlets that work on multiple registers.

Conventional Wisdom

Conventional wisdom, a term coined by economist John Kenneth Galbraith, summarizes basic shared understandings of a group of people. As he writes, "It will be convenient to have a name for the ideas which are esteemed at any time for their acceptability, and it should be a term that emphasizes this predictability. I shall refer to these ideas henceforth as the conventional wisdom" (8). In short, it reflects the basic idea that society operates according to a number of (typically) unchecked assumptions, some of which are true and some of which are not. As an economist, Galbraith in the present might point to beliefs like "housing is always a stable investment" or "the stock market always goes up over time." Conventional wisdom reflects the relative permanence of culture; a culture needs some stability of thought in order to exist, and discourse, rhetoric, and argument all rely on this stability of meaning.

Rhetoricians study conventional wisdom (along with related concepts such as commonplaces and the *sensus communis*) for several reasons. First, conventional wisdom forms the basis of rhetorical invention; arguments can be created based on shared intellectual ground. Second, critics can look to conventional wisdoms to understand how problematic cultural beliefs exist and persist in language. Similar to Foucault's concept of discursive formations, conventional wisdoms can provide a way to understand ideological dimensions of a culture (323). Finally, a critic can examine the state of conventional wisdom more broadly to understand how a culture discusses and manages common issues. As such, an understanding of the speed with which conventional wisdom changes is necessary to best understand public discourse and knowledge.

In part due to speed, meaning is always already contested. For example, during each mass shooting in the United States, myriad stories burst forth online and on cable news not only trying to explain the event, but offering contesting frames relating to gun rights, political ideology, conspiracies, and a variety of other factors. Meaning is instantly blurred on a mass cultural scale. As Odette Yousef writes for *NPR*:

> Even before details were known about the shooter who killed 19 children and two school faculty at Robb Elementary School in Uvalde, Texas, fringe media were awash in rumors, conspiracy theories and misinformation. Some posts incorrectly identified the shooter, while others posited without evidence that the massacre was a government-orchestrated "false flag" operation. With the tragic events following closely on the heels of another mass shooting in Buffalo, N.Y., the online discussions reverted to unfounded narratives and scapegoats that have become all too familiar as the country grapples with the continued toll of gun violence.

As outlined here, a variety of ideologically loaded meanings advance quickly among different audiences and groups.

Though Yousef highlights that this occurs on fringe media, it is undeniable that fringe media has become much less fringe in recent years. In an analysis of the Buffalo mass shooting, the *New York Times* highlighted the mainstreaming of the far-right, racist replacement theory:

> [R]eplacement theory, once confined to the digital fever swamps of Reddit message boards and semi-obscure white nationalist sites, has gone mainstream. In sometimes more muted forms, the fear it crystallizes — of a future America in which white people are no longer the numerical majority — has become a potent force in conservative media and politics, where the theory has been borrowed and remixed to attract audiences, retweets and small-dollar donations. (Confessore and Yourish)

The authors quote Chris Stirewalt, a former Fox News political editor, who describes the rapidness of this mainstreaming via television personalities:

"Cable hosts looking for ratings and politicians in search of small-dollar donations can see which stories and narratives are drawing the most intense reactions among addicted users online. [Social media sites and internet forums are] like a focus group for pure outrage" (qtd. in Confessore and Yourish). In sum, fringe theories emerge almost instantly and move quickly into mainstream discourse, muddying the waters of conventional wisdom and blurring the meanings of important national events, ideas, and people.

These examples demonstrate up-tempo discourse in action. As a result of this, large-scale connotation and conventional wisdom do not have a chance to form in any meaningful way. Or, put differently, micro-connotations and conventional wisdoms form almost instantly among varieties of subgroups. The speed of culture creates a universe of connotations that make coherent public conversation and discussion nearly impossible, at least on the large scale of a democratic nation. Information comes quickly and through myriad conflicting prisms, including echo chambers, message boards, political news organizations, infotainment, and public figures. There is no rhythm, but rather chaos. Up-tempo discourse creates a dizzying effect on the culture writ large: what is true? Whom to believe? The faster these questions are answered in like-minded groups, the greater the difficulty for meaningful democratic deliberation.

Up-Tempo Discourse and the Charge for Change

This essay sought to sketch out an understanding of rhetorical contexts in the (post) pandemic era. Contemporary communication is defined by the rapid sharing of information and the quickness with which meaning is developed, contested, and discarded. Though I focused primarily on examples that illustrated problems with speed and communication, that is only one dimension. Up-tempo discourse is not inherently problematic. It provides a way to understand the public sphere as one in constant and rapid flux, where connotation and conventional wisdom are incredibly unstable at all times. For critics, this creates a need to understand the increasingly transient nature of meaning. For advocates, this requires a better understanding of how to create a rhetorical foothold in an environment that is like shifting quicksand. What is normal in the present, it is clear, is unrelenting and rapid change. This is the ground on which rhetoricians now stand. Both problems and opportunities abound.

Works Cited

Confessore, Nicholas, and Karen Yourish. *The New York Times*, 15 May 2022, https://www.nytimes.com/2022/05/15/us/replacement-theory-shooting-tucker-carlson.html. Accessed 10 Oct. 2022.

Foucault, Michel. *The Birth of Biopolitics: Lectures at the College de France, 1978–1979*. Translated by Graham Burchell, Palgrave MacMillan, 2008.

Galbraith, John Kenneth. *The Affluent Society*. Houghton Mifflin Harcourt. 1998.

Gallagher, Fergal. "Tracking Hydroxychloroquine Misinformation: How an Unproven COVID-19 Treatment Ended Up being Endorsed by Trump." *ABC News*, 22 Apr. 2020, https://abcnews.go.com/Health/tracking-hydroxychloroquine-misinformation-unproven-covid-19-treatment-ended/story?id=70074235. Accessed 10 Oct. 2022.

Gibbs, Anna. "After Affect: Sympathy, Synchrony, and Mimetic Communication," *The Affect Theory Reader*, edited by Melissa Gregg and Gregory J. Seigworth, Duke UP, 2010, pp. 186–205.

Ivie, Robert. "Rhetorical Aftershocks of Trump's Ascendency: Salvation by Demolition and Deal Making." *Res Rhetorica*, vol. 4, no. 10, 2017, pp. 61–79. doi:10.29107/rr2017.2.5.

Karatzogianni, Athina, and Andrew Robinson. "Virilio's Parting Song: The Administration of Fear and the Privatisation of Communism through the Communism of Affect." *Media Theory*, vol. 3, no. 2, 2019, pp. 161–78.

Menczer, Fillip, and Thomas Hills. "The Attention Economy." *Scientific American*, vol. 323, no. 6, 2020, pp. 54–61. doi:10.1038/scientificamerican1220-54.

Pazzanese, Christina. "Battling the 'Pandemic of Misinformation.'" *The Harvard Gazette*, 8 May 2020, https://news.harvard.edu/gazette/story/2020/05/social-media-used-to-spread-create-covid-19-falsehoods/. Accessed 10 Oct. 2022.

Roose, Kevin, and Matthew Rosenberg. "Touting Virus Cure, 'Simple Country Doctor' Becomes a Right-Wing Star." *The New York Times*, 2 Apr. 2020, www.nytimes.com/2020/04/02/technology/doctor-zelenko-coronavirus-drugs.html. Accessed 15 Sept. 2022.

Sweeney, Chris. "Fighting the Spread of COVID-19 Misinformation." *Harvard T. H. Chan School of Public Health*, www.hsph.harvard.edu/news/features/fighting-the-spread-of-covid-19-misinformation/. Accessed 22 Sept. 2022.

Virilio, Paul. *Speed and Politics*. Translated by Mark Polizzotti, Semiotext(e), 2006.

Virilio, Paul. *The Administration of Fear*. Translated by Ames Hodges, Semiotext(e), 2012.

Vosoughi, Soroush, et al. "The Spread of True and False News Online." *Science*, vol. 359, 2018, pp.1146–51.

Wagner, Brooke E, et al. "Recreational Screen Time Behaviors during the COVID-19 Pandemic in the US: A Mixed-Methods Study among a Diverse Population-Based Sample of Emerging Adults." *International Journal of Environmental Research and Public Health*, vol. 18, no. 9, 2021, doi: 10.3390/ijerph18094613. Accessed 28 Sept. 2022.

Yousef, Odette. The Uvalde Shooting Conspiracies Show How Far-Right Misinformation Is Evolving." *NPR News*, 26 May 2022, https://www.npr.org/2022/05/26/1101479269/texas-uvalde-school-shooting-misinformation-conspiracy-far-right. Accessed 10 Oct. 2022.

10 *Conocimiento* in the Landscapes of Housing Insecurity

Jason Michálek

Abstract

During threats of COVID, communities of people experiencing homelessness have been uniquely afflicted with relatively uncommon troubles. This essay considers current scholarship on mediated deliberations around homelessness, interrogating the implications of this case study in order to offer promising methods of digital assembly that could productively facilitate better resolution to such community issues. It outlines the elements of conflict and efforts of digitally assembled community action that reveal how true compassion can emerge through allocentric public assembly. Exploring coalitional assembly and grounded mutual aid efforts, it demonstrates how State action does not subvert the power of community but rather necessitates alternative public assemblies.

Context

During the ongoing threats of COVID, communities of people experiencing homelessness have been uniquely afflicted with a convergence of relatively uncommon troubles. In Bloomington, Indiana, these phenomena came to a stasis when unhoused people occupied a city park space to individually shelter in tents—close to community services but also unhidden from public gaze. In the optical awareness of the public eye, this collective assembly challenged the community of people who mostly self-identify as "progressive" and "compassionate" to account for the image of actual Others.

Here, a sentiment from Benedict Anderson's critique of nationalist identities highlights the obscurity of a unified and fixed public perception. The critical focus of Benedict Anderson reminds us that "[Community] is imagined because the members of even the smallest nation will never know most of their fellow-members, meet them, or even hear of them, *yet in the minds of each lives the image of their communion*" (6, emphasis mine). When we speak of imagined multitudes, we homogenize them into our conceptions that precede and exceed perceptions.

That's what's problematic about referring to "the homeless" and essentialized "homeless people." In other words, we see with our egos what we fear as the Other. Instead of colonizing conceptions of preconceived citizenry, we can gain more insights from what Gloria Anzaldúa has identified as "seven ojos de luz"—or "eyes of light" (Anzaldúa and Keeting 545). Thus we share a public imaginary as a common/place to which we can all pander. However, to move beyond imagination to what *actual* communion could look like, we need to see the assemblages of communities with new eyes. And yet, even when we gaze with our eyes in the light of day, we can fail to build bridges that would allow us to *come* to know—*truly know*—what it is we are perceiving.

In this essay, I draw from a grounded case study of people experiencing homelessness in Bloomington, Indiana. I outline the elements of conflict as well as the efforts of digitally assembled community to offer a landscape of actions that not only avoids neutrality but reveals how true compassion can emerge through the continuity of allocentric public assembly. I use examples of coalitional assembly and grounded mutual aid efforts to show how State action does not subvert the power of community. I end by offering ways of adapting methods based in Anzaldúa's concept of *conocimiento* to facilitate better communication that builds bridges, opens to diverse but collaborative communities, and fosters place as a presumptive outcome of persuasion, listening, conversation, and expression.

Exigence

On the night of March 4, 2021, Bloomington City Council held a Zoom meeting to consider a proposed ordinance that would allow sleeping in designated areas of city property—particularly Seminary Park, the site unhoused residents had been occupying the past winter, despite the periodic evictions of the city. Among the events leading up to this ordinance were the deaths of a few well-known members of the unhoused community, drafting of a local homeless bill of rights, and deployment of countless efforts to improve the community and situation of housing insecurity by a coalition of housing advocates, the Bloomington Homeless Coalition—or BHC, that I later discuss in greater depth.

As a place of digital assembly, the platform of Zoom reproduces the structures of a physical *topos* of assembly; however, this particular example demonstrates how re/production of community amplified the illusory constraints of digitized belonging. For instance, with chat disabled and public comment severely controlled by the city staff, the technologies of discipline were structured to mutate the community into something the government pre/scriptively regulated. The example of one exchange between a speaker from the public and a member of the council was an instance of misregulation in which multiple members of the public were given speaking permissions. Even among the limitations of the meeting and the controls of accessibility to assembly, participants were able to call attention to conventions to raise awareness of the artifice of hyperreality and public access.

When an unseaming glitch prompted a council member to say, "I'm hearing multiple voices," one of the audio-only participants explained that citizens had constructed a sound system in a physical public park in order to provide virtual accessibility to the unhoused residents who lacked a foundational room of their own. The indictment juxtaposed with State acknowledgement of "multiple voices" provides meta-commentary on the polysemy of public convergence and the effects of silencing Others to hear only some. When people can call out the separation of publics in the community with the ways the Zoom meeting is operating, the interruption draws attention to the divide between the publics and their apparent constitutive relation to State regulators. It is in this divide that alternative publics can emerge.

Framework

In scholarship addressing community conversations around homelessness[8] Whitney Gent demonstrates how neutrality is a barricade to addressing conflicts and controversies in legislated spaces. The problem with neutrality is that it "pretends to balance power by calling people to bracket their identities and interests during deliberation, but makes this impossible by denying systemic explanations for difference" (241). If we imagine bridges merely as passive structures that are equally open and inclusive to all, we are stuck in

---

8. I use the term "homelessness" to emphasize that lack of belonging in a community is not necessarily connected to houses, and that the alienation from feelings of "home" can be enacted discursively, politically, and digitally as well as with physical structures.

neutral and fail to cross beyond our own boundaries. More specifically, when people can appeal to an imagined *res publica* as a common being that everyone is born into, the imagined community barricades the bridges we might form to link differences in active community building efforts.

As a contrast, Leon and Pigg have applied Gloria Anzaldúa's concept of *conocimiento* to develop a networked rhetoric that can grapple with "dwelling places that . . . are multiple, dense, and resist reduction" (273). This network has been present in the operations of the Bloomington Homeless Coalition and continues to invite people to consider and encounter Others beyond their limited likeness. A networked form of conocimiento forces different community members to experience their differentiation and develop a fellow feeling of dissimilarities in a perpetual and ongoing noticing. This network is not merely conceptual or digital, but rather radically depends on the social relation between human bodies and information as it is incorporated into technologies.

In a more direct presentation of the concept prior to the digital network application, Anzaldúa's primary conceptions involve processes of decolonizing from dominant cosmologies of fitting into the public imaginary—that is both reductive in the formation of knowledge and submissive to a false hierarchy that preferences science and rationality. Instead, conocimiento involves "opening all your senses, consciously inhabiting your body and decoding its symptoms" in order to "challenge official and conventional ways of looking at the world, ways set up by those benefiting from such constructions" (Anzaldúa 542). The high concept form of embodied ways of knowing involves simultaneous healing at the cultural and individual level in an ongoing process where "bits of your self [*sic*] die and are reborn in each step" (546). For the purposes of this analysis, the grounded application of the concept coupled with a networked approach can have critical implications for advancing the work of community reparations in intersectional and digitally mediated forms.

I offer a caveat here *cum* Anzaldúa that building such bridges is praxical. They can neither be as physically material as concrete structures, nor as imaginatively metaphorical/metaphysical as a rainbow bridge of consciousness, but rather they must rely upon and maintain networks of linkages that are actively traversed transversally. Similar to the concept of the rainbow bridge with its spectrum of perceptive awareness, Anzaldúa's concept offers ways of seeing together, anew, and nonlinearly if applied in action. In other words, it is *border crossing* as an active verb, and the kinship/familiarity is formed through utilizing digital connections that enable re/formation of togetherness. The fact that we're networked—digitally, socially, and otherwise—is precisely what enables mutual aid to materialize in collective forms. To demonstrate an instantiation of this, we'll turn now to the BHC.

Case Study

In a cleanup effort organized and orchestrated by the BHC several months prior to the city council meeting, coalition members actively worked to ameliorate community concerns that would later re-emerge as critiques about the occupation of the more centralized Seminary Park. The focus of the cleanup was Switchyard Park, a less centralized city property that is currently more often utilized by families and dog owners, but also a park that was constructed on previously undeveloped property that the unhoused community had used to develop encampments.

The BHC deploys a mutual aid model that is co-operative with other networks in the area—including the Facebook group for Monroe County Mutual Aid and People's Market, an alternative market that regularly coordinates sponsored Community Supported Agriculture boxes that are delivered to requesting customers with no expectation of payment or validation of need. In particular, the latter market has continually worked to develop ways to distribute nutrient-dense foods to vulnerable communities that lack capital or access to the abundance of resources that constitutes that reality. By bridging connections with communities of residents in poverty and convening resources within the community to resolve impoverished conditions, the coalition and its partners maintain a dynamically responsive position from which to draw upon and nurture active collaborations based in collective forms of conocimiento.

As a material example, a virtual flyer circulated via social media advertised locations and purposes of "Little Free Closets"—old newspaper dispensers that were reformed for the purpose of supplying free clothes as mutual aid. The flyer described suggested clothing to stock—some of which was pictured in the graphic. This document was not generated by the BHC, but members of the coalition helped to regularly circulate the digital content and the coalition worked with multiple mutual aid groups to stock the listed locations. Though the other visual elements in the flyer portray a more lighthearted tone—such as a clip art duck with an umbrella—the information conveyed had material and effective implications for addressing the changing exigencies of the people in extreme precarity during the winter months by connecting the actualized community through digital bridges.

While any social media user could've circulated such a graphic, it was the purposeful efforts of coalitions working with the people in exigent need that helped to address the changing needs of those in precarity. By approaching the issue in a frame of conocimiento and updating the information available to the public, it was the network of efforts that created a meaningful perspective. As a mediating group of communication between the general public and the people in need, the networked positionality of the BHC effectively fostered persuasion, listening, conversation, and expression. Rather than "hearing multiple voices" regarding the homeless as homogenized as the city council performatively enacted, the coalition distilled the voices of actual people experiencing homelessness and presented the importance of their lived experiences content in a way that created visibility for marginalized segments of the community. These efforts offered ways for the broader community to extend true compassion that addressed their needs directly by crossing the borders of their different positions in the community in ways that challenged conventions and actively sought to resist the individualizing othering imposed by capitalist systems.

Takeaway

From the example of the dismissive comments of the city council as contrasted with the circulated communications of the Bloomington Homeless Coalition, this case study provides one example of how networked community offers more substantive ways to "suffer with" vulnerable segments of a community through true compassion. While it's true that community is nonlinear and emergent—and maybe even seven metaphorical eyes are too few to see all that is articulated in the assemblages of coalitions and communities—a public can become more informed through recursive mediations of knowledge production and circulation that are afforded by technologies. The dynamic efforts of the BHC suggests that when we show up, we build bridges. And when we speak up, we traverse bridges. And when we grow up (and grow our connections), we strengthen bridges.

A networked form of conocimiento is established and maintained through processes of perpetuity, coming together at the root level again and again. Even in the less visible modes of influence—like the side alleys and back channels—are what substantially nurtures communal sentiments of both belonging and alienation. These sentiments are constantly emerging and shifting. If an issue with imagined community is that it's *never* encountered, the generative contrast of conocimiento arises because community is *constantly* encountered.

Through coalitions that exceed governmental regulations, governmental participation from citizens engaged on the ground, and dispersed community efforts, conocimiento allows a consciousness-raising effort that is never settled but always responsive to the needs of the community because it operates *in community*. We shift because we live together. And if that leaves us unsettled, we can embrace the nomadic ability to thrive untethered to static dwellings in exchange for dwelling mobility and articulate our being by mobilizing with each other.

It is the Us that shifts, at varying levels of transitivity: listening to, sharing with, and being [for] each Other.

Works Cited

Anderson, Benedict. *Imagined Communities: Reflections on the Origin and Spread of Nationalism*. Verso Books, 2006.

Anzaldúa Gloria, and AnaLouise Keating. *This Bridge We Call Home: Radical Visions for Transformation*. Routledge, 2002.

Gent, Whitney. "When Homelessness Becomes a 'Luxury': Neutrality as an Obstacle to Counterpublic Rights Claims." *Quarterly Journal of Speech*, vol. 103, no. 3, 2017, pp. 230–50, doi:10.1080/00335630.2017.1321133.

Leon, Kendall, and Stacey Pigg. "Conocimiento as a Path to Ethos." *Rethinking Ethos: A Feminist Ecological Approach to Rhetoric*. Southern Illinois UP, 2016, pp. 257–78.

11 THE SHEEPDOG ETHOS: ARMED CITIZENSHIP AS CARING LABOR

Daniel A. Cryer

ABSTRACT

A growing body of research investigates the identities taken on by people who regularly carry firearms, yet one common identity that carriers adopt – the "sheepdog" – has been frequently mentioned by scholars of gun cultures but not closely analyzed. This paper examines the origins of the sheepdog ethos in the work of Army Lt. Col. Dave Grossman, a leading scholar in the psychology of killing and a prolific trainer of police, arguing that one primary purpose of this ethos is to cast armed citizenship as a type of care work. In Grossman's writing and public speaking, widely accepted meanings of "care" and "love" are changed to serve as justifications for armed public life. This essay further analyzes the sheepdog ethos from the perspective of an ethic of care, finding that while it is admirably attuned to the real physical work of caring for others, the sheepdog's grounding in identity and moral hierarchy inhibits sheepdogs' attentiveness to those it claims to care for and their ability to assess whether their brand of armed care is effective.

Scholars studying the concealed carry of firearms have usefully coined terms that refer to gun carriers and the subcultures they occupy, helping to clarify the roles that armed citizenship plays within gun cultures and US society more broadly: carriers are *citizen-protectors* (Carlson) or *mobile sovereigns* (Anker) implementing *DIY security* (Light), while the shift from hunting to personal protection as a leading motivator for gun ownership is *gun culture 2.0* (Yamane). Less common, however, are scholarly analyses of the books and essays comprising much of pro-gun literature to examine the origins and effects of the names carriers give themselves. One influential identity within carry culture, mentioned by many scholars but not deeply explored, is the *sheepdog*, in which carriers see themselves protecting good, harmless people ("sheep") from evil criminals ("wolves").

What I will call the *sheepdog ethos* originates in the work of Army Lt. Col. Dave Grossman, first in his influential book *On Killing*, then more fully fleshed out in the essay "On Sheepdogs, Wolves, and Sheep" in the follow-up volume, *On Combat*. The term has since gained wide currency. Carlson points out that carriers in Michigan "explicitly identify themselves as 'sheepdogs' who protect the 'sheep' from the 'wolves'" (66) and that these terms were used by NRA-sponsored instructors in their classes. There are currently gun shops or training facilities with *sheepdog* in the name in at least nine U.S. states, and self-defense training seminars using the term include Sheepdog Response run by former UFC fighter Tim Kennedy, and Sheepdog Seminars, which offer defensive training for churches. In the film *American Sniper*, based on the autobiographical book by Navy SEAL sniper Chris Kyle, the main character's father gives a dinner table speech to a young Kyle and his brother laying out the societal roles played by sheepdogs, sheep, and wolves.

This paper argues that in referring to themselves as sheepdogs, carriers define armed citizenship as a type of care work, enacting a deep and rhetorically effective change in the language and ethics of gun ownership. As care work, the practice of living as a sheepdog gives a moral framework to a lifestyle organized around preparedness for violence. Violence is not incompatible with coherent moral systems or even with ethics of care, and some theorists of care and care ethics discuss how violence in certain circumstances can be caring (Held 138–39). But when Grossman's sheepdog ethos is compared with more rigorous care ethics, the ways in which the sheepdog both lives up to and falls short of care become clear. Further, a rhetorical analysis of Grossman's construction of the sheepdog ethos, particularly one that proceeds from the standpoint of care ethics, allows us to focus on the demagogic, identity-based nature of Grossman's claims. This paper provides a brief overview of Grossman's work and his construction of the sheepdog ethos as a form of caring labor, then assesses the sheepdog ethic using Joan Tronto's formulation of care ethics.

The Sheepdog as Care Worker

Dave Grossman is among the most prominent figures advocating armed citizenship in the United States. His credibility comes from years of scholarship and public speaking on the psychology of violence and killing, his academic appointments at West Point and the University of Arkansas, and his background as an Army Ranger. *On Killing* is widely cited by scholars studying violence (Collins) and gun culture (Blanchfield, Messner) as a seminal psychological study of perpetrators of lethal violence. In the past two decades, Grossman has become one of the country's leading trainers and motivational speakers for police and armed citizens. According to Radley Balko, author of *Rise of the Warrior Cop*, Grossman "has trained more US police officers than anyone else" and "more than anyone else, has instructed cops on what mindset they should bring to their jobs." Balko says Grossman's seminars "teach cops how to escalate, how to see the world as their enemy and how to find the courage to kill more people, more often."

In his books and public speaking, Grossman characterizes modern life as war and his audience as warriors. He tells them that, as warriors, they hold society together. If a society lost all of its doctors, teachers, engineers and mechanics, Grossman says, it could survive, but "if we went but a single generation without the warriors who are willing to confront human aggression every day, then within the span of that generation" civilization would fall (Grossman and Christensen xxii). Importantly, when Grossman's warrior chooses violence, it always comes from "a deep love for [his] fellow citizens," so deep that "[h]e hurts, suffers, and weeps for those he is sworn to protect" (Grossman and Christensen 187). It is this deep love that defines the sheepdog.

Grossman's essay "On Sheep, Wolves, and Sheepdogs" appears in his book *On Combat*. In the most general terms, the essay divides humanity into three categories defined by their relationship to violence and care. Most people are sheep: they "are not capable of hurting each other, except by accident or under extreme provocation" (180–81). Wolves are evil people who prey on the sheep. They are "aggressive sociopaths" who "feed on the flock without mercy" (181). Sheepdogs, as police officers, soldiers, or lawfully armed civilians, protect sheep by enacting violence upon the wolves, who deserve it. Sheepdogs are like wolves because they are capable of hurting others, but their caring nature sets them apart. Their self-discipline and love allow them to direct violence only where it is necessary, so their aggression is a gift to humanity (181).

Care for others defines the sheepdog so fundamentally that a lack of care simply means that person cannot be a sheepdog, consigning them by default to the role of sheep or wolf. Grossman says, "[T]he sheepdog must not, cannot and will not ever harm the sheep" (182). Betraying unrealistic notions of police accountability, he continues: "Any sheepdog who intentionally harms the lowliest little lamb will be punished and removed" (182). According to

Grossman, even sheep are uncaring when compared to the sheepdog. What defines sheep above all is "denial" that wolves will prey on them, and this denial amounts to a death sentence for the people they love, because the "price" paid for being a sheep is that, "[w]hen the wolf comes, you and your loved ones are going to die if there is not a sheepdog there to protect you" (184). Unlike sheepdogs, sheep do not care enough about those close to them to see the world's evils clearly. This lack of clarity not only puts them and others in danger, but also leads them to "scorn and disdain" the sheepdog (185), meaning that the sheepdog's "deep love" for the flock goes unreturned.

Grossman's depiction of caring public labor that upholds social order yet remains unappreciated aligns with feminist theorizations of care work. As a philosophical concept, care is relational and emotional, and because it is relational, care is more than a feeling or a disposition: it is a "practice" that "involves both thought and action" (Tronto 108). Care work is labor that requires care for people in need, whether for pay or as private unpaid labor like caring for one's children. Nancy Folbre has defined unpaid care work as "labor undertaken out of affection or a sense of responsibility for other people, with no expectation of immediate pecuniary reward" (75). Researchers have noted that care work is generally undervalued yet is also a type of work that allows other work to be done. Whether paid or unpaid, the benefits of caring labor extend beyond the isolated caregiver and recipient. The successfully parented child becomes a productive member of society; the well-taught student gains knowledge she applies to her profession and those it serves.

The sheepdog ethos casts carrying a gun in public as a form of masculine care work. According to Grossman, sheepdogs move through the world ready to protect sheep, who are unable to protect themselves. This form of care is not simply a feeling or disposition, but a program of action that involves carrying a deadly weapon and using it if necessary. Despite this, in Grossman's view, the sheepdog's work goes unappreciated. Because of the general public's fear of violence and lack of understanding of its place in the social order, they "scorn and disdain" the sheepdog (Grossman and Christensen 185). Like other care work, the work of the sheepdog has benefits far beyond the act of protection. According to Grossman, it is *the* labor that makes civilization possible.

The religious symbolism of sheep, wolves, and the implied shepherd who commands the sheepdog adds powerful resonances of caring labor to Grossman's themes of love and sacrifice. As constructed by Grossman, the sheepdog takes on characteristics of the biblical shepherd. Bible scholars point out that the image of the shepherd was long associated with risk and violence because of the potential dangers associated with shepherding. In the Old Testament, David uses his experience as a shepherd to argue for his fitness to fight Goliath (Hylen 386), saying to Saul, "Your servant used to keep his father's sheep, and when a lion or a bear came and took a lamb out of the flock, I went out after it and struck it, and delivered the lamb from its mouth; and when it arose against me, I caught it by its beard, and struck and killed it" (New King James Version, 1 Sam. 17:34–35). The metaphor of the shepherd expresses the competence and moral uprightness that comes from a willingness to risk bodily harm when those one cares for are threatened—what one scholar refers to as "the shepherd's risk-taking love" (Hylen 397).

Grossman's use of biblical imagery is especially clear in his most recent book, *On Spiritual Combat*, a daily devotional intended as a companion to the Bible, covering "spiritual warfare" in the same manner that his earlier books deal with "the physical battlefield" (12). Grossman urges readers to "tap the strength that is drawn from our deep, Christian-warrior roots. [...] Proclaim it now throughout the land: I am a sheepdog under the authority of the Great Shepherd!" (22). In this way, Grossman equates a willingness to engage in violence, and even to take a life, with Christian tradition.

The Sheepdog in the Four Phases of Care

The sheepdog ethos is an ethic meant to guide carriers' actions. But how does it compare to a more rigorously developed ethics of care? Joan Tronto's four phases of care are useful for this task because they treat care as a concrete process of action and as a political matter of public importance. Her four phases of care are "caring about, noticing the need to care in the first place; taking care of, assuming responsibility for care; caregiving, the actual work of care that needs to be done; and care-receiving, the response of that which is cared for to the care" (127). From these arise four corresponding elements of care ethics: "attentiveness, responsibility, competence, and responsiveness" (127). The second and third phases concern the actions of the caretaker and, seen in its best light, Grossman's sheepdog ethos performs these tasks well. The first and fourth phases concern the caretaker attending and responding to the perceptions and wishes of the cared-for, and it is in these phases that the sheepdog most seriously falls short of ethical care.

Seen through Tronto's framework in its best possible light, the strength of the sheepdog ethos is in its orientation toward concrete action, which happens primarily in the second and third phases of caring, "taking care of" and "caregiving." Responsibility in the "taking care of" phase means recognizing that because one is capable of meeting a recognized need, one *should* meet that need. In Grossman's formulation of the sheepdog, a small group of people in any society is willing and able to enter the toxic realm of violence. Because violence must sometimes be fought with violence, societies need these individuals to use their "gift" (Grossman and Christensen 181) for the greater good. Further, Tronto's "caregiving" phase requires competent execution. Competence in armed citizenship is multi-faceted, involving physical training and mental preparation, but one virtue of Grossman's work is its thoroughness in describing what he calls the "toxic, corrosive, destructive" realm of human violence (Grossman and Christensen 7), from the first inklings that a fight is imminent to the psychological effects of killing on the killer. Even if his message is muddled by his encouragement of violence in his police trainings, across his body of work Grossman communicates the seriousness of violent confrontation, showing that real violence is, despite what we see in staged versions, hard, ugly, and destructive of all involved. While such a message—or any message—cannot make an armed citizen competent, an understanding of it seems to be an essential component of any armed person's toolbox.

Yet even as Grossman's sheepdog framework sets realistic expectations for the demanding physical work of armed citizenship, its lack of responsiveness to those it labels "sheep" compromises its claims to ethical care. Tronto's first phase of care is "caring about," which "involves the recognition in the first place that care is necessary" (106) and requires a high degree of empathy. It is on these grounds of empathy and attentiveness that the sheepdog first falls short of an ethic of care. At no point in Grossman's vast body of work is there any acknowledgment that those he designates as sheep should have a say in how they are cared for. Doubtless many whom he labels as sheep would prefer not to be watched over by an armed civilian, or called sheep at all.

Further intensifying the problem of inattentiveness in the case of the sheepdog is what Tronto calls disdain for care-receivers, a not uncommon pitfall of caring labor. Those requiring care can be seen as helpless, lacking autonomy, even pitiful or inferior (120). Grossman tries to hedge against this type of disdain when he says he "mean[s] nothing negative by calling [people] sheep," and "there is nothing morally superior about the sheepdog" (183). But what defines the sheep above all for Grossman is denial that evil exists in the world, while the defining aspect of the sheepdog is an understanding of societal violence and a willingness to engage it to protect others. The sheepdog is the hero, an identity to aspire to, while the sheep is helpless and pitiful, a tempting but ultimately weak identity to which one should not succumb. Grossman says, "If you are a warrior who is legally authorized to carry a weapon and you step outside without that weapon, then you become a sheep, pretending that the bad man will not come today. [. . .] [I]f you are authorized to carry a weapon, and you walk outside without it, just take a deep breath, and say this to yourself . . . 'Baa'" (186). Grossman's sheepdog as caregiver, then, succumbs to the problem of disdaining the care-receiver and fails the test of attentiveness, without which the care of the sheepdog is a kind of forced caring. It projects a need for care onto sheep and insists that it proceed on the sheepdog's terms.

But the sheepdog ethos is also more than an ethic; it is a worldview centered in violence and identity, and in basing his claims in identity Grossman evades empirical questions about the accuracy of sheepdogs' and sheep's perceptions of the world. If one group is constitutionally incapable of or unwilling to perceive danger and another group is uniquely able to perceive and confront those dangers, then questions of empirical accuracy are answered in advance. In other words, sheepdogs can ignore any concerns sheep might have not because the sheep's arguments have been fairly represented and refuted, but because they are sheep, defined by denial, making their perceptions irrelevant. Patricia Roberts-Miller notes that a defining feature of demagoguery is an appeal to identity to the exclusion of policy debate and empirical inquiry (6–8, 16). Her point is not that demagoguery is always unacceptable—indeed, she argues that nearly everyone is demagogic at one time or another—but that demagoguery becomes dangerous when employed by powerful people or encoded in the reasoning of large groups. Grossman's societal taxonomy of sheepdogs, wolves and sheep makes carrying a necessity for sheepdogs not only for self-defense but for moral standing, and it delegitimizes empirical reasons that sheep might have for not carrying or not owning guns at all. But there is a great deal of empirical support for keeping guns out of the home, including findings that carrying makes one more likely to be shot during a violent encounter (Branas et al.) and that gun ownership correlates with higher rates of suicide (Miller et al). The sheepdog's lack of attentiveness causes him to miss empirically provable reasons for not carrying, even as this blind spot can increase the likelihood of his own injury or death.

The sheepdog framework's problems with attentiveness and fixation on identity would also seem to compromise its *responsiveness*, the ethical principle at stake in Tronto's final phase of care-receiving, or "the response of that which is cared for to the care" (127). "Care-receiving" says that any care claiming to be ethical must include avenues for assessing its effectiveness. What indicators can the caregiver point to showing that the need for care has been met? Because Grossman argues that a societal shift towards more people carrying guns in public is also a shift towards a more caring public life—a claim that is far from self-evident—it is reasonable to expect an accounting of whether and how such a shift amounts to effective care. Grossman's identity-based argument, however, does not offer a realistic look at the dangers sheepdogs pose to sheep and keeps him from addressing the "conditions of vulnerability and inequality" (Tronto 134) that responsiveness is meant to correct. Grossman frames sheepdogs' trustworthiness with a deadly weapon as simply part of who they are and harming sheep as something they would never do. Speaking of "the gift of aggression" that sheepdogs possess and give to the world, he says, "They would no more misuse this gift than a doctor would misuse his healing arts" (Grossman and Christensen 181). Grossman defines the question of sheepdogs' potential to harm sheep as one controlled by identity and choice; since sheepdogs would not choose to harm sheep, sheep will not be harmed.

Compared to more rigorous theories of violence, assumptions like this appear unrealistic and naive. Collins, for example, who draws extensively on Grossman's *On Killing*, emphasizes the situational nature of violence. Even as Collins acknowledges that a small percentage of people—the "violent few"— are responsible for a disproportionate amount of violence (370–74), he argues that we should not focus on types of people when looking for the causes of or solutions to violence. "Better," he says, "to proceed on the assumption that all humans are basically alike and that situational dynamics over very specific periods of time determine where individual fighters will be on the continuum" of violent behavior (70). "Not violent individuals," he summarizes, "but violent situations; and also, not fearful individuals but fearful positions in situations. And thus across the board" (70). Fiske and Rai also frame violence in a manner at odds with Grossman's identity-based framework, and which further suggests that widespread adoption of the sheepdog ethos could lead to more violence. According to them, violence and how it is viewed in any given culture is best explained not by "some trait or state of the individual perpetrator" (274), but by the culture's governing model(s) of social relations. Relational models that emphasize unity of an in-group against out-groups, or moral hierarchies in which "[s]uperiors [...] feel a sense of pastoral responsibility toward subordinates and are motivated to lead, guide, direct, and protect them" (19) make violence *more* acceptable rather than less for managing social relationships, and hence more likely (260). If one major purpose of Tronto's "responsiveness" phase of caregiving is to judge care's effectiveness, then the care of the sheepdog is, at best, highly suspect on the grounds that it perceives the nature of violence as proceeding almost entirely from individual traits rather than from human situations and relations, and on the grounds that it proposes a social model with underlying assumptions likely to point us toward more violence rather than less.

In sum, subjecting Grossman's formulation of the sheepdog to an ethic of care reveals an admirable willingness to take on the physical work of protection and, in some ways, a clear-eyed sense of just how toxic violent situations can be. But it is almost completely unconcerned with the perspectives and experiences of the care-receiver, a state of affairs in which real ethical caregiving cannot take place. As a consequence, it seems reasonable for those researching gun cultures to approach with skepticism any claims of care and love justifying armed citizenship. In the face of such claims we can ask several questions that grow from a familiarity with an ethics of care: What leads you to believe that you are caring for people in the manner they prefer to be cared for, rather than imposing your brand of care onto them? If you believe you have reason to disregard their wishes, is that on the basis of a fair representation of their views? How do you know that the care you provide is working? Moral frameworks for violence that can't provide answers that align positively with rigorous conceptions of care can more accurately be called domination concealing itself in the language of love.

Works Cited

American Sniper. Directed by Clint Eastwood, Warner Brothers, 2014.

Anker, Elisabeth. "Mobile Sovereigns: Agency Panic and the Feeling of Gun Ownership." *The Lives of Guns*, edited by Jonathan Obert, Andrew Poe and Austin Sarat, Oxford UP, 2019, pp. 21–42.

Balko, Radley. "A Day with 'Killology' Police Trainer Dave Grossman." *Washington Post*, 14 Feb. 2017, https://www.washingtonpost.com/news/the-watch/wp/2017/02/14/a-day-with-killology-police-trainer-dave-grossman/. Accessed 15 Oct. 2021.

Blanchfield, Patrick. "Prosthetic Gods: On the Semiotic and Affective Landscape of Firearms in American Politics." *Gun Studies: Interdisciplinary Approaches to Politics, Policy, and Practice*, edited by Jennifer Carlson, Kristin A. Goss and Harel Shapira, Routledge, 2019, pp. 196–210.

Branas, Charles C, Theresa S. Richmond, Dennis P. Culhane, Thomas R. Ten Have, Douglas J. Wiebe. "Investigating the Link Between Gun Possession and Gun Assault." *American Journal of Public Health*, vol. 99, 2009, pp. 2034–40.

Carlson, Jennifer. *Citizen-Protectors: The Everyday Politics of Guns in an Age of Decline*. Oxford UP, 2015.

Collins, Randall. *Violence: A Micro-Sociological Theory*. Princeton UP, 2008.

Fiske, Alan Page, and Tage Shakti Rai. *Virtuous Violence: Hurting and Killing to Create, Sustain, End, and Honor Social Relationships*. Cambridge UP, 2015.

Folbre, Nancy. "Holding Hands at Midnight: The Paradox of Caring Labor." *Feminist Economics*, vol 1, 1995, pp 73–92.

Grossman, Dave. *On Killing: The Psychological Cost of Learning to Kill in War and Society*. Revised ed., Back Bay, 2009.

Grossman, Dave, and Loren W. Christensen. *On Combat: The Psychology and Physiology of Deadly Conflict in War and in Peace*. 4th ed., Killology Research Group, 2012.

Grossman, Dave, and Adam Davis. *On Spiritual Combat: 30 Missions for Victorious Warfare*. Broadstreet, 2020.

Held, Virginia. *The Ethics of Care: Personal, Political, and Global*. Oxford UP, 2006.

Hylen, Susan E. "The Shepherd's Risk: Thinking Metaphorically with John's Gospel." *Biblical Interpretation*, vol. 24, 2016, pp. 382–99.

Light, Caroline E. *Stand Your Ground: A History of America's Love Affair with Lethal Self-Defense*. Beacon, 2017.

Messner, Michael A. "Guns, Intimacy, and the Limits of Militarized Masculinity." *Gun Studies: Interdisciplinary Approaches to Politics, Policy, and Practice*, edited by Jennifer Carlson, Kristin A. Goss and Harel Shapira, Routledge, 2019, pp. 224–40.

Miller, Matthew, Deborah Azrael, and Catherine Barber. "Suicide Mortality in the United States: The Importance of Attending to Method in Understanding Population-level Disparities in the Burden of Suicide." *Annual Review of Public Health*, vol. 33, 2012, pp. 393–408.

Roberts-Miller, Patricia. *Rhetoric and Demagoguery*. Southern Illinois UP, 2019.

Tronto, Joan C. *Moral Boundaries: A Political Argument for an Ethic of Care*. Routledge, 1993.

Yamane, David. "The Sociology of U.S. Gun Culture." *Sociology Compass*, 16 June 2017. https://doi.org/10.1111/soc4.12497. Accessed 15 October 2022.

12 Redefining the Climate Crisis as a "Security" Threat: The Biden Administration's Progress and Limitations in Addressing This Charge to Change

Heidi E. Hamilton

Abstract

Since taking office, the Biden Administration has consistently defined climate crisis as a "security" threat. This change in rhetoric in one way provides a charge for the United States, a call to action through the national security apparatus. However, this security rhetoric focuses the problem on traditional national security threats, such as resource-based conflicts and military readiness, and thus also confines US responses within a militarized mindset. Instead, the scope of "security" needs to be expanded both to encompass a framing of "human security" and to consider sustainable, not just military, solutions.

This essay examines Biden Administration rhetoric that discusses the climate crisis as a security threat. It first draws out distinctions in how this rhetoric changes from past approaches that did not define climate in this way. Then, the essay employs feminist foreign policy theory, specifically critiques by Women, Peace, and Security (WPS) advocates as a framework to suggest a further charge for change, asking for not only defining climate crisis within the definition of security, but also looking at definitional moves to change what the US means by security itself. Employing this framework looks at ways in which the Biden Administration's rhetoric limits definitional changes as well as potential places in the rhetoric that provide places to start changing not only conceptions of security, but also approaches to the climate crisis.

"Whenever climate catastrophe strikes, our interconnected world is less secure. What to do about it, though, depends upon your definition of security" (Susskind). For advocates of the Women, Peace, and Security (WPS) agenda, Susskind, executive director of MADRE, an international women's human rights organization, speaks to the concern over how national security discourse securitizes climate crisis. The WPS agenda refers to a series of United Nations Security Council Resolutions (UNSCR). PeaceWomen, a program of the Women's International League for Peace and Freedom, indicates that "[t]hese resolutions make up the Women, Peace and Security Agenda. They guide work to promote gender equality and strengthen women's participation, protection and rights across the conflict cycle, from conflict prevention through post-conflict reconstruction." Increasing numbers of advocates of the WPS agenda argue that given its substantial effects "it is impossible for WPS advocates to work toward, or even talk about, peace and security without centering" the climate crisis (Cohn and Duncanson 749).

The Biden administration, upon taking office, consistently defined climate crisis as a "security" threat. This change in rhetoric provides a charge for the United States, a call to action through the national security apparatus. However, this security rhetoric focuses the problem on traditional national security threats, such as resource-based conflicts and impacts on military readiness, and thus confines US responses within a militarized mindset whose mindset often ignores structural inequalities and excludes measures that address resource management and conflict mediation. For example, instead of a militarized mindset, the scope of "security" needs to be expanded to encompass a framing of "human security" and to consider sustainable, not just military, solutions.

This essay examines Biden administration rhetoric that discusses the climate crisis as a security threat. It briefly draws out distinctions in how this rhetoric changes from past administrations' approaches, instead prioritizing dealing with the climate crisis. The latter part of the essay then employs feminist foreign policy theory, specifically critiques by WPS advocates, as a framework to suggest a further charge for change, not merely defining climate crisis within the definition of security but considering definitional moves to change what the US means by security itself. Employing this framework reveals ways in which the Biden administration's rhetoric limits definitional changes to security, as well as potential places that provide openings to start changing not only conceptions of security, but also approaches to the climate crisis.

Climate Crisis and Security Rhetoric

To begin, the Biden administration clearly names the climate crisis as a security issue. This naming, although not completely new, prioritizes the climate crisis in ways different than past administrations. Back to President Clinton, administrations have been linking climate change to national security, although assuming a slower rate of climate change (Bump). For example, the Obama administration's 2015 U.S. National Security Strategy indicated that "Climate change is an urgent and growing threat to our national security" (White House, "National Security Strategy" 12). The Trump administration undercut these steps, withdrawing from the Paris Agreement and focusing on promoting domestic energy sources, rather than including climate change, in its National Security Strategy (Chemnick).

Immediate actions by President Biden after taking office defined the climate crisis as a security issue, rhetorically suggesting an emphasis not existing before. On January 27, 2021, he signed the executive order "Tackling the Climate Crisis at Home and Abroad." Part I of that executive order states, "Climate considerations shall be an essential element of United States foreign policy and national security" and "This order builds on and reaffirms actions my Administration has already taken to place the climate crisis at the forefront of this Nation's foreign policy and national security planning" (United States 7619). His comments prior to the signing reinforce this message. Biden states, "this executive order I'm signing today also makes it official that climate change will be at *the center* of our national security and foreign policy" (italics added).

Forough Amin and Alessandro Gagaridis' theory of securitization aids in understanding this rhetorical framing. As Amin and Gagaridis posit that "political issues can be converted into security issues (securitized) through discourse" (62), they also argue this securitization goes beyond just addressing an issue:

> States are not only concerned with managing security problems, but they can also create those problems in line with their interests. By securitizing a political issue, states represent it as a matter of high urgency and priority and, thereby, seek to convince their populations or the international community to mobilize extraordinary resources for dealing with it. . . . Successfully securitizing a subject means being able to legitimize the securitized version of it, and this, in turn, depends on how persuasive that constructed version is. (62)

Successfully naming something a security issue through a successful speech act then also transforms the way of dealing with them (Trombetta 588).

Biden's rhetoric attempts this securitization, and statements by other administration officials continue this securitization process. At an April climate change summit, Secretary of Defense Lloyd Austin remarked, "Today, no nation can find lasting security without addressing the climate crisis. We face all kinds of threats in our line of work, but few of them truly deserve to be called existential. The climate crisis does." Secretary of State Antony Blinken states, "Pick a security challenge that affects the United States. Climate change is likely to make it worse." In both statements, not only is the explicit linkage between national security and the climate crisis made, but the importance of this linkage is stressed through describing it as an "existential" threat or arguing that *all* other security challenges are affected by it. The Director of National Intelligence Avril Haines's language is more direct, indicating the need to "view climate change as an *urgent* national security priority" (italics mine).

THE WPS AGENDA AND FEMINIST FOREIGN POLICY

In order to analyze further how this move toward securitization not only defines the climate crisis as a security threat, but also reinforces militarized understandings of security, I turn to the work of advocates of the WPS agenda and feminist foreign policy scholars. The platform for the WPS agenda rests on ten United Nations Security Council Resolutions (UNSCR), starting with UNSCR 1324 and ending most recently with UNSCR 2493 (United States Institute of Peace). The agenda is described as consisting of four pillars "ensuring women's participation in governance and peace and security fields, preventing conflict and violence, protecting women's and girls' rights in conflict, and assuring appropriate and just relief and recovery for survivors of conflict" (Smith). WPS advocates may include those working with UN agencies and in civil society through non-governmental agencies, but also those engaging in scholarly work, under the umbrella of feminist foreign policy or feminist international relations (IR) theory. Feminist IR theory studies the gendered nature of foreign policy, and by extension, foreign policy discourse. How feminist IR theorists examine definitions of security is most relevant to the analysis of Biden administration climate crisis rhetoric. Traditional realist definitions of security center on the state. Jacqui True points out that security is "examined only in the context of the presence and absence of war, because the threat of war is considered endemic to the sovereign state-system where security is zero-sum and by definition national" (234). This focus on externally imposed violence "ignore[s] other forms of insecurity and their gendered dimensions" (Ackerly and True 252). This understanding fits the concerns held by securitization theorists. Trombetta points out that "[t]he label security brings with it a set of practices and a way of dealing with a problem that characterizes an issue as a security issue. . . . Security is about survival, urgency and emergency" (588).

Feminist IR scholars instead reconceptualize security. Ann Tickner argues for a broader idea of national security: "thinking about military, economic and environmental security in interdependent terms suggests the need for new methods of conflict resolution which seek to achieve mutually beneficial, rather than zero-sum, outcomes" (63). Jill Steans discusses conceiving of human security instead. A focus on human security not only focuses on the range of threats to humans, not just states, but also allows for human agency in confronting these threats, rather than only state action (Tripp).

This feminist IR work distinguishes between securitization that reinforces a risk-based discourse reifying realist notions of security and justifying state-based and military actions and securitization that may expand understandings of *what* security entails and *who* acts to ensure security. Specifically, this work has paid increasing attention to the militarization of security threats around the climate crisis. Regarding environmental and climate security, Trombetta notes, "By securitizing nontraditional issues, the incongruence of a specific logic of security appears . . . In this framework, the construction of both threats and rules by which security is carried out are open to a process of social construction and transformation" (591). In other words, while securitization often reinforces narrow conceptions of security and legitimizes militarized solutions, the potential exists to construct understandings of security issues that expand the range of solutions.

Constructing Climate Crisis as Security Threat

In this section, Biden administration rhetoric is examined more closely. Beyond naming climate crisis as a national security issue, how that issue is defined, who is called upon to act, and what actions should be taken will be explored. In doing so, drawing upon the feminist IR literature and WPS advocates, I look at ways in which this construction confines security to a militarized mindset and ways in which it enables transformations of the security framework.

Confining Security to a Militarized Mindset

In three ways, Biden administration rhetoric, which defines the climate crisis as a security threat, reinforces narrow, militarized conceptions of security.

First, the climate crisis is constructed primarily as a *military* threat. For WPS advocates, this construction increases risks. Cohn and Duncanson argue that while the risks of conflict from climate breakdown needs to be considered, viewing climate crisis as a threat to individual states' national security leading to a militarized response misunderstands the social and economic causes and perpetuates harmful outcomes (752). Administration rhetoric constructs this military threat in three ways: through the overall threat scope, through increasing migration, and through threats to the military itself. The overall scope of the threat is characterized. Blinken remarks, "Climate change exacerbates existing conflicts and increases the chances of new ones—particularly in countries where governments are weak and resources are scarce." Haines makes threat considerations even more explicit, "How increasingly disruptive extreme weather events driven in part by climate change can trigger crop failures, wildfires, energy blackouts, or infectious disease outbreaks with enormous economic and political impacts that are capable of changing a country's long-term trajectory. How droughts can lead to scarce resources that trigger conflicts and exacerbate violent extremism. How shifting coastlines will affect sovereign borders."

Biden administration officials discuss the security threat posed by climate crisis induced migration, again framing it in confrontational terms. Austin states, "Closer to the equator, rising temperatures and more frequent and intense extreme weather events in Africa and Central America threaten millions with drought, hunger, and displacement. As families risk their lives in search of safety and security, mass migration leaves them vulnerable to exploitation and radicalization, all of which undermine stability." His focus ends on the stability issue, which presumably poses the risk to the US, not concern over people starving. Blinken expresses similar comments:

> Climate change can also be a driver of migration. . . . When disasters strike people who are already living in poverty and insecurity, it can often be the final straw, pushing them to abandon their communities in search of a better place to live. For many Central Americans, that means trying to make it to the United States - even when we say repeatedly that the border is closed, and even though the journey comes with tremendous hardships, especially for women and girls who face heightened risk for sexual violence.

Blinken's comments do voice more concern for the human cost of migration, even as he brings up US borders. (The way he voices those concerns is problematic, however, and will be addressed later.)

Officials also characterize the security threat to the military more directly. President Biden remarks that "the Defense Department reported that climate change is a direct threat to more than two thirds of the military's operational critical installations." Haines provides a specific example, explaining "the flooding of US bases in certain locations, such as the Marshall Islands, will continue to increase, potentially creating challenges for military readiness." Invoking the Marshall Islands here is particularly remarkable because no acknowledgement is made of effects on the nation itself, where sea level changes may force entire populations to be relocated from their homeland. The securitizing move places the focus entirely on the climate crisis vis-à-vis the US military. As Austin illustrates, the end point is about us: "From coast to coast and across the world, the climate crisis has caused substantial damage and put people in danger, making it more difficult for us to carry out our mission of defending the United States and our allies." This securitizing move risks enhancing the danger. Susskind argues, "In this militarized way of thinking, the danger lies not in crop failures but in the uprooted migrants seeking safety at our borders. The threat is not the drought, but the armed groups controlling water supplies. This definition of national security divides us and diverts attention from addressing a global crisis that will require us to work together as allies, not enemies, to solve."

In the remarks securitizing the climate crisis, a second limitation is exposed. When the effects on people, especially women, are mentioned, they are characterized as victims who need to be protected. WPS advocates caution on focusing on the protection and not the participation pillar within the WPS agenda, which "could translate into a paternalistic focus on women's vulnerability and erase the structural insecurity that perpetuates these inequities in the first place. Painting women as victims solely in need of protection from the effects of the climate crisis depoliticizes gendered power relations" (Papworth). Blinken's statement, previously quoted, acknowledges the unique impact on women and girls, but frames that in the context of nation-state (i.e., the US) action to protect, rather than empower. Haines similarly mentions vulnerable populations and even the climate crisis' intersection with factors such as economic prosperity, but fell short of suggesting any participatory role for women, just indicating there would be new vulnerabilities.

Third, the securitizing moves rely largely on top-down solutions, including work with other nations. This provides a limited range of solutions. Kurnoth et al. point out that "bilateral and multilateral diplomacy drive the climate security agenda from 'top-down.'" Instead, what is needed is to "strengthen bottom-up processes that engage civil society, locally led organisations, youth, and other, often still excluded, drivers of change" (Kurnoth et al.). Biden announced, "Today's executive order will help strengthen that commitment by working with other nations to support the most vulnerable to the impact of climate change and to increase our collective resilience.

That includes a summit of world leaders that I'll convene to address this climate crisis." Blinken similarly states, "We'll seize every chance we get to raise these issues with our allies and partners, and through multilateral institutions" before proceeding on to talk specifically about NATO. Both statements emphasize the work at a nation-to-nation level, even as they suggest action will be taken to protect others, not necessarily involved in decision-making processes.

Enabling Transformations of the Security Framework

These securitizing moves, and the restriction of the climate crisis to a more militarized understanding, are not surprising. However, administration rhetoric also constructs security in two ways that provide opportunities to expand security discourse. First, while a large focus of the security discourse is on the conflict risks and effects on military readiness, at times, security is broadened to human security. First defined as a concept in the United Nations Development Programme 1994 annual report, "Human security shifted the focus of security from the state to the individual" (Trombetta 593). Human security thus entails a broader perspective, looking at food security, water issues, energy supply (Trombetta 593), protection from disease, and provision of shelter (Cohn and Duncanson 750). Susskind indicates, "feminist foreign policy orients security as fundamentally about care." Moves toward this understanding occur a few times. Biden, talking generally about action on the climate, states, "we're talking about the health of our families and cleaner water, cleaner air, and cleaner communities." Blinken, talking about the larger effects, also discusses the very real effects on human lives, and the disproportionate effects:

> Unless we turn this around, it's going to get worse. More frequent and more intense storms; longer dry spells; bigger floods; more extreme heat and more extreme cold; faster sea level rise; more people displaced; more pollution; more asthma. Higher health costs; less predictable seasons for farmers. And all of that will hit low-income, black and brown communities the hardest.

So, human security costs are mentioned amid the larger militarized security costs. Additionally, statements that approach finding solutions also open up the security discourse. This occurs both in terms of the type of actions and who might also be involved in finding solutions. In terms of type of action, Trombetta argues that "the instruments to provide stability require effort to promote both mitigation and adaption to environmental impact and change" (593). Furthermore, "A focus on emissions has the merit of involving industrialized countries and avoiding the removal of their responsibility suggested by the discourse on environmental conflicts, which focused on the global south, its inadequacy and responsibility" (Trombetta 597).

Within administration rhetoric is a continuing discussion thread over reducing emissions, particularly mentioning the US rejoining the Paris Climate Agreement (U.S. Office of the Press Secretary). President Biden stresses the portion of the executive order that emphasizes clean energy: "a modern, resilient climate infrastructure and clean energy future." Thus, the fact that the executive order combined both domestic and foreign policy responses also allowed for the framing of mitigation and adaptation solutions to occur around the security rhetoric. Haines makes those connections clearer, saying "we can also help the world understand the impact that climate change is having on our lives to catalyze ambition and perhaps most of all, to identify opportunities to promote adaptation and mitigation." And while the focus is largely on US action, and working with multilateral partners, a nod to a larger range of partners occurs. Blinken remarks, "We will enlist states, cities, businesses large and small, civil society, and other coalitions as partners and models." While obviously still placing the US as the leading actor, this moves to suggest more actors could be part of the solution to the security issue.

Conclusion

In many ways, prioritizing the climate crisis as a security threat is a major advancement. While past administrations began that defining (except for the Trump administration), the Biden administration prioritized it in additional ways. Doing so allows for more urgent responses on the part of the United States, looking at the larger global picture. While a few possibilities occur to expand how the US defines and approaches security threats, much of this securitizing rhetoric remains confined to a narrow conception of security concerns defining threats within a military mindset, which also narrows the range of solutions available and prevents a focus on measures that enhance care for human security. To return to Susskind's quote from the start, how we define security, how securitization occurs, will affect how we respond to the existential threat of the climate crisis.

Works Cited

Abdenur, Adriana, Mavesha Alam, Adam Dav, Cristal Downing, and Mosello, Beatrice. "How Can Climate Considerations be Better Integrated into the Women, Peace, and Security Agenda?" *The Global Observatory*, 15 Oct. 2021, theglobalobservatory.org/2021/10/how-can-climate-considerations-be-better-integrated-into-the-women-peace-and-security-agenda/

Ackerly, Brooke A., and Jacqui True. "Studying the Struggles and Wishes of the Age: Feminist Theoretical Methodology and Feminist Theoretical Methods." *Feminist Methodologies for International Relations*, edited by Brooke A. Ackerly, Maria Stern, and Jacqui True, Cambridge UP, 2006, pp. 241–60.

Amin, Forough, and Alessandro Gagaridis,. "'I Deeply Regret that Some Perceive My Being Here as Political': Rhetorical Analysis of Netanyahu's Speech on the Iran Nuclear Deal as a Securitizing Move." *International Journal of Language Studies*, vol. 13, no. 3, 2019, pp. 61–86.

Austin, Lloyd. "Secretary Austin Remarks at Climate Change Summit." 22 April 2021. Department of Defense, www.defense.gov/News/Transcripts/Transcr pt/Article/2582828/secretary-austin-remarks-at-climate-change-summit/.

Biden, Joseph. "Remarks by President Biden before Signing Executive Actions on Tackling Climate Change, Creating Jobs, and Restoring Scientific Integrity." 27 Jan. 2021. White House, www.whitehouse.gov/briefing-room/speeches-remarks/2021/01/27/remarks-by-president-biden-before-signing-executive-actions-on-tackling-climate-change-creating-jobs-and-restoring-scientific-integrity/.

Blinken, Antony. J. "Tackling the Crisis and Seizing the Opportunity: America's Global Climate Leadership." 19 Apr. 2021. Department of State, https://bit.ly/3NNtjFa.

Bump, Philip. "The Long History of Linking Climate Change to American Security." *Washington Post*, 20 May 2015, www.washingtonpost.com/news/the-fix/wp/2015/05/20/the-long-history-of-linking-climate-change-to-american-security/

Chemnick, Jean. "Trump Drops Climate Threats from National Security Strategy." *Scientific American*, 19 Dec. 2017, www.scientificamerican.com/article/trump-drops-climate-threats-from-national-security-strategy/

Cohn, Claire, and Claire Duncanson. "Women, Peace and Security in a Changing Climate." *International Feminist Journal of Politics*, vol. 22, no. 5, 2020, pp. 742–62.

Haines, Avril. "DNI Haines Remarks at the 2021 Leaders Summit on Climate." 22 Apr. 2021. www.dni.gov/index.php/newsroom/speeches-interviews/speeches-interviews-2021/item/2208-dni-haines-remarks-at-the-2021-leaders-summit-on-climate.

Kurnoth, Hannah Elisabeth, Beatrice Mosello, and Jenna Greve. "Stronger Together." *Climate Diplomacy*, 14 Jun. 2021, climate-diplomacy.org/magazine/conflict/stronger-together.

Papworth, Evyn. "Looking Beyond Conflict to Address Climate Change Impacts in the Women, Peace and Security Agenda." *The Global Observatory*, 19 Mar. 2021, theglobalobservatory.org/2021/03/looking-beyond-conflict-address-climate-change-impacts-in-wps-agenda/

PeaceWomen. "Security Council Opens Debate: Sexual Violence in Conflict," April 2019." 23 April 2019, www.peacewomen.org/security-council/security-council-open-debate-sexual-violence-conflict-april-2019

"Press Briefing by Press Secretary Jen Psaki, Special Presidential Envoy for Climate John Kerry, and National Climate Advisor Gina McCarthy." *The White House*, 27 Jan. 2021, https://bit.ly/3CJYfjg. Interview Transcript.

Smith, Elizabeth. "Scope for Improvement: Linking the Women, Peace and Security Agenda to Climate Change." *Stockholm International Peace Research Institute*, 5 Jun. 2020, https://bit.ly/3plhAEm.

Steans, Jill. *Gender and International Relations: Issues, Debates and Future Directions*. Polity Press, 2006.

Susskind, Yifat. "The Climate Crisis Needs a Feminist Response, not a Military One." *Grist*, 9 June 2021, grist.org/fix/climate-crisis-feminist-response-military-national-security/

Tickner, Ann. J. "Hans Morgenthou's Principles of Political Realism: A Feminist Reformulation." *International Theory: Critical Investigations*, edited by James Der Derian, Palgrave Macmillan UK, 1995, pp. 53–74.

Tripp, Aili Mari. "Toward a Gender Perspective on Human Security." *Gender, Violence, and Human Security: Critical Feminist Perspectives*, edited by Aili Mari Tripp, Myra Marx Ferree, and Christina Ewig, New York UP, 2013, pp. 3–32.

Trombetta, Maria Julia. "Environmental Security and Climate Change: Analysing the Discourse." *Cambridge Review of International Affairs*, vol. 21, no. 4, 2008, pp. 585–602. DOI: 10.1080/09557570802452920

True, Jacqui. "Feminism." *Theories of International Relations*, edited by Scott Burchill & Andrew Linklater, St. Martin's P, 1996.

United States, Executive Office of the President [Joseph Biden]. Executive Order No. 14008 "Tackling the Climate Crisis at Home and Abroad." *Federal Register*, vol. 86, no. 19. 21 Jan. 2021.

United States Institute of Peace. "What Is UNSCR 1325? An Explanation of the Landmark Resolution on Women, Peace and Security," n.d., www.usip.org/gender_peacebuilding/about_UNSCR_1325

White House. "The National Security Strategy of the United States." Feb. 2015. Washington: President of the United States.

13 THE 'WAR ON CHRISTMAS' AND PREVENTIVE WAR

Patricia Roberts-Miller

ABSTRACT

This paper examines the puzzling hyperbole of self-described "conservatives" who reframe normal policy disagreements as war. It argues that the rhetoric of being at war is in service of a policy agenda, oriented toward making a minority political/religious ideology hegemonic. Paradoxically, then, these rhetors are trying to use the claim of being victims of a war oriented toward their extermination in order to justify policies oriented toward the cultural/political extermination of the Other. While this strategy is often identified as "projection" (Burke, Roberts-Miller, Skinnell) this paper argues that it is more usefully understood as preventive war.

In 2015, Starbucks released a slightly revised holiday cup. Like previous years, it was red, but without Christmas trees, reindeers, or Christmas ornaments. Several people took the removal of Christmas trees and reindeers from the cups as trying "to take Christ and Christmas off of their brand new cups" (Itkowitz). Despite it being a fairly muddled rhetoric (neither the Christmas tree nor reindeer symbolize Christ, for instance), the notion of there being a "war on Christmas" was already common in certain circles, and promoted by media outlets like Fox (Media Matters "Fox News") and Breitbart (Kassam). That same year, Donald Trump promised, "I guarantee if I become president, we're going to be saying 'Merry Christmas' at every store" (Schleifer). The fantasy that there is a conspiracy to destroy America, and it is signified by trivial aspects of holiday practices, goes at least as far back as the 1959 John Birch panic over the sale of UNICEF Christmas cards that didn't mention Christmas (Kregeloh). In 2004, the Committee to Save Christmas was formed in response to clerks at Macy's and Bloomingdale's saying "Happy Holidays" instead of "Merry Christmas," and the plaint has been a constant since (Goldberg 161–63).

It's tempting to ridicule the hyperbole of someone claiming we have to "save" Christmas from a clerk saying "Happy Holidays," let alone insist that removing reindeer from Starbucks cups is part of a conspiracy to promote partial birth abortion and gay marriage (O'Reilly, qtd. in Wildau), but it's important to note that this reframing of normal policy disagreements as signifiers of war permeates self-described "conservative" media. According to such pundits and politicians, there are wars on: America (Coulter), business (Lin), Christians (Media Matters "Fox News"), Christmas (Gibson), conservatives (Hasson), the family (Stoll), men ("Coming War," Venker), the police (Grassley, MacDonald), religion (Gregg), Republicans (Knefel), the rich (Perkins), the right (Hanson), statues (Robertson), suburban property values (Limbaugh), Trump (Goodwin), the unborn (Cassidy), white males (Lifson), white people (Cegielski), "you and your family" (O'Reilly, qtd. in Stabile). And who is it that is at war with all these groups? A capacious and homogenized group of "Liberals," "Democrats," "Biden's voters," "the woke mob," feminists, political correctness, secular progressives.

The majority of Americans identify as Christian (Pew), the richest Americans still hold almost 70 percent of the US net wealth ("Distribution"), and the "war on police" is little more than holding them accountable to law (Thomson-DeVeaux et al.). As of the 2022 elections Republicans have twenty-three state government trifectas (Democrats have fourteen, "State Government"). In the 2020 elections, fifteen states voted Republican for president, governor, state senate, state house, US Senate, *and* US House (eight states voted Democrat for all those positions; Wikipedia), and white men are still dominant in politics and business despite being a minority (Villarreal, Guynn). So, if there's a war on those groups, it's singularly ineffective.

The number of supposed wars is absurdly capacious—"liberals" seem awfully busy—and the evidence that there is war is often tenuous, incoherent, or unintentionally funny. John Gibson uses the example of George and Laura Bush sending out cards that "included best wishes for a holiday season" as a sign that they are worried about offending someone (rather than that they are being considerate), and he goes on to say, "The fear of offending someone with a declaration of one's own faith is clear evidence of the war" (190). One of the blurbs for Gibson's book claims that "we must hide behind closed doors to celebrate a traditional holiday." O'Reilly's assertion that Grant's making Christmas an official holiday had to do with "acknowledging the country's Judeo-Christian tradition," the equation of Jesus and reindeer, and various other odd claims invite us to dismiss this demagoguery as too ridiculous to take seriously. However, I will argue that we should take the framing of "war" for normal policy disagreements very seriously, and seriously consider that some people take it literally.

The politics as war frame is not meaningless rhetorical flourish; frames cut off some things, and focus attention on others. Depending on the kind of war that is imagined, this frame limits or cuts off normal democratic practices of deliberation and negotiation, and it focusses attention on in-group danger. As will be argued in the first section of this paper, war radicalizes a community to the degree that people are persuaded they are faced with an implacable enemy determined on in-group extermination. A radicalized base will support radical policies of out-group control and suppression, advocating or justifying aggression and coercion against the "enemy." Briefly, the degree of choice in a war constrains the degree to which a community will permit or value deliberation and policy argumentation—the more choice, the more such democratic practices are valued, and the less choice, the more that those practices are seen as dangerous, even treasonous. The more that proposed aggression is a war of choice, the harder it is for advocates to engage in effective argumentation. Thus, the kind of war that's being advocated matters for scholars of rhetoric. So, the question is: if there is a war on Christmas, Christians, men, and so on, what kind of war is it?

For scholars of rhetoric, one useful way to think of wars is in terms of how much choice a nation has about the war. In a war of self-defense, there is no choice—the war has already been started by the enemy. Because the victim of aggression is generally seen as justified in responding in kind, rhetors advocating such a response are likely to be successful—consider how the rhetorical situation for FDR changed between December 5 and December 8 of 1941. Especially if the aggressor is determined on extermination, advocating counter-aggression is likely to be a popular case. More important, advocating taking time to deliberate thoroughly is likely to be unpopular, perceived as cowardice or treachery. Further, political and military leaders and combatants are generally granted "moral license"—formal and informal norms of fairness, procedure, and so on are suspended. As will be discussed, because wars of self-defense are rhetorically straightforward, and because of that granting of moral license, rhetors often claim that aggression is self-defense, even when that characterization is less than plausible.

Sometimes it is obvious that an enemy aggression is imminent, and therefore a nation or group decides to engage in *preemptive* aggression. A preemptive war or action is "an attack initiated on the basis of incontrovertible evidence that an enemy attack is imminent" (qtd. in "Preemptive War Doctrine"). Jack Levy and William Thompson emphasize the importance of perception for this kind of action: "Preemption involves a military attack in response to the virtual certainty that the adversary is about to strike" (46). One of the more famous instances of a preemptive attack was Sir Francis Drake's 1587 raid on the port of Cadiz, where the Armada was gathering for an invasion of England ("Preemptive"). In 1914, both Russian mobilization and German invasion of Belgium were preemptive (Van Evera 41). Napoleon's 1815 march to Belgium was preemptive, since he believed an invasion on the part of the coalition was imminent (Lebow 106). Preemptive aggression is a kind of "anticipatory self-defense," and, hence, generally perceived as just.

A *preventive* war is similar to preemptive aggression, in that both preemptive and preventive actions are grounded in the conviction that war with the Other is inevitable. The difference is, as Robert Jervis says, one of time. A preemptive action is "an attack against an adversary that is about to strike," whereas preventive action "is a move to prevent a threat from fully emerging" (40). Groups engage in preventive war when they believe that there is a "closing window of opportunity," and that this moment is the most advantageous. The Japanese bombing of Pearl Harbor in 1941 is one of the more famous examples. More rhetorically challenging than either preemptive aggression or self-defense, a successful case for preventive war depends largely on the extent to which advocates can persuade their audience that war with the other is unavoidable—that the Other is already planning to attack, albeit not imminently.

Often, preventive aggression is reframed as preemptive. Scholars generally agree that the 2003 invasion of Iraq was preventive, but advocates of invasion often tried to frame it either as self-defense (accusations Saddam Hussein was involved with the 9/11 attack) or preemptive (the Weapons of Mass Destruction narrative). When Earl Warren advocated mass imprisonment of people of Japanese ancestry, he was advocating preventive coercion. But he presented it as a preemptive measure, insisting that sabotage was imminent. When it was pointed out to him that there had been no instances of sabotage, he said the absence of sabotage "convinced [him] more than any factor," and "I take the view that that is the most ominous sign in our whole situation" (qtd. in Roberts-Miller 95).

Diplomacy, deliberation, and policy argumentation are all limited in conditions where aggression toward an enemy is generally perceived as self-defense, preemptive, or preventive. In the first case, negotiating with the enemy seems to be submitting, and at least some degree of surrendering (for instance, whereas there was some possibility of the UK negotiating with Argentina regarding the Falklands/Malvinas Islands, such a course of action became politically impossible once Argentina sent troops of occupation). If people believe that their situation justifies either preemptive or preventive aggression, then they believe that diplomacy and deliberation cannot resolve the conflict—war is, as said above, unavoidable because the Other is determined on it. To put it more clearly, in such situations, "the conflict" is not the consequence of negotiable disagreements, but the consequence of the Other's implacable hostility (that is, who They are) or an essential incompatibility of the two groups (that is, who we both are). That is, the rhetoric advocating or justifying such aggression shifts the stasis from policy issues to identity.

The fourth kind of war might be called a war of *pure choice*. The Other does not present an existential threat (imminent or long-term), and has no intention of attacking us. In wars of pure choice, it is possible to resolve any conflicts through diplomacy, deliberations, or policies far short of coercion. The exception is if the aggressor (that is, the group that wants to start a war of aggression against another) wants to exterminate the Other, either politically (for example, Russia's 2022 invasion of Ukraine), or physically (Germany's 1939 invasion of Poland). Obviously, neither Ukraine nor Poland would negotiate to the satisfaction of the aggressor. More common is when the aggressor wants to gain a specific resource or territory (the 1846–1848 war between the US and Mexico), regime change (the 1898 Spanish-American War), or favorable foreign/economic policies (the Opium Wars).

The case for a war of pure choice is the most rhetorically difficult, and so it is rare that a rhetor tries to make that case (the only exception I've found is Alexander the Great at the Beas); instead, rhetors claim they had no choice, reframing the aggression as preventive, preemptive, or self-defense. Thus, for instance, Hitler's invasion of Poland—which would trigger war with France and Great Britain—was rhetorically defended as action forced on Germany by Allied belligerence and Polish aggression (Hitler).

It's worth noting that Hitler may have sincerely believed that his invasion was preventive, and not pure choice. As Horace Rumbold, the British ambassador to Germany, noted in a 1933 telegram, Hitler believed that nations were always at war with one another: "Any living organism which ceases to fight for its existence is, [Hitler] asserts, doomed to extinction. A country or a race which ceases to fight is equally doomed" (49). In short, Hitler began a war of pure choice, believing it was preventive, and defended it rhetorically as self-defense. That someone sincerely believes he is always already at war with the Other doesn't make it true.

There is one more point to be made about war before returning to the rhetoric of politics as war. Most wars, according to the nineteenth-century military theorist Carl von Clausewitz, have political motives and political ends. What he calls "normal" wars are oriented toward specific goals, such as gaining territory or resources; when those goals have been achieved, the war can end. The more limited the goals, the more limited the war (see especially 86–88). There are, he acknowledges, some instances of "absolute" war, in which the goal is to "destroy the adversary, to eliminate his existence as a State" (qtd. in Howard). That is, political *or* physical extermination. There is no place for deliberation or diplomacy in such a war; the aggressor is determined on complete subjugation (politicide or genocide), and therefore there aren't policy changes that might end the war. Similarly, the object of such aggression is faced with political or physical extermination, and so the only question to be deliberated is how self-defense might be conducted.

In sum, to the extent that rhetors can persuade their base that an evil and implacable Other essentially determined on our physical or political extermination is already at war with us, they can demonize deliberation, characterize dissent as treason, and gain moral and political license to engage in a war of political or physical extermination against anyone who can be painted as a willing or duped ally of that Other. And they can do so by, perhaps somewhat paradoxically, depoliticizing policy conflict. That is, instead of policy conflicts being about policies that are subject to reasonable deliberation, bargaining, negotiating, and so on, and about which there is much uncertainty and more than two sides, those conflicts can be taken to signify a war of extermination between two and only two groups.

Thus, back to the beginning question: what kind of war is the war on Christmas? The actions in this "war" range from the trivial (an individual saying "Happy Holidays" rather than "Merry Christmas" or a private company making decisions about cups) to policy questions that are important, but well within the realm of normal policy conflict, resolvable through normal democratic practices. Gibson's *The War on Christmas* is largely about lawsuits regarding the separation of church and state; i.e., First Amendment questions. To what extent should we promote celebrations of Christmas as a religious versus secular holiday? Should taxpayers subsidize sectarian religious education? Should students be required to listen to sectarian sermons? Should the government endorse not just one religion, but one way of thinking about that religion? Should some religious sects get preferential treatment in public spaces? Framing policy disagreements about the separation of church and state as skirmishes in an already active war of extermination on "religion" and "Christmas" puts those issues out of the realm of deliberation and policy argumentation.

Gibson doesn't acknowledge that there are legitimate policy disagreements. He says, "It's really a war on Christianity" (160). An editorial in *The Washington Times* says, "The War on Christmas is a war on America." Oddly enough, the article goes on to make Christmas secular (that is, it takes the Christ out of Christmas):

> In many ways, Christmas is as much an American holiday as a Christian holiday. (No trees or tinsel in Bethlehem.) Today, only 63 percent of Americans call themselves Christians, while 93 percent celebrate Christmas. In other words, almost a third of those who celebrate Christmas are non-Christians. More than Thanksgiving, Memorial Day or the Fourth of July, Christmas unites us as a people. Anything that brings Americans together, the left fears—like the flag, the national anthem and statues of our heroes. (Feder)

Bill O'Reilly explains the goal of the "war on Christmas" as part of a plot to remake America: Secular progressives realize that America as it is now will never approve of gay marriage, partial birth abortion, euthanasia, legalized drugs, income redistribution through taxation, and many other progressive visions because of religious opposition. But if the secularists can destroy religion in the public arena, the brave new progressive world is a possibility (Wildau). O'Reilly's list of policy desiderata is odd in several ways, as though everyone who says, "Happy Holidays" advocates partial birth abortion. It also ignores that several of these "progressive visions" are advocated by religious people, many of whom are Christian and celebrate Christmas. O'Reilly's imagined political world is a stark binary of identity, as though all policy commitments are equally bifurcated. When Gibson appeared on O'Reilly's show, Gibson said, "Every time a supermarket checker or store clerk greets you with ['Happy Holidays'] instead of 'Merry Christmas,' you have met another soldier in the War against Christmas" (qtd. in Cassino). Taken literally, the notion of a war on Christmas is pernicious nonsense. It posits as "Christian" practices that are relatively recent, not universal among Christians, and not particularly central to a Christian understanding of advent. A Christian might say "Happy Holidays" because there are many holidays between November and February, or because they take seriously the "do unto others" rule and therefore strive to treat people of other faiths as they wish to be treated. Even if a person says "Happy Holidays" because they do not celebrate Christmas, they are not invading Poland while doing it. There is not a Festivus Army.

What does Gibson think Christians should do? Go to war against liberals. He says, "The Christians are coming to retake their place in the public square, and the most natural battleground in this war is Christmas. The war on Christmas is joined" (186). Gibson is not literally calling for a shooting war. However, taking the equation of politics and war literally doesn't necessarily require a shooting war—the notion of all disagreements being part of a literal war with Satan and Satanic forces has an unhappily long history in American politics (Roberts-Miller "The Mask").

Were the imagined "war on Christmas" the only war in which liberals supposed to be engaged, the rhetoric, albeit demagoguery, would be nothing more than irritating. But it isn't the only war against conservatives. Advocating policies and practices of tolerance and inclusion regarding sex and gender is a sign that "dangerous, lawless forces are at work" in a "war on the family" (LaBissoniere). The activities of Black Lives Matter "and their white Marxist brethren in Antifa" (which include making NASCAR more inclusive—not usually articulated as a goal of BLM) are part of a war on white people, one that might end with white middle-class Americans being treated as Jews were by Nazis (Cegielski). Tom Perkins, in a letter in the *Wall Street Journal*, also makes the Nazi analogy, calling attention to "the parallels of fascist Nazi Germany to its war on its 'one percent,' namely its Jews, to the progressive war on the American one percent, namely the "rich" (Perkins). US House Representative Greg Steube went on Newsmax in the summer of 2022 to say that the warrant for Trump's Mar-A-Lago estate was proof that "We have entered totalitarian regime in the Biden Administration that is set on declaring war on conservatives" ("We Have Entered," see also "Oversight"). According to Thomas Lifson, writing for *The American Thinker*, that white males without a college degree now have the same mortality rate as Black Americans is not the consequence of poor health coverage or changes in the economy, but that "political correctness kills" by making white males feel bad—it's a war on white males. I could go on, but the point is that disagreements about policy—what should we do about persistent and pervasive racial disparities, what rights regarding privacy and marriage should we recognize, what has the economy done to the non-college educated working class, should NASCAR be more inclusive, what should we do about policing, and so on—are characterized as a war on the good by the evil. Policy questions are reframed as signifiers of a war on an imagined "us," and therefore are not complicated questions to be deliberated, but signs of that war of extermination.

The capacious and yet homogeneous group is not advocating policies out of principle, but out of an irrational and intransigent hostility to the good. Ann Coulter ends her book *Treason*: "The left's anti-Americanism is intrinsic to their entire worldview. Liberals promote the rights of Islamic fanatics for the same reason they promote the rights of adulterers, pornographers, abortionists, criminals, and Communists. They instinctively root for anarchy and against civilization. The inevitable logic of the liberal position is to be for treason" (202).

Newt Gingrich says that "the left" has no sense of right and wrong: "The irreligious left attacks the church to take authority away from God and give power to the government. In doing this they redefine right and wrong" (232). If we're threatened by war on the part of a completely immoral Other determined on exterminating "us," then we are justified in anything we do that involves denying that Other any political power.

Dinesh D'Souza, in the ironically titled *The Big Lie*, argues for using media, the legal system, and defunding to make the Democratic Party a permanent minority party (see especially 239–47). Marjorie Taylor Greene drew attention for her "national divorce" comment, but less attention was paid to how she clarified her point. She was arguing for a view called "ascendant in the Republican Party"—that red states would pass laws so objectionable to liberals that they would move to already blue states. And, should a Democrat move to a red state:

> "Well once they move to a red state, guess what, maybe you don't get to vote for five years. You can live there, and you can work there, but you don't get to bring your values that you basically created in the blue states you came from by voting for Democrat leaders and Democrat policies." (qtd. in Ford)

That partisan sort would give the GOP control of the electoral college and the Senate; it would enable what's called "competitive authoritarianism" (Levitsky). GOP politicians are open about using voter suppression, gerrymandering, legislative rejection of the popular vote, and insurrection to win elections (Wines, "Spindell," Herenstein, "Voting Laws"). These violations of democratic norms seem justified to people who have been radicalized by the fantasy of "liberals" already at war with Americans, Christians, whites, conservatives, and so on. The rhetoric of war, applied to everything from whether Starbucks has a reindeer on its cups to whether civil rights are human rights, legitimizes a preventive and not entirely metaphorical war against people who disagree about policies.

WORKS CITED

Cassidy, Ernst, "Senate Republicans Push to End Biden DoD's War on the Unborn | U.S. Senator Bill Cassidy of Louisiana," *www.cassidy.senate.gov*, 15 Mar. 2023,www.cassidy.senate.gov/newsroom/press-releases/cassidy-ernst-senate-republicans-push-to-end-biden-dods-war-on-the-unborn.

Cassino, Dan. "How Fox News Created the War on Christmas." *Harvard Business Review*, 9 Dec. 2016, hbr.org/2016/12/how-fox-news-created-the-war-on-christmas.

Cegielski, Jim. "The War against White People." *Laurel Leader-Call*, 9 Dec. 2021, www.leader-call.com/opinion/columnists/the-war-against-white-people/article_070a1c04-b7df-11ea-b4b8-c3e6e33ee5f9.html.

von Clausewitz, Carl. *On War*. Translated by Michael Howard and Peter Paret, Princeton UP, 1989.

"The Coming War on Men." *National Center for Public Policy Research*, 16 Dec. 2020, nationalcenter.org/ncppr/2020/12/16/the-coming-war-on-men/.

Coulter, Ann H. *Treason : Liberal Treachery from the Cold War to the War on Terrorism*. Three Rivers Press, 2004.

"Distribution of Wealth in the U.S. 2020." *Statista*, 23 Jan. 2023, www.statista.com/statistics/299460/distribution-of-wealth-in-the-united-states/.

D'Souza, Dinesh. *Big Lie : Exposing the Nazi Roots of the American Left*. Washington, DC, Regnery Publishing, 2017.

Feder, Don. "The War on Christmas Is a War on America." *The Washington Times*, 8 Dec. 2022, www.washingtontimes.com/news/2022/dec/18/war-on-christmas-is-war-on-america/.

Ford, Matt. "It's Not a "National Divorce." It's a Call for One-Party Authoritarian Rule." *The New Republic*, 25 Feb. 2023, newrepublic.com/article/170776/marjorie-taylor-greene-national-divorce-one-party-authoritarian-rule.

Gibson, John. *The War on Christmas : How the Liberal Plot to Ban the Sacred Christian Holiday Is Worse Than You Thought*. Sentinel, 2006..

Gingrich, Newt. *Defeating Big Government Socialism : Saving America's Future*. Center Street, 2022.

Goldberg, Michelle. *Kingdom Coming : The Rise of Christian Nationalism*. Norton, 2007.

Goodwin, Michael. "The Media's Road to Ruin Its Own Credibility in War on Trump." *New York Post*, 5 Feb. 2023, nypost.com/2023/02/04/the-medias-road-to-ruin-its-own-credibility-in-war-on-trump/.

Grassley, Chuck. "Grassley: Let's End the War on Cops | United States Senate Committee on the Judiciary," *www.judiciary.senate.gov*, 10 May 2021, www.judiciary.senate.gov/grassley-lets-end-the-war-on-cops.

Gregg, Samuel. "The Woke War on Religion." *The Spectator World*, 27 July 2020, thespectator.com/topic/woke-war-religion/.

Guynn, Jessica, and Jayme Fraser. "How Diverse Is Corporate America? There Are More Black Leaders but White Men Still Run It," *www.usatoday.com*, USA Today, 16 Feb. 2023, www.usatoday.com/in-depth/money/2023/02/16/white-men-corporate-america-diversity/11114830002/.

Hanson, Victor Davis. "Why Target Tucker Carlson? It's Part of the Left's War on the Right." *The Hill*, 9 Aug. 2019, thehill.com/opinion/civil-rights/456803-why-target-tucker-carlson-its-part-of-the-lefts-war-on-the-right/.

Hasson, Peter J. *The Manipulators : Facebook, Google, Twitter, and Big Tech's War on Conservatives*. Regnery Publishing, 2020.

Herenstein, Ethan, and Thomas Wolf. "The 'Independent State Legislature Theory,' Explained." Brennan Center for Justice, *www.brennancenter.org*, 6 June 2022, www.brennancenter.org/our-work/research-reports/independent-state-legislature-theory-explained.

Hitler, Adolf. Address by Adolf Hitler—September 1, 1939." *Avalon.law.yale.edu*, 2008, avalon.law.yale.edu/wwii/gp2.asp.

Howard, Michael. *Clausewitz: A Very Short Introduction*. Oxford UP, 2002.
Ingraham, Christopher. 2016. "The 'Smoking Gun' Proving North Carolina Republicans Tried to Disenfranchise Black Voters." *Washington Post*, 29 July 2016.
Itkowitz, Colby. "Who Is Josh Feuerstein, the Man behind the Starbucks Red Cup Frenzy?" *Washington Post*, 10 Nov. 2015, www.washingtonpost.com/news/acts-of-faith/wp/2015/11/10/who-is-josh-feuerstein-the-man-behind-the-starbucks-red-cup-frenzy/.
Jervis, Robert. "Mutual Assured Destruction." *Foreign Policy*, no. 133, Nov. 2002, pp. 40. *EBSCOhost*, https://doi-org.ezproxy.lib.utexas.edu/10.2307/3183553.
Kassam, Raheem. "War on Christmas: Starbucks Red Cups Are Emblematic of the Christian Culture Cleansing of the West." *Breitbart*, 5 Nov. 2015, www.breitbart.com/europe/2015/11/05/war-on-christmas-starbucks-new-red-cups-are-emblematic-of-the-christian-culture-cleansing-of-the-west/.
Knefel, John. "Fox News Is Laying the Groundwork for the Next Insurrection—or Worse—by Telling Its Viewers Biden Is Waging War on Them Personally." *Media Matters for America*, 13 Sept. 2022, https://www.mediamatters.org/fox-news/fox-news-laying-groundwork-next-insurrection-or-worse-telling-its-viewers-biden-waging-war.
Kregeloh, Hubert. *There Goes Christmas?*! American Opinion: Massachusetts, 1959.
LaBissoniere, John. "The "Respect for Marriage Act": Is It Truly Respectful?" *Beyond Today*, 8 Mar. 2023, www.ucg.org/beyond-today/beyond-today-magazine/the-respect-for-marriage-act-is-it-truly-respectful.
Lebov, Richard Ned. *Why Nations Fight—Past and Future Motives for War*. Cambridge UP, 2010.
Levitsky, Steven, and Lucan A Way. *Competitive Authoritarianism : Hybrid Regimes after the Cold War*. Cambridge UP, 2010.
Levy, Jack S, and William R Thompson. *Causes of War*. Wiley-Blackwell, 2010.
Lifson, Thomas. "Stunning Evidence That the Left Has Won Its War on White Males," *www.americanthinker.com*, 26 Mar. 2017, www.americanthinker.com/blog/2017/03/stunning_evidence_that_the_left_has_won_its_war_on_white_males_.html.
Limbaugh, Rush. "Biden Will Renew Obama's War on Suburban Property Values." *The Rush Limbaugh Show*, 26 Oct. 2020, www.rushlimbaugh.com/daily/2020/10/26/biden-will-renew-obamas-war-on-suburban-property-values/.
Lin, Tom C. W., "Business Warfare" (February 3, 2022). 63 *Boston College Law Review* 1 (2022), Temple University Legal Studies Research Paper No. 2022–04, Available at SSRN: https://ssrn.com/abstract=4025269.
MacDonald, Heather. "Team Biden Finally Admits There's a War on Cops." *New York Post*, 28 Apr. 2022, nypost.com/2022/04/28/team-biden-finally-admits-theres-a-war-on-cops/.
Massie, Chris. "Rep. Brooks: Dems' "War on Whites" behind Some Criticism of Sessions | CNN Politics." *CNN*, 11 Jan. 2017, www.cnn.com/2017/01/11/politics/kfile-mo-brooks-war-on-whites/index.html.

Media Matters. "Fox News Contributor Says There Is a 'War on Christians' in America." *Media Matters for America*, 9 Dec. 2022, www.mediamatters.org/fox-news/fox-news-contributor-says-there-war-christians-america.

Media Matters. "Fox Host: "The War on Christmas [Is] Off to an Early Start" on Starbucks' Coffee Cups." *Media Matters for America*, 9 Nov. 2015, www.mediamatters.org/fox-friends/fox-host-war-christmas-early-start-starbucks-coffee-cups.

O'Reilly, Bill. "The War on Christmas Centralizes." *Fox News*, 24 Mar. 2015, www.foxnews.com/transcript/bill-oreilly-the-war-on-christmas-centralizes.

"Oversight Project Announces Litigation Blitz against FBI: 'Double Standard-Driven War on Conservatives Must Stop.'" *The Heritage Foundation*, 6 Mar. 2023, www.heritage.org/press/oversight-project-announces-litigation-blitz-against-fbi-double-standard-driven-war.

Perkins, Tom. "Progressive Kristallnacht Coming?—Letters to the Editor." *Wall Street Journal*, 24 Jan. 2014, www.wsj.com/articles/SB10001424052702304549504579316913982034286.

Pew Research Center. "Modeling the Future of Religion in America." *Pew Research Center's Religion and Public Life Project*, 13 Sept. 2022, www.pewresearch.org/religion/2022/09/13/modeling-the-future-of-religion-in-america/.

Philo, Kaila. "Texas GOP Proposes Bill to Allow Sec of State to Overturn Election Results in State's Largest Blue County." *TPM–Talking Points Memo*, 30 Mar. 2023, talkingpointsmemo.com/news/texas-gop-proposes-bill-to-allow-sec-of-state-to-overturn-election-results-in-states-largest-blue-county.

"Preemptive War Doctrine." *Encyclopedia of United States National Security*, edited by Richard J. Samuels, vol. 2, SAGE Reference, 2006, pp. 592–93. *Gale eBooks*, link.gale.com/apps/doc/CX3452700497/GVRL?u=txshracd2598&sid=bookmark-GVRL&xid=d139fc21.

Roberts-Miller, Patricia. "The Mask of War and the War of Masks: The Fabricated Culture War Gets Deadly." *Javnost (Ljubljana, Slovenia)*, vol. 30, no. 1, 2023, pp. 1–17, https://doi.org/10.1080/13183222.2023.2168954.

—. *Rhetoric and Demagoguery*. Southern Illinois UP, 2019.

Robertson, Michelle. "Fox News' Tucker Carlson Slams Northern Calif. Town in 'War on Statues.'" *San Francisco Chronicle*, 3 Apr. 2018, www.sfchronicle.com/bayarea/article/fox-news-tucker-carlson-arcata-mckinley-statue-cal-12802558.php.

Rumbold, Horace. "Sir H. Rumbold (Berlin) to Sir J. Simon (Received May 3), No. 425. *Documents on British Foreign Policy, 1919–1939*. Second Series, Volume V. Her Majesty's Stationery Office, 1956. 47–55.

Schleifer, Theodore. "Trump: Maybe We Should Boycott Starbucks?" *CNN*, 10 Nov. 2015, www.cnn.com/2015/11/09/politics/donald-trump-starbucks-boycott-christmas/index.html.

"Spindell's Crowing Is Despicable." *Nujournal.com*, 2 Feb. 2023, www.nujournal.com/opinion/2023/02/02/spindells-crowing-is-despicable/.

Stabile, Angelica. "Tucker Carlson: Kenosha Riots Prove Urban Unrest Is "Class War Masquerading as a Race Conflict.'" *Fox News*, 25 Aug. 2020, www.foxnews.com/opinion/tucker-carlson-kenosha-riots-class-war.

"State Government Trifectas—270toWin." *270toWin.com*, 2023, www.270towin.com/content/state-government-trifectas.

Stoll, Ira. "How the Left Wages War on the Family." *Reason.com*, 26 Jan. 2015, reason.com/2015/01/26/how-the-left-wages-war-on-the-family/.

Thomson-DeVeaux, Amelia, et al. "Why It's So Rare for Police Officers to Face Legal Consequences." *FiveThirtyEight*, 4 June 2020, fivethirtyeight.com/features/why-its-still-so-rare-for-police-officers-to-face-legal-consequences-for-misconduct/.

Van Evera, Steven. *Causes of War: Power and the Roots of Conflict*. Cornell UP, 2013.

Venker, Suzanne. "The War on Men." *Fox News*, 12 Mar. 2015, www.foxnews.com/opinion/the-war-on-men.

Villarreal, Alexandra. "White Male Minority Rule Pervades Politics across the US, Research Shows." *The Guardian*, 26 May 2021, www.theguardian.com/us-news/2021/may/26/white-male-minority-rule-us-politics-research.

"Voting Laws Roundup: December 2021 | Brennan Center for Justice," *www.brennancenter.org*, 21 Dec. 2021, www.brennancenter.org/our-work/research-reports/voting-laws-roundup-december-2021.

"We Have Entered a 'Totalitarian Regime' That Is 'Declaring War' on Conservatives." *YouTube*. Newsmax. 10 Aug. 2022, https://www.youtube.com/watch?v=89XGQICu_C

Wikipedia Contributors. "Political Party Strength in U.S. States." *Wikipedia*, Wikimedia Foundation, 13 Dec. 2019, en.wikipedia.org/wiki/Political_party_strength_in_U.S._states.

Wildau, Gabe. "FOX Hypes Stories to Claim 'Christmas under Siege.'" *Media Matters for America*, 10 Dec. 2004, www.mediamatters.org/fox-nation/fox-hypes-stories-claim-christmas-under-siege.

Wines, Michael. "Some Republicans Acknowledge Leveraging Voter ID Laws for Political Gain." *The New York Times*, 16 Sept. 2016, www.nytimes.com/2016/09/17/us/some-republicans-acknowledge-leveraging-voter-id-laws-for-political-gain.html.

Part III: Eternal Issues of Rhetoric in Our Kairotic Moment

14 Sleuthing Toward Bethlehem: Hitler's Theory of Reading and Learning and the Enduring Appeals of Confirmation Bias

Ryan Skinnell

Abstract

In *Mein Kampf*, Hitler famously expounded his theory of reading and learning thusly: "The art of reading as of learning is this: to retain the essential, to forget the non-essential." This essay contends that Hitler's theory of learning and reading can be understood as a sort of evidentiary detective work in which the committed Nazi was always on the lookout for ideas, historical examples, and theories that proved the truth of Nazism. Hitler's method is interesting in that it works from the same premise as a detective novel, which takes a "crime" as the basis for gathering evidence. Constituting and reconstituting the crime is a crucial part of the persuasive process, which Hitler does by constituting and reconstituting the evidence. Consequently, Hitler's process is inductive but *looks* deductive. As such, non-falsifiable claims appear logical and rational, and as a consequence, the process makes confirmation bias into a cardinal virtue.

In his execrable autobiography, *Mein Kampf*, Adolf Hitler famously expounded his theory of reading and learning thusly: "The art of reading as of learning is this: *to retain the essential, to forget the non-essential*" (14, emphasis in original). Of course, Hitler is long dead, and for that we can all be grateful. But as I discuss below, his theory of reading and learning remains unfortunately relevant nearly a century after he wrote *Mein Kampf*, particularly for understanding the recent resurgence of authoritarianism, neofascism, and conspiracism at the center of national and international politics.[9]

People who knew Hitler as a young man affirmed that he was a voracious reader of a wide range of texts. His boyhood friend, August Kubizek, for instance, wrote that "Books were his whole world!" (183). As historian Timothy Ryback details in *Hitler's Private Library*, the Führer owned, and seems to have read, thousands of books—including those that expounded worldviews completely antithetical to his own. By most accounts, Hitler was an exceptionally well-read genocidal dictator.

But as his theory of reading and learning illustrates, he had a peculiar way of reading, which is my concern here. People who knew Hitler affirmed that he read a lot, but they also affirmed that he had a habit of reading for information that confirmed and fortified his beliefs. In fact, it was not so much a *habit* of reading as a method. Hitler simply disregarded anything that might cause him to reflect on, reconsider, or reject his "granite beliefs."

He writes in *Mein Kampf*, "I know people who 'read' enormously, book for book, letter for letter, yet whom I would not describe as 'well-read.' True, they possess a mass of 'knowledge,' but . . . they lack the art of sifting what is valuable for them in a book from that which is without value, of retaining the one forever, and, if possible, not even seeing the rest . . ." (35). Throughout his life, and certainly after he'd gone into politics in the 1920s, Hitler was openly contemptuous of people who read carefully and considered alternate points of view.

He continues, "a man who possesses the art of correct reading will—in studying any book, magazine, or pamphlet—instinctively and immediately perceive everything which in his opinion is worth permanently remembering, either because it is suited to his purpose or generally worth knowing" (36). In other words, knowledge, right opinion, and rigid belief preceded reading and learning. Reading and learning provided the incontrovertible proof a person needed to sustain what he already believed.

In Hitler's worldview, then, confirmation bias was a cardinal virtue, and his theory of reading and learning—what I think of as his forensics—was his preferred method for upholding it. Hitler was helpful enough, or narcissistic enough, to set down his forensic reading and learning method for future generations in his autobiography, but as a method it obviously exceeds him.

---

9. On the global resurgence of authoritarianism in the twenty-first century, see Repucci and Slipowitz.

In fact, fascists and other authoritarians were, and are, notorious for rejecting evidence that contradicts their beliefs (e.g., Skinnell, "Deceiving" and "Two Truths").

I want to take this argument a step further and suggest that Hitler's forensic method can be profitably understood as a sort of evidentiary detective work. In Hitler's view, the committed Nazi was always on the lookout for clues—actions, historical examples, philosophies—that proved the incontrovertible truth of Nazism. Reading and learning were the detective's tools.

A brief aside here—this forensic method of reading and learning is not totally unlike certain writing and speech pedagogies that encourage students to settle on a thesis and then locate evidence to support it. There are reasonable arguments for thesis-driven pedagogies, especially given the constraints of time and attention in a one or two-semester required course, and they are obviously not my main consideration here. It's hard for me, however, not to think about the pedagogical implications of Hitler's method for people who do what we do for a living. But I digress.

There is perhaps no better illustration of Hitler's forensic method of reading and learning than his engagements with the infamous *Protocols of the Elders of Zion*. *The Protocols* was an anti-Semitic pamphlet, initially produced and disseminated by Russian intelligence services at the beginning of the twentieth century, which propagated a centuries-old conspiracy theory about Jewish bloodthirstiness and world conquest (see Landes and Katz; Siegel). *The Protocols* was supposedly the meeting minutes taken from a secret conference in the late 1890s—the first Zionist Congress in Basel, Switzerland. According to the text, the conference was attended by a cabal of Jewish elders who laid out a blueprint for world domination and Christian subjugation.

The Protocols laid out a lurid theory of Jewish world domination that included everything from controlling the world's economy by fomenting disputes among subjugated classes to stealing and eating Christian babies as part of their religious rituals. Virtually nothing in the text is original—it takes centuries of anti-Semitic tropes and conspiracies, packages them together in a "secret" document that was supposedly written by Jewish leaders themselves, and frames it as a revelation. Everything in *The Protocols* is, unequivocally, bullshit.

Unlike its contents, the history of *The Protocols of the Elders of Zion* as a text is complex and disputed. But its lack of authenticity as a record of a nefarious Jewish plot is indisputable. It was a fake, a forgery, much of it plagiarized from fictional texts written decades before the conference was supposed to have taken place. It was definitively debunked no later than 1920. Nevertheless, since *The Protocols* reinforced one of the oldest, most prominent, and most destructive anti-Semitic conspiracy theories in Western history, it played a central role in Nazi rhetoric long after it was discredited.

In fact, Hitler and most high-ranking Nazis knew *The Protocols* was a forgery. Hitler said as much in *Mein Kampf* (307–08) and Joseph Goebbels wrote in 1924, even before he became an important figure in the Nazi Party, that "I believe in the inner, but not the factual, truth of *The Protocols*" (qtd. in Longerich 40). Randall Bytwerk, one of the foremost authorities on Nazi rhetoric, has shown that top Nazi leaders believed the spurious authorship and other details of *The Protocols* were irrelevant ("Believing"). Leaning on Hitler's forensic method of reading and learning, the Nazis sleuthed out evidence that confirmed their biases and disregarded the rest. Based on the clues they uncovered, they saw the pamphlet as incontrovertible, if not necessarily factual, proof of the "inner truth" about Jewish world domination. The Nazis even bought exclusive rights to *The Protocols* in 1929, and it is still in wide circulation (see, e.g., US Department of State).

I think most people will agree that Nazis and fascists are bad, and it would not be an unfair critique to point out that in proving that the (evil) Nazis used bad evidentiary methods is a little like starting with a thesis and piling on the evidence. But my goal isn't to reinvent or reinforce the "Nazis are bad" common sense. It is, rather, to establish that Hitler's forensic method existed as a preliminary step to understanding how it actually worked, and works, rhetorically. Because rhetoricians have to wonder, what are we to make of people wittingly using evidence they know is bad *to convince even themselves* to believe certain things about the world?

In *Awful Archives*, Jenny Rice raises complementary questions about evidence by analyzing conspiracy theories. As she puts it, she "needed some way to understand this thing we call evidence, and how it acts in the most faulty, flimsy, or fallacious arguments" (13). More pointedly she asks, "Why do traditional modes of argument often fail in the face of claims that rely on bad evidence?" (15).

Rice is specifically interested in how evidence is constituted in public discourse and how different kinds of—and different registers of—evidence can be circulated to support what seem like absurd conspiracy theories. She takes an enviably empathetic view of the people she's studying to try and make sense of how ordinary people become invested in narratives that seem from the outside to be beyond the pale. One conclusion she draws is that rhetoricians need to "expand our concepts of evidence as an affective process, as opposed to a static artifact" (13). Rice is after rhetorics/theories of evidence that don't, on the one hand, stand up to rational inquiry and argumentation, but that well-meaning people nevertheless believe deeply in the truth of because they support their predetermined beliefs. In other words, she contends that evidence isn't just true or false, right or wrong. Rather evidence makes people feel certain ways—it's wrapped up in community-building, identity-formation, and passionate belief. There is, in an important sense, a kind of good faith in treating evidence in these terms. For the people Rice is interested in, they genuinely believe in the fidelity of their evidence, even if it may fail to stand up to rational-critical interrogation.

I am all in on Rice's argument, in case that's not clear, and Hitler's forensic method is likewise premised on finding the evidence he needed to prove what he already believed. But unlike the people Rice studies, Hitler and the Nazis knew they were using bad evidence. So another question arises: how can we understand this thing we call evidence and its role in public discourse when the people citing it *know* it's faulty, flimsy, or fallacious?

There is a certain sense in which Hitler's gumshoe theory of evidence accumulation provides a distinctive answer. Of course, it illustrates Rice's point about the affective, accumulative *enargeia* of evidence. Goebbels didn't think *The Protocols* was actually true, but he still *felt* like it was. Even though they knew it was a forgery, the evidence worked for Goebbels, Hitler, and others in the mode of affective process. But Hitler's forensics adds a curious wrinkle that makes our detective metaphor particularly helpful.

In a classic detective novel, one thing is almost certainly true—there is a crime. In the best ones, it's a murder, though it can sometimes be a heist or even a mystery about what the mystery is. In some cases, the invention of a crime becomes the mystery that needs solving. But whatever the ultimate crime, readers can be assured that Sherlock Holmes and Easy Rawlins never end up saying, "Whoops. Guess there wasn't really a problem after all. My mistake!" The crime is the inexorable premise without which there is no mystery and therefore no detective.

What makes Hitler's forensic method so interesting is that he works from the same premise as a detective novel. There was a crime. Indeed, "a crime" is the grounding for most (dare I say all) conspiracy theories. In the case of *The Protocols of the Elders of Zion*, the crime is "Jews are evil." He then proceeds to find evidence to explain and support the point in much the same way Holmes or Rawlins begins with a body and finds evidence to explain how it got there.

Unlike the dead body, however, Hitler's crime isn't self-evident, though he treats it as such. That is, Holmes and Rawlins start with an actual body and look for clues to explain it. They are constrained by the physical proof of the initial crime as well as by the clues that derive from it. Hitler also starts with a premise and also goes searching for clues, but he invented the crime and he can shift it as his needs dictate because there is no actual body. Jews are all-powerful, Jews are weak, Jews blend in, Jews stand out, Jews are Bolsheviks, Jews are capitalists. Constituting and reconstituting the crime is a crucial part of the persuasive process, which Hitler does by constituting and reconstituting the evidence to fit. Consequently, Hitler's process is inductive, but it *looks* deductive. It looks like he's drawing his conclusions from evidence in the world, but he's candidly not.

As it happens, looking deductive is powerfully, affectively persuasive. Deduction is rational and logical. It draws reasonable inferences from the accumulation of evidence. Rice contends that "the proliferation of 'evidence' in conspiracy discourse refigures individual pieces of data into a qualitatively coherent whole" (28). So, too, Hitler's forensics. As such, non-falsifiability seems . . . looks . . . feels . . . logical and rational. What this means on one hand is that even evidence we know is bad can carry a so-called inner truth, especially for someone who grounds their method in knowing and believing before reading and learning.

But it also means that audiences, even those who fancy themselves—ourselves—logical and rational are not magically protected from bad evidence that we know is bad. When we are invested in a particular belief or set of beliefs, it can be remarkably easy to convince ourselves that the process of finding evidence looks logical and rational, and from there, it can be easy to imagine that the right answer, which is of course the one that we hold, is immune to reflection, reconsideration, or rejection.

Works Cited

Bytwerk, Randall L. "Believing in 'Inner Truth': The Protocols of the Elders of Zion in Nazi Propaganda, 1933–1945." *Holocaust and Genocide Studies*, vol. 29, no. 2, 2015, pp. 212–29.

Hitler, Adolf. *Mein Kampf.* Translated by Ralph Mannheim, Mariner Books, 1999.

Kubizek, August. *The Young Hitler I Knew.* Translated by Geoffrey Brooks, Frontline Books, 2011.

Landes, Richard, and Steven T. Katz, eds. *The Paranoid Apocalypse: A Hundred-Year Retrospective on the* Protocols of the Elders of Zion. NYU Press, 2012.

Longerich, Peter. *Goebbels: A Biography.* Translated by Alan Bance, Jeremy Noakes, and Lesley Sharpe, Random House, 2015.

Repucci, Sarah, and Amy Slipowitz. *Freedom in the World 2022: The Global Expansion of Authoritarian Rule.* Freedom House, 2022. freedomhouse.org/sites/default/files/2022-02/FIW_2022_PDF_Booklet_Digital_Final_Web.pdf.

Rice, Jenny. *Awful Archives: Conspiracy Theory, Rhetoric, and Acts of Evidence*, Ohio State UP, 2020.

Ryback, Timothy W. *Hitler's Private Library: The Books That Shaped His Life*, Knopf, 2008.

Segel, Binjamin W. *A Lie and a Libel: The History of the Protocols of the Elders of Zion.* Translated by Richard S. Levy, Nebraska UP, 1996.

Skinnell, Ryan. "Deceiving Sincerely: The Embrace of Sincerity-as-Truth in Fascist Rhetoric." *The Rhetoric of Fascism*, edited by Nathan Crick, U. of Alabama P, 2022, pp. 222–40.

—. "Two Truths and a Big Lie: The 'Honest' Mendacity of Fascist Rhetoric." *Journal of the History of Rhetoric*, vol. 25, no. 2, 2022, pp. 175–97. doi:10.5325/jhistrhetoric.25.2.0175.

US Department of State. *Report on Global Anti-Semitism*. Bureau of Democracy, Human Rights, and Labor, 2005. https://2009-2017.state.gov/j/drl/rls/40258.htm.

15 From Plato to Paulo Freire: Re-Exploring Ann Berthoff's Pedagogical Theory and Its Rhetorical/Philosophical Roots in Light of Contemporary Challenges

Andrew L. Sigerson

Abstract

Berthoff's body of work has a theorized pedagogical history going back to Plato; she is likewise recognized for bringing Freire to a US audience, offering unique interpretations of Freirean concepts that have been instructive in implementing his pedagogy. Berthoff envisions her scholarship as a productive "begin where they are" approach that raises discursive consciousness: Freire understands his students not merely as deprived citizens of the Global South, but "as culture makers, historical subjects, and children of God" (*Meaning* 9). The potential for change rests within them; however, a well-informed revolutionary pedagogy can provide the tools to harness the power of their active minds and dialectical capacities for meaning-making via "the word." Berthoff demonstrates that the development of these capacities is ideally served by writing, granting rhet/comp centrality in the "charge for change"—but in a manner that differs from other US iterations of critical pedagogy in its firm basis in a philosophy of language. Berthovian and Freirean pedagogies can help form fresh perspectives on critical literacy for our students—*beginning* where they are, "as language animals endowed with the form-finding and form-creating powers of mind and language" (9), but not *ending* there.

Ann Berthoff and Philosophies of the Word

This piece aims to constructively explore the premise that Paulo Freire's pedagogy of critical literacy, which is often glossed using his aphorism "the word and the world" and is foundational to today's educational theory/practice, shares key traits with the unique writing pedagogy of Ann Berthoff, a founding mother of the field of rhet/comp; namely, both rest firmly on a philosophy of language. Specifically, their philosophies align with Peircean/triadic semiotics, the stimulating yet underappreciated pedagogical implications of which will be elucidated below. Peircean semiotics—US philosopher C.S. Peirce's pioneering theory of signs—differs from the more widely-recognized Saussurean, dyadic model of the sign as *signified-signifier* in that for Peirce, the sign is triadic (triangular versus linear, structurally), with the third point accounting, in broad terms, for interpretation (Berthoff, *Sense* 2). Pedagogically, this philosophy of language is foundational to Freire's work (implicitly) and Berthoff's (explicitly), allowing them the freedom to take advantage of language and its productive limits, whose "formal completeness . . . make possible the apprehension of the world and meaning-making" through (re)interpretation of signs (Berthoff, *Barricades* 5–6). Both scholars hold students' existing language and their discursive and rhetorical potential to be a generative tool and productive pedagogical starting point, as opposed to an obstacle or a locus of oppression (5).

Berthoff and Freire in North America

In an important way, it is through their philosophical/dialectical approaches that Berthoff and Freire surpass the fields that they helped spawn—rhet/comp and critical pedagogy, respectively, which often overlap, especially regarding questions of literacy. Their pedagogical praxes, underlain by philosophically informed, clear-headed theory and productive broad and innovative arrays of classroom approaches and possibilities, still have not been fully utilized or built upon or, indeed, even robustly comprehended. Unfortunately, a tendency has existed surrounding both thinkers not only to be misunderstood, but to be picked over and largely left behind, in the case of Berthoff, or in the case of Freire, left spawning a field of adherents with a recognized tendency to interpret his pedagogy in an awkwardly unbalanced fashion (George 100–105).

Both scholars' successes and travails in terms of rhet/comp can be viewed from a perspective of shifts that took place in the field in the late twentieth century involving a foregrounding of ideology and even outright political posturing (which will be discussed below); due to the natures of their respective pedagogies, this led to the marginalization of Berthoff and the ascension of Freire, at least in name. Up to the present day, a conspicuous lack of awareness of each author's philosophical grounding, and especially the philosophy of language central to the methods and praxis of each, has been observable in our field, as exhibited by Paige Arrington (6) in her doctoral dissertation on Berthoff's marginalization and its significance to our discipline. It is, in fact, in terms of what has been missed or passed over that this pair comes nearest to one another in both theory and practice; it is also where their greatest regenerative power lies for our field.

Pedagogies of Knowing, Philosophies of Language

Berthoff often alludes to the influence of Peircean/triadic semiotics on her teaching, citing Peirce frequently, while Freire does not; indeed, it is unclear whether Freire was well-acquainted with Peirce's work. Nevertheless, both scholars base their pedagogies on harnessing students' powers of perception, abstraction, and interpretation via signs—*words*—to develop their discursive powers of thought and communication in their *worlds*, producing more empowered citizens. Both, though often having worked in starkly different contexts, recognize as an elemental precept that literacy and writing education be a "means of discovering the mind assuring that language is not seen as a set of slots, not as an inert code . . . but a means of *naming* the world, of holding the images by whose means we . . . recognize the forms of our experience; of reflecting on those images, as we do on other words" (Berthoff, *Sense* 25). Consequently, both, if not always addressing the same educational contexts, essentially see the role of teachers as follows:

> . . . to assure that language is continually exercised . . . so that students will learn to abstract in the discursive mode; they will learn to generalize. They will thus learn to "think abstractly" because they will be learning how meanings make further meanings possible . . . And, . . . in [our] pedagogy of knowing, [to give] our students back their language so that they can reclaim it as an instrument for controlling their becoming. (Berthoff, *Sense* 26)

Peircean semiotics, which holds interpretation (*interpretant* in his sign-model) to be a third component of the sign itself (Peirce 11), is of obvious relevance to this pedagogical mandate, as "in the triadic conception of the sign, the symbol user, the knower, the learner is integral to the process of making meaning" (Berthoff, *Sense* 21). Berthoff even posits that "[Peirce's triangle], by thus representing the mediating function of interpretation, can serve as an emblem for a pedagogy of knowing" (21), the latter being a term used by both Freire and Berthoff to describe their pedagogies.

Knowing before Revolution

Hailing from the Global South, having grown up with and taught destitute laborers in Brazil and Chile, and, indeed, being in exile from a right-wing dictatorship when he arrived in North America (Díaz 20), Freire's political grounding is inevitable. Berthoff too, though, views the consolidation of political consciousness as an outcome of her pedagogy: "Education does not substitute for political action, but it is indispensable to it because of the role it plays in the development of critical consciousness. That, in turn, is dependent on the transforming power of language" (*Sense* 121). Nevertheless, in the same way that vital, empowering aspects of Berthoff's writing pedagogy were passed over due to wrong-headed evaluations of her philosophically-grounded and sometimes challenging approaches as apolitical or even "retrograde" (Arrington 51), the centrality of the philosophy of language underlying Freire's pedagogy (not to mention the fact the he *was* a philosopher [Díaz 1]) has likewise often been misunderstood or overlooked in favor of his perceived political background, a novelty for a mainstream literacy educator working in the US. Amidst disciplinary shifts and misunderstandings, both scholars' "pedagogies of knowing," a term that Freire first used to describe his own work in 1985 (*Politics* 55) and Berthoff in turn incorporated to describe her similar approaches in a North American context, were largely lost, though related concepts from Freire such as conscientization have remained firmly, if at times superficially, in the pedagogical lexicon.

Pedagogies of knowing, however, are the defining features of the scholars in question from a contemporary point-of-view. Freire first describes this concept focusing on the teacher's relationship with their students:

> The first type of educator . . . is a knowing subject, face to face with other knowing subjects. [They] can never be a mere memorizer, but a person constantly readjusting [their] knowledge who calls forth knowledge from [their] students. For [them], education is a pedagogy of knowing. . . . For the educator who experiences the act of knowing together with [their] students . . . dialogue is the sign of the act of knowing. [They] are aware, however, that not all dialogue is in itself the mark of a relationship of true knowledge. (*Politics* 55)

The dialogue to which Freire refers is one oriented toward the nature of *knowing* itself, manifested through a pointed focus on the medium by which we come to know, reflect upon how we know, and transform what we know: language.

Berthoff, meanwhile, in her foreword to Freire and Macedo's *Literacy*, seizes upon the concept of a pedagogy of knowing—which she goes on to make her own throughout her work, using it more frequently than Freire does himself—and describes it in direct relation to Freire's political relevance and critical pedagogy:

> If education is to serve other than as an instrument of oppression, it must be conceived of as a "pedagogy of knowing." Education for freedom is not simply a matter of encouraging teaching that has a political flavor; it is not a means of transmitting received ideas, no matter how "good"; it is not a matter of extending the teacher's knowledge to the uneducated or of informing them of the fact of their oppression. Teaching and learning are dialogic in character, and dialogic action depends on the awareness of oneself as knower, an attitude Freire calls conscientization. (Foreword xiii)

Again, this "awareness of oneself as a knower" is inextricably linked to awareness of one's language use and its possibilities—a conception of literacy focused on understanding how we know and make meaning via *the word*.

It follows that both scholars' approaches are aimed at discursive empowerment of students, guided by a philosophy of language that corresponds to the pedagogical imperative that "we have to learn to write, but we're born composers" (Berthoff, *Sense* 91). The task of the teacher, Peirce's "sense of learning," is to raise students' consciousness of how they come to know through the mind's capacity for perceiving and abstracting, thinking and meaning-making, with reflection on this process eventually leading to the ability to generalize (to abstract in discursive terms) and perform other higher-order acts of knowing as a direct manifestation of heightened literacy (*Sense* 20–21). Both scholars' pedagogies, then, begin with perception of our worlds through signs—words—and the ensuing acts of abstraction, interpretation, and discursive action that define human thought and communication, and consciousness-raising regarding these processes.

Their pedagogies are not only philosophical in that they are built upon a philosophy of language and the primacy of the word, of rhetoric—which Berthoff claims is what humans possess in place of omniscience (*Meaning* 43)—as a tool for seeing, meaning-making, interpreting, and reflecting; further, they are philosophical in terms of the epistemological consequence that follows, that is, that we know and can change the world through signs, as the world is, in fact, entirely composed of signs. Freire captures this central tenet of Peircean/triadic semiotics in his recounting of a Chilean laborer who concluded, while attending Freire's "culture circle," that without humans there would be no world, explaining, "There would be no one to say: 'This is a world'" (*Pedagogy* 119). Berthoff, echoing Freire's student, states that "all our experience is mediated, and . . . the fact of the matter is that there are no data and no facts until and unless we formulate them" (*Sense* 93). Both affirmations point to the essential role of (re)interpretation of signs—of literacy—in not only comprehending but *forming* human knowledge.

Rhetoric and Philosophy (or Lack Thereof)

In light of what has been described above, Berthoff and Freire's convergent pedagogies merit closer examination within the broader rhetorical field, both historical and contemporary, regarding their fundamentally philosophical orientations. Indicative of said philosophical orientation, each views the development of literacy as a dialectical process, especially in terms of the interplay between students—beginning where they are—their teachers, and the broader social contexts in which they operate. Within said contexts, both pedagogues aim to enhance their students' capacity to direct discourse toward higher purposes and understanding, harkening back to Plato. This section, then, addresses the question of a philosophical conception of literacy in terms of the long history of rhetoric as an academic subject and the more recent history of our field of rhet/comp, comparatively. This discussion is crucial for a broader consideration of what the pedagogies in question may have to offer amidst the social, ecological, and intellectual challenges of today (how they may function as or supplement, in other words, *critical pedagogies*). As Berthoff states, "the bond between teaching and philosophy is immemorial, and the study of the relationship between language and thought . . . is necessarily carried forward . . . by a recognition of our life as social creatures" (*Barricades* 10–11); yet philosophy is notably absent from most contemporary, mainstream pedagogies.

Plato's Seminal Interrogation of Rhetoric: Rhetoric and Philosophy

As Plato considers whether rhetoric might be made legitimate, he contemplates a positive possibility, that is, that a true rhetoric might rise above cheap forms of oratory and exceed inspired poetry, even (244b–245a), to become philosophical in nature. Interestingly, Berthoff echoes this questioning of rhetoric in our era when comparing her students' familiarity with persuasion, which is "the air we breathe," to argumentation, which they have rarely observed in contemporary life: she identifies this as a modern problem and a pedagogical priority (*Sense* 25). Rhetoric being philosophical, as Plato has Socrates explain repeatedly, would mean being oriented toward a public, dialectical exploration of knowledge and truth. For example, Socrates describes to Phaedrus a higher purpose of discourse in response to the question of what sort of speech could be said to be composed artfully:

> . . . [discourse] capable of helping itself as well as the [person] who planted it, [that] is not barren but produces a seed from which more discourse grows in the character of others. Such discourse makes the seed forever immortal and renders the [person] who has it as happy as any human can be. (276e–277a)

Crucially for rhetoric, this seed of enlightened discourse serves those who seek to learn and share it in a manner that could be described as nutritive or even righteous, as opposed to self-serving or merely ornamental. This is not presented simply as a type of rhetoric, but rather as what rhetoric *is*, if it be admissible to humanity after scrutiny and interrogation as a legitimate art, a legitimate object of study and learning.

A decisive interpretation of Plato's ultimately favorable view of rhetoric as philosophical is put forward by Quintilian, who writes of the *Gorgias*, "It is obvious . . . that Plato does not think that rhetoric is a bad thing, but that real rhetoric can be attained only by the just and good person" (2.15.28). He continues, referring to the *Phaedrus* in turn:

> [Plato] makes it even clearer . . . that this art cannot be perfect without a knowledge of justice also. . . . His attack was directed, however, against the class of men who made bad use of their facility in speaking. . . . The teachers of rhetoric also seemed unsatisfactory to Plato, because they separated rhetoric from justice and preferred the credible to the true: he says so also in the *Phaedrus*. (2.15.29–2.15.32)

Through the concepts of justice and truth, Quintilian alludes to the necessary union of rhetoric and philosophy: *What is just? What can be held to be true?*

Berlin's Rehearsal of Plato: Rhetoric and Ideology

In terms of recent, important interrogations of rhetoric writ large, as well as modern rhet/comp, the work of James Berlin must come to mind. As a key figure in the field in the late twentieth century, Berlin's pioneering historiographies of rhetoric and writing instruction in the US during the past two centuries, both in extensively researched monographs and focused articles, have played an important role in orienting the field up to the present, notably in terms of how we conceive of the way in which writing is taught and its social and political implications. Indeed, there is little doubt as to whether Berlin, a learned rhetorician, was conscious of the parallels between his field-defining interrogations of rhetoric in the 1980s and Plato's foundational contemplations of rhetoric in the fourth century BCE. Notably, though, Berlin's work evolved into a markedly political undertaking, as can be observed in his 1988 article "Rhetoric and Ideology in the Writing Class" (differing from more focused earlier work, where he can be seen to praise Berthoff extensively).

There is irony in Berlin's rehearsal of Plato in that he eschews philosophy altogether, replacing it with an admittedly nebulous concept of *ideology* (478). It is with such a move that Berthoff and Freire's respective pedagogies begin to lose their transformative steam in terms of literacy instruction. Berlin rehearses Plato without philosophy, while at the same time offering a muffled echo of Aristotle in his pervasive, typically dichotomous schemes of rhetorical classification. But if we were to consider writing/literacy as a primary tool for thought and meaning-making in the manner of Berthoff and Freire—as a primary discursive extension of Freire's *Animal symbolizum* for knowing and fostering change that can be taught and refined (Berthoff, Foreword xiii)—then we would not flinch at the prospect of deliberately improving students' linguistic abilities. Furthermore, especially considering the increasingly multilingual spaces in which we teach, we might follow the example of contemporary foreign language teachers in addressing higher-level discursive capacities in a manner expedited, engaging, and socially oriented toward the sphere of academia in particular, in the case of rhet/comp: this in order to increase students' capacity for accessing and contributing to higher learning and social change in short order, along with justifying our own existence.

In Berlin's scheme, though, which remains largely representative of the contemporary field, we must firmly establish an understanding of how we are influenced by ideology, rather than how we come to know through increased literacy, and self-consciously proceed from there. This is presented as a crucial element of contemporary writing instruction, and it comes as no surprise that he christens his rhetoric "social-epistemic" (488). It is not an understanding of knowledge and its formation, interpretation, and expression through language that matters so much as perceiving the ideology that underlies how knowledge is conceived of and communicated. Absent of this notion, any rushed act of knowing in an educational context would be putting the cart before the horse. "Knowledge is power" takes on a pall of suspicion: the task of the day becomes fending off the entrenched power of what is taken to be knowledge (ideology), for which language is merely a servant Berthoff's philosophical writing pedagogy was not deemed sufficiently critical to continue with this new direction in rhet/comp, and her field-defining work was eventually sidelined, including by early supporters such as Berlin (Arrington 51–52); Freire's work, meanwhile, was taken up enthusiastically in view of its political content without fully considering, if at all, its underlying philosophy of language (Arrington 6).

LITERACY HOW? SHARED SEMIOTICS AND THE (UN)LIKELY CONVERGENCE OF BERTHOFF AND FREIRE

Interestingly, both Plato and Berlin begin their key tracts on rhetoric by questioning not whether, but rather *how* rhetoric ought to be envisioned and taught. This paper examines Berthoff in like form, beginning with the philosophy of language that shapes her pedagogy as well as Freire's. Returning to Peirce, who directly influenced Berthoff and by extension the contemporary field of rhet/comp, we see the world composed entirely of signs, as mentioned previously; meaning is arrived at not merely via the relationship between signified and signifier, which Saussure rightly identifies as arbitrary, but also via interpretation. Thus, the arbitrary nature of signs is not a problem of language, rendering it subservient to dominant ideologies—a notion stemming from Saussurean linguistics that has been hugely influential during the past century (Culler 28, 96), perhaps even to the detriment of the humanities (Berthoff, *Barricades* 8)—rather, the arbitrary nature of signs, their ability to be endlessly (re)interpreted, is a necessity, in Peirce's conception (Culler 188–189). Signification is *only possible* because of interpretation, hence its implication in the sign as a third component (*interpretant*)—again, this is Peirce's triadic, as opposed to dyadic, model (Peirce 11). As alluded to previously, Peirce goes so far as to define the *sense of learning* based on semiotics: the "process of interpreting signs—the habit of reflecting on interpretations, of drawing out implications of one or another representation; the 'plural consciousness' [that] allows differing interpretations to be formulated and brought to the test," in Berthoff's words. Her writing pedagogy directly follows from this notion of learning (*Sense* 5).

Freire's pedagogy, again, rests upon the same premise: while we all have the ability for perception, abstraction, and interpretation, the ability to employ self-reflection through language awareness and formulate, problematize, and operationalize our ideas is a pedagogical goal that teachers and students can reach together. Broadly, the objective is that students be ready to "[reflect] and [act] upon the world in order to transform it," the activity of theory/practice that Freire defines as his famed "praxis" (*Pedagogy* 76). Freire, who worked in environments bereft of educational opportunity, began here with the generative word—the naming and manipulating of *words* to consciously interpret and reinterpret his students' *worlds*. Meanwhile, Berthoff, working in an urban, working-class US writing instruction context, aimed at making students comfortable with complexity and the centrality of language in helping us to organize reality and make meaning out of it—in helping us to know (*Meaning* 12). It follows that a key principle of literacy education is that higher-level discourse helps us give structure to complexity and better understand and act in our worlds, which Berthoff does not shy away from approaching in lexico-grammatical terms:

> Words cluster . . . [and] clusters of words turn into syntax: it is the discursive character of language, its tendency to 'run along'—and that's what discourse means—language's tendency to be syntactical brings thought along with it. It is the discursive, generalizing, forming power of language that makes meanings from chaos. (*Meaning* 38)

The differences briefly illustrated here between the pedagogical contexts and contents of the approaches of Berthoff and Freire, who nonetheless share converging visions of literacy and philosophies of language, could be generative of new conceptions of critical pedagogy for this century, drawing attention to the enduring relevance of language education as such in the context of a productive awareness of and attention to students, their language, and their worlds.

Reimagining and Reviving: Looking Back to Uncover New Possibilities

This piece calls for reimagining and reviving Berthovian pedagogy as an under-utilized, perhaps unrecognized species of critical pedagogy that, while often overlapping with Freirean pedagogy in foundations, goals, and possible implementations, may in fact serve better in various developing and developed world contexts today, both North and South. The variations in time, place, and historical context involved in such considerations, rather than muddling the possibility of Berthoff or Freire's enduring value, represent productive differences that can generate new possibilities for us as literacy educators.

In particular, Berthoff's more robust focus on higher-level discursive tools such as understanding how we know through syntactic forms; paragraphing and paraphrasing and their formative and interpretive power; and dialectical note-taking, for example, for which she provides many guidelines and examples throughout her work (especially in *Forming/Thinking/Writing* [1982], which is intended for this purpose), could be adapted to help form the toolbox of writing teachers who wish to approach critical pedagogy by fostering the critical discursive abilities of their students in today's world. *Critical* here, it should be noted, would refer more to students' enhanced skill sets at the end of the writing course than teachers' perceptions of the condition in which they enter the writing course.

It is simultaneously pragmatic and utopian to imagine the *charge for change* being ignited in the writing classroom, as opposed to burning out in the writing classroom. *Charge* can refer to an action, but it can also refer to an emergent rhetorical power and responsibility that merely begins with us as literacy educators, meeting our students as unique and talented "language animals" already full of productive abstractions and rhetorical energy that we can help them to channel into powerful discursive tools. This broad goal is captured in a quote from Freire that Berthoff reports from his talk at UMass–Boston (her home ground), which is strongly reminiscent of Socrates's statement to Phaedrus, cited above, regarding the true aim of discourse:

> For me, philosophically, existentially, the fundamental task of human beings should be reading the world, writing the world; reading the words, writing the words. If we did that consciously, with critical consciousness, of course we would be active, willing, choosing subjects of history. Then we could speak freely about our presence in the world. (qtd. in *Meaning*, 126).

Reviving and reimagining Berthovian pedagogy while continuing to re-envision Freirean pedagogy can help take us there.

Works Cited

Arrington, Paige. *Ann Berthoff from the Margins*. 2019. Georgia State U, PhD Dissertation.

Berlin, James. "Rhetoric and Ideology in the Writing Classroom." *College English*, vol. 50, no. 5, 1988, pp. 477–94.

Berthoff, Ann. *The Making of Meaning*. Boynton/Cook, 1981.

—. Foreword. *Literacy: Reading the Word and the World*, by Paulo Freire and Donaldo Macedo, Bergin & Garvey, 1987, pp. xi–xxiii.

—. *The Sense of Learning*. Boynton/Cook, 1990.

—. *The Mysterious Barricades: Language and Its Limits*. U of Toronto P, 1999.

Culler, Jonathan. *On Deconstruction*. Cornell UP, 1982.

Díaz, Kim. "Paulo Freire." *Internet Encyclopedia of Philosophy*, https://iep.utm.edu/freire/#H7. Accessed Apr. 1, 2022.

Freire, Paulo. *The Politics of Education*. Bergin & Garvey, 1985.

—. *Pedagogy of the Oppressed: 50th Anniversary Edition*. Translated by Myra Bergman Ramos, Bloomsbury, 2018.

George, Ann. "Critical Pedagogies." *A Guide to Composition Pedagogies*, 2nd edition, edited by Gary Tate, et al., Oxford UP, 2014, pp. 77–93.
Peirce, C.S. *The Essential Peirce, Vol. 1*. Edited by Nathan Houser and Christian Kloesel, Indiana UP, 1992.
Plato. *Phaedrus. The Complete Works of Plato*. Edited by John M. Cooper, Hackett, 1998, pp. 506–56.
Quintilian. *The Orator's Education, Books 1–2*. Translated by Donald A. Russell, Harvard UP, 2001.

16 Ibn Sina on Style: A Dialogue between Aristotelian Rhetoric and Arabic Poetics

Maha Baddar

Abstract

This article outlines some of the major changes introduced to Greek and Neo-Platonic theories of style by Ibn Sina to introduce scholars of cultural rhetorics to the development of these traditions in the medieval Arabic tradition. In his extensive theory of style that spans five chapters, Ibn Sina references specific aspects of Greek rhetoric and poetics to show their incompatibility with Arabic, contrasts oral and written discourse, and raises difficult questions such as the adequacy of the use of metaphorical expressions in rhetorical discourse alongside a discussion of context and decorum. One of the main aspects of Ibn Sina's theory of style is the focus on Arabic poetics as one of the foundations for style in Arabic. As a result of the spread of literacy in the medieval Arabic-speaking world, Ibn Sina's theory of style expands on the rules of written discourse, especially legal documents.

I say, habit and customs mandate issues that cannot be fully mastered in creating speech, conjugating it, presenting it as rhymed prose, and so forth. It is worth noting that the Greeks in this category used cases that we did not learn, or stop at, and we do not believe they are beneficial today. Arabs have different rules to make prose closer to poetic composition.

—Ibn Sina

Abu 'Ali Ibn Al 'Abdullah al-Hussein Ibn Sina (known in the West as Avicenna; 980–1037 CE) is the most influential thinker of medieval and early modern times. In fact, medieval philosophy is categorized into what came before and what came after Ibn Sina. He was born near Bokhara in what is known today as Uzbekistan. Even though Persian was his first language, he wrote mostly in Arabic, the lingua franca of the Islamic Empire at the time. His *Canon of Medicine* was taught in Europe in the Latin translation up until the seventeenth century. However, in his own autobiography, Ibn Sina dismisses medicine as an easy art that he mastered at a young age. It is in fact questions of philosophy that Ibn Sina grappled with throughout his life. He wrote hundreds of books (some of which are extant) on topics that covered fundamental questions on logic, ethics, politics, law, knowledge, the intellect, communication, psychology, and metaphysics. Ibn Sina's work is part of the Medieval Arabic Translation Movement, which means that he had access to Greek and Neo-Platonic thinking as well as the Arabic translations and commentaries on Aristotle and Plato.[10]

Ibn Sina outlines an innovative theory of rhetoric, including a theory on style, in his *Rhetoric*, titled *Rhetorica* (written ريطوريقا in Arabic letters) which is part of the volume on logic from his encyclopedic work *al-Shifa,'* or *the Cure*. *Al-Shifa'* is a multi-volume work that covers many branches of knowledge following the Aristotelian classification of knowledge. The logical arts follow the order of the *Organon*.[11] However, the reader is cautioned not to be misled by this organizational gesture into thinking that the content of Ibn Sina's logical works was a commentary on Aristotle.

Of interest to scholars of cultural and comparative rhetorics is Ibn Sina's original contributions to rhetorical theory stemming from his adamant refusal to be merely another commentator on Aristotle. Ibn Sina was not interested in commenting on Aristotle like his predecessors (such as al-Kindi and al-Farabi) and even descendants (such as Ibn Rushd). He was an independent, innovative thinker who earned the title *al-Sheikh al-Ra'ees* (or the master). When asked by his biographer Abu Ubayd al-Juzjani to comment on Aristotle's work, Ibn Sina's response was:

---

10. For a detailed account of the Medieval Arabic Translation Movement see Gutas, *Greek Thought, Arabic Culture*.

11. The Alexandrian school added Aristotle's *Rhetoric* and *Poetics* to his logical curriculum, called it the *Organon* and used the Neo-Platonic philosopher, Porphyry's (234-305 CE) *Isagoge*, or *Introduction*, as an introductory treatise to the collection of logical works. The Arabic philosophical tradition inherited the same structure from the school of Alexandria, hence treating rhetoric and poetics as logical arts and referring to the *Isagoge* as part and parcel of the Aristotelian logical curriculum.

I have neither the time nor the inclination to occupy myself with close textual analysis and commentary. But if you [pl.] would be content with whatever I had readily in mind [which I have thought] on my own, then I could write for you [pl.] a comprehensive work arranged in the order which will occur to me" (qtd. in Gutas, *Avicenna* 103–04).

Ibn Sina's *Rhetoric* is testimony to the accuracy of the above statement. A close reading of the book shows two innovative rhetorical theories of political rhetoric and of style rooted in Islamic culture and the rules of the Arabic language, respectively. The book also includes a more extensive account of the syllogism and the enthymeme that shows that syllogistic reasoning was central to his worldview and approach to knowledge-making. This account is in alignment with the new position awarded to rhetoric as part of the logical curriculum. He mentions in his *Introduction* to the volume of logic in *al-Shifa*: "The relation of this field of study [that is, logic] to inner reflection, which is called 'internal reasoning' is like the relation of grammar to the explicit interpretation, which is called 'external reasoning' and like the relation of prosody to the poem" (qtd. in McGinnis 28). Additionally, the examples and the topoi throughout the book are derived from and of relevance to the medieval Arabic Islamic world, as Ibn Sina continuously reminds us.

In Part Four of his *Rhetoric*, Ibn Sina introduces a theory of style that shows awareness of Greek, Arabic, and Persian elements of style. He combines the rules of Arabic eloquence rooted in pre-Islamic poetry, *ilm al-balagha*, with *fann al-khataba*, the Arabic art in dialogue with Aristotelian rhetoric and the Neo-Platonic commentary tradition on it. He also incorporates Persian elements, not surprisingly, as an act of homage to his first language. The two different arts, the *ilm al-balagha* and *fann al-khataba* are based on different rhetorical traditions that inform the discursive practices of two different languages and cultures. Ibn Sina incorporates many elements from *ilm al-balagha* in his theory of style because he was creating a theory of style for Arabic speakers and writers. As a result, he repeatedly mentions the incompatibility between certain aspects of the Arabic and Greek rhetorical traditions because of the morphological and syntactic differences between the two languages. He rejects certain Greek stylistic rules and replaces them with Arabic ones. Such adaptations were applicable to areas of style related to grammar, the use of metaphor, the differences between spoken and written utterances, and decorum.

The content of Ibn Sina's theory of style is part of his *Rhetoric*, but many of the rules of eloquence are derived from Arabic poetics, the reader will notice. Even though Ibn Sina has an independent book on poetics in the same volume from *al-Shifa*,' the many references to poetics are necessary in his book on rhetoric because one cannot write a book on Arabic style while ignoring the rules of Arabic poetry. The reader of his Rhetoric, as a result, will witness Ibn Sina negotiating rules that belong to one field, poetics, and applying them to another, rhetoric, while simultaneously negotiating the rules of eloquence from the Greek and Arabic rhetorical traditions. In the process, many references to poetry are made throughout the *Rhetoric*, at times to compare poetry to rhetoric, and at other times to contrast the two fields. The following passage highlights the influence of poetics on Ibn Sina's theory of style:

"و اعلم أن اختلاف النغم عند محاكاة المحاكى إنما يكون من وجوه ثلاثة: الحدة و الثقل و النبرات. و المنازعون من الخطباء يكتسبون هذه الملكة من مراعاة المنازعين من الشعراء فما كان أعمل في أغراضهم نقلوه إلى صناعاتهم" (199).

"Difference in intonation is characterized by three aspects: pitch, emphasis and tone. Rhetors who argue acquire this skill through emulating poets: they copied what worked for poets to their art of rhetoric" (Baddar 33). Ibn Sina clearly distinguishes rhetoric and poetry and does not haphazardly converge the rules of both fields. He says:

وقد يعرض لمستعمل الخطابية شعرية كما يعرض لمستعمل الشعر خطابية. و إنما يعرض للشاعر أن يأتي بخطابية و هو لايشعر إذا أخذ المعاني المعتادة و الأقوال الصحيحة التي لا تخييل فيها و لا محاكاة ثم يركبها تركيب موزونا. وإنما يعتز بذلك البله و أما أهل البصيرة فلا يعدون ذلك شعرا. فإنه ليس يكفي للشعر أن يكون موزونا فقط. و هذا الإنسان في حكم اللص لأنه يسرق ظننا بغير وجوب و لا أشباه وجوب. (204)

> It is accidental to use poetic rhetoric or rhetorical poetry. It is possible for a poet to use rhetoric while not reciting poetry if regular meanings and proper sayings free of imagination or simile are put together in a rhyming pattern. However, this is foolish, and perceptive people do not consider this to be poetry. It is not sufficient for poetry to rhyme only. The person who does this is similar to a thief because they unnecessarily steal assent. (Baddar 35)

While discussing the difference between poetry and prose, Ibn Sina claims that rhyming statements with proper meaning do not qualify as poetry because they do not appeal to the imagination, the key feature of poetry that distinguishes it from rhetoric. On the other hand, poetic rhetoric, when used, is made up of persuasive utterances that convey acceptable, persuasive content.

Certain stylistic decisions serve the goals of both rhetors and poets in Ibn Sina's theory on style. He highlights the importance of word-choice to accomplish the goals of rhetoric and poetics, namely persuasion and imagination respectively. He says,

"و أما الإقناع في الخطابة و التخييل في الشعر فيختلف في المعنى الواحد بعينه بحسب الألفاظ التي تكسوه. (199)

"On the other hand, with persuasion in rhetoric and imagination in poetry, one meaning can have several interpretations depending on the choice of utterance that covers it" (Baddar 33).

The reader of Ibn Sina's section on style from his *Rhetoric* will notice the focus on the individuality of language and the difficulty of transferring rules from one language to another. Ibn Sina shows the reader that different languages have different rules and that the sound patterns of Greek poetry, for example, are not applicable or helpful for improving the composition of utterances in other languages. To prove his point, Ibn Sina falls back on his Persian background, adding yet another layer to his complex theory of style. He says,

"و كذلك فإن القول المنثور قد يجعل بالمدات موزونا كالخسروانيات فإنها تجعل موزونة بمدات تلحقها. " (223)

"[P]rose can sound metered through the use of elongation. For example, the use of *Khusrawaneyat* [a Persian genre of poetry] are metered through elongations that follow them." He contrasts this with Arabic where the focus is on melody rather than meter. After showing that languages such as Persian and Arabic use stylistic elements other than meter, he persuades his reader not to follow the Greek tradition and that meter is not integral for Arabic writers and speakers by saying,

"ثم لليونانيين في هذا الباب أحوال لم نحصلها و لم نقف عليها و ما نراها نحن ينتفع بها اليوم." (224)

"It is worth noting that the Greeks in this category used cases that we did not learn, or stop at, and we do not believe they are beneficial today. Arabs have different rules to make prose closer to poetic composition" (Baddar 39). Ibn Sina clarifies in another passage that the grammatical rules of one language are not transferable to another. He says,

"أن يراعي أمر التأنيث والتذكير ما كان بعلامة و ما لم يكن بعلامة حتى لا يقع فيه غلط. والوجه الخامس أن يراعي أمر الجمع و التثنية و الوحدان والتصاريف التي تختص بها ". (215)

"It is important to note that different languages have different rules, so nothing said about these rules is universal or absolute" (Baddar 38). To support his claim, he recommends that writers and speakers of Arabic "accurately use feminine and masculine references, be it ones that have a clear feminine suffix or not (تاء التأنيث) in order to avoid error" and "to follow the rules of plural, duplication and singular following the appropriate conjugations that are specific to each one of them"¹² (215). Rules of gender and number are specific to the Arabic nouns and are used here to illustrate the non-transferability of the rules of one language to another.

The discussion of the use of metaphor in oral and written discourse in Ibn Sina's *Rhetoric* far exceeds its counterpart in Aristotle's text in both length and complexity. For starters, Ibn Sina is clearly undecided about the use of metaphor in rhetorical discourse. Isolated passages about metaphor throughout Part Four of the book are in fact contradictory because they range from discouraging the use of metaphor altogether to stating that its use should be mandatory in certain contexts.[13] A close reading of Ibn Sina's passages about metaphor shows that the reasons Ibn Sina offers for rejecting or using metaphor depend ultimately on the speaker's rhetorical situation. Metaphor plays a minor if not a non-existent role in rhetoric, or so claims Ibn Sina on more than one occasion. Why, then, does he make repetitive references to metaphor when discussing style in rhetoric? To start with, since metaphor is integral to poetry, he finds himself having to address its compatibility with rhetoric because his theory of style is rooted in poetics, after all. The awkwardness lies in the fact that on more than one occasion Ibn Sina declares the incompatibility between metaphor and rhetoric, yet he finds himself recommending the use of metaphor in certain situations related to decorum and sensibility. He rejects metaphor on this basis:

"و استعمال الاستعارات و المجاز في الأقوال الموزونة أليق من استعمالها في الأقوال المنثورة." (203)

---

12. In addition to the singular and plural rules, Arabic has a rule for when a noun refers to two things.

13. Ibn Sina's biographer states that he wrote most of *al-Shifa'* in record time while in hiding. The text clearly did not undergo a thorough revision and many parts of it read like lecture notes that have been added to the written text. This may explain some of the contradictory statements concerning metaphor among other things. The reader should keep this in mind while tackling the text. None of this should take away from the value the book adds to the study of the history of rhetoric and the development of rhetorical theory after Aristotle.

"Using metaphor and imagery in statements with meter is more appropriate in poetry than using them in prose" (Baddar 35). In some sections he goes as far as completely discouraging the use of metaphor on the ground that it deceptive and that all deception is unacceptable:

و ليعلم أن الاستعارة في الخطابة ليست على أنها أصل بل على أنها غش ينتفع به في ترويج الشئ على من ينخدع و ينغش ويؤكد عليه الإقناع الضعيف بالتخييل كما تغش الأطعمة و الأشربة بأن يخلط معها شئ غيرها لتطيب به أو لتعمل عملها فيروج أنها طيبة في أنفسها . (203)

> It should be known that use of metaphor in rhetoric is not a foundational element, but a kind of artifice used to promote something to those who are deceived and cheated by weak persuasion and imagination. This is similar to cheating food and drink by adding something to make it taste better or to make it seem to possess good qualities and is thus promoted as good and pure (Baddar 35).

Despite the direct refusal of the use of metaphor in the above passage, Ibn Sina resorts to recommending its use when discussing the importance of word-choice in rhetoric. In a long passage explaining why the rhetor should use certain words but not others in certain rhetorical situations, such as courtship, he borrows from the Arabic poetic genre of *gazal* and recommends the use of metaphor to do justice to the beauty of the beloved:

وللقول الانتقالي الاستعاري في تأثيره مراتب. فإنه قال الغزل في صفة بنان الحبيب: إنها وردية كانت أوقع من أن يقول: حمر و خصوصا أن يقول: قرمزية. فإن قوله في الاستعارة للحمر "وردية" قد يخيل معها من لطافة الورد و عرفه ما لا يخيله قوله "حمر" مطلقا . (208)

> A metaphorical transitional expression has different levels in influencing the audience. For example, in a courtship poem describing the beloved's fingers, it is more realistic to describe them as rosy rather than red or crimson. Metaphorically using "rosy" to refer to a shade of red invokes in imagination the pleasantness of a rose; such a connotation would never be invoked in the audience's imagination by using "red" (Baddar 37).

In specific rhetorical situations, Ibn Sina even concedes that the use of metaphor is not only acceptable, but imperative. This is, again, in relation to word-choice. He says:

فيجب أن تبدل الألفاظ المفردة بالأقاويل. و قد يبدل الاسم بالقول إذا كان الصريح يستبشع مثل الاسم لصريح لفرج النساء فالأحسن أن يبدل فيقال: عورة النساء و كما يبدل اسم الحيض بدم النساء و يبدل الاسم الصريح للجماع بلمس النساء. و ربما بدل الاسم بالصفة المفردة فيقال بدل الاسم الصريح للجماع: الوطء و بدل اسم ذلك الذي لهن: العورة. و ربما تركت الصفة و فزع إلى التشبيه و الاستعارة . (217)

A noun could be replaced by a statement if saying the noun directly may be offensive such as the reference to a woman's vagina; in this case it is better to substitute it by using "a woman's private parts" instead. One should also substitute the reference to menstruation by saying "women's blood" and the direct reference to intercourse by saying "touching women." A noun could be substituted by a specific attribute such as substituting intercourse by "lying down with." The same applies to referring to genitals. It is also possible to not use an attribute and resort to using simile and metaphor (Baddar 38).

While not applicable to his twenty-first century readers, this passage not only provides an adequate example for the use of metaphor but is also proof that Ibn Sina's claim that different times, languages, and the cultures associated with them have different rules for style and decorum is indeed accurate.

Borrowing from Arabic poetics was not the sole influence from his immediate linguistic and cultural context on his theory of style. A topic covered by Ibn Sina that was not covered extensively by Aristotle is related to the advancement in literacy in the Islamic empire in the medieval era. Ibn Sina covers an extensive account stylistic elements that work specifically for written discourse. But first, here is how he contrasts spoken and written discourse:

اعلم أن اللفظ المكتوب ينبغي أن يكون أشد تحقيقا و استقصاء في الدلالة و اللفظ المخاطب به يكون أشد اختلاطا بأخذ الوجه و النفاق المذكورين سواء كان خلقيا و انفعاليا. و المنافقون الآخذون بالوجوه شديدو الحرص على قراءة الكتب النافعة في أخذ وجوه و الكتاب على قراءة الكتب النافعة في تجويد اللفظ. و الشعراء أيضا كذلك. و ما يسمع و لا يقرأ فلا يتصدى لنقد الفكر و لا يلزم من تصحيحه ما يلزم من تصحيح المكتوب. و لهذا كان كثير من الكتاب المهرة لا يجيدون الإقناع بالمخاطبة و كثير من الخطباء المقنعين المفلقين لا يحسنون أن يعملوا بأيديهم إقناعا. و السبب في ذلك أن المنافقة شديدة الموافقة في المنازعات و المفاوضات. و تشبهها أحوال أخرى مثل إهمال الرباطات باختصار أو تكرير القول الواحد استظهارا. و ليس من شئ من هذا بملائم للكتابة . (233)

You should know that the written utterance should be verified and well-scrutinized for accurate signification. On the other hand, the spoken utterance is more inaccurate because of the use of deception and the tendency to attract the audience's attention that were previously mentioned. This could be accomplished through ethical or emotional means. Such deceptive speakers are very adept at reading books on how to attract an audience's attention and books on improving styles. Poets do the same. What is heard but not read is easily forgotten so it is not subject to critical thinking and it is not necessary to correct it the way written discourse is. This is why many good writers do not excel at persuasion in speeches while many creative, persuasive speakers are not good at working with their hand [writing] to persuade. The reason is that deception works well in arguments and negotiations as well as in other cases where conjunctions are ignored through summarizing and repeating the same words from memory. None of this is appropriate for writing (Baddar 41).

Ibn Sina repeatedly mentions deception as a potential danger associated with oral discourse and does not remove manipulation from the oral rhetoric equation. This is not easy to do when committing the discourse to the permanent medium of writing.

Factors such as manipulating the audience's emotions and relying on the audience's inability to remember everything the speaker says contribute to the potential for deception in spoken discourse. Written discourse, on the other hand, allows the reader to closely examine the discourse for fallacies and deception and the preservation of the discourse in the written medium solves the problem of lapses in the audience's memory. Ibn Sina therefore emphasizes that written discourse should follow these basic rules:

و أما اللفظ المرئي أى المكتوب الذي ليس بمسموع فمنه الرسائل و لايحتاج فيها إلا إلى القراءة ومنها السجلات التي يخلدها القضاة و الخطباء و لا يطلب فيها غاية التعظيم و التفخيم للكلام فإنه مبغوض بل أن يكون جزءا من الكلام مهذبا. و إذا اشتمل على التحميد و العظة فينبغي أن تكون العبارة عنه على ما بينا فيما سلف. و يجب أن يكون أشد الكلام تقويما. لأن السجل أشرف من الرسالة و أبقى و أشد احتياجا إلى الغرض. فينبغي أن تكون ألفاظه مشهورة غير غريبة ليس من المشهورات السفسفية. و لا ينبغي أن تكون فيها إضمارات كثيرة فإنها تردها إلى الغربة عن الشهرة والاختصار يفقدها الغرض في أمثالها. ولابد من أن تخلط بها أيضا أشياء لطيفة من التعبيرات المعتادة و قليل من الغريبة و شئ من الوزن الخطابي على الجهات المقنعة المذكورة. (235–36)

As for the seen discourse, i.e., the written, not the spoken discourse, which includes epistles, it only requires reading. This discourse also includes records that judges and rhetors make permanent. Such discourse does not require exaggeration or glorification; this is despised. Instead, a part of the discourse should be refined. If it includes praise and advice, utterances should follow the same criteria.

> It should be closely corrected because an official record is more distinct than a letter. It is also more permanent and more needed to fulfil the purpose of the rhetor. Therefore, its terms should be well-known, not unfamiliar or strange, and it should be free of vulgar terms. It should not include ellipses because it makes the discourse regress into being unfamiliar, and such abbreviation makes it lose its purpose. It should still be combined with agreeable gestures such as familiar variations as well as a few unfamiliar ones and some rhetorical meter in the persuasive sections (Baddar 42).

Here, Ibn Sina highlights the importance of revision, something not possible while spontaneously delivering an oral speech, as well as the permanent nature of the written word, a state that substitutes the canon of memory, not only for the writer but the reader as well. It is a state that allows for examination and reflection on the part of the reader, hence reducing the chances of the writer's use of fallacies.

Written documents that occupy Ibn Sina's attention are legal ones, which is understandable considering his focus on deliberative rhetoric throughout the book. The following is a passage where he, in a timeless gesture, cautions against ambiguity and recommends variety in written discourse:

> و من التغييرات الحسنة أن يتحدث عن أمر بحيث ظاهره لا يكون حجة على القائل و يعتقد في الضمير أنه إنما يعني به معنى ما بلا شك فيه من غير أن يكون أقر به. ومن ذلك عكسه: و هو أن يقول القائل بقوله على ظاهره و كأنه يقر به بأن غرضه ذلك المعنى لكن الأحوال تدل على ما أريد به ظاهره وربما كان السبب فيه اتفاق الاسم. (230)

> Pleasant variation includes referring to a noun using a pronoun in such a way that the reference to the noun is inferred. That way the speaker can avoid having to mention the noun explicitly. The opposite is also a pleasant kind of variation; in this case, the speaker will say something explicitly, but it will be clearly inferred from the context that the opposite is the intended meaning. This could be accomplished through the use of a similar noun (Baddar 41).

Alongside variation, simplicity or complexity of style in writing is recommended by Ibn Sina based on the writer's context. Awareness of context and audience dictate what he promotes as stylistically adequate. He uses an example from poetic genres to show rhetors how to adjust their style to their rhetorical situation when he says:

و يكون المتكلفون و المتفصحون في كل عصر محاولين للتفيهق في بذلة الكلام. و ليس يحسن هذا في كل موضع و لا أيضا في كل شعر. فكثيرا ما يجب أن يستعمل مثل هذا في غير الشعر و كثيرا ما يجب أن يستعمل في الشعر. فإن الأشعار القصار و الخفاف التي ينحى بها نحو المعاني الهزلية والضعيفة يجب أن لا تفخم فيها الألفاظ بل يؤتى بالبذلة. (201)

> Those in charge of eloquence in every time period exert effort to understand mundane speech. This does not work in every situation or with any kind of poetry. Oftentimes, similar effort it used with discourse other than poetry. Short and light poems that deal with weak and ludicrous meanings should not be made grand but, banal ones should be used instead (Baddar 34).

Organization is a topic elaborately discussed in Part Four of the book, especially in relation to written discourse. For example, there is a detailed discussion of formatting a sentence using of linking words and conjunctions to help orient the reader. There is also a discussion of how one part of a document should lead to the one following it in a coherent way. For the former case he says:

و أن يراعي حقه من التقديم و التأخير فإنه يجب أن يقول: لما كام كذا كان كذا فإن حق " لما " أن يقدم. ويقول: كان كذا لأن كذا كذا فإن تقديم "لأن" قبل الدعوى سمج. أقول و لم يأتمر بهذا فرفوريوس صاحب أيساغوجي. و أن يدخل رباط بين رباط و بين جوابه إلا في بعض المواضع

> One should pay attention to what comes early on or later in a sentence. For example, a speaker should say, "when 'x' happened, 'y' happened." It is necessary to not postpone the second clause with the use of "when." Another example is saying, "such and such happened as a result of 'x.'" In this example, using "as a result of" before the clause is dull. I say, Porphyry did not recommend this in the *Isagogue*. He did not recommend the use of an additional conjunction between two clauses already connected by a conjunction except in certain cases (213–14).

The passage does not cover a simple grammatical rule; it is rooted in logic and uses a reference to the *Isagogue* as an example, hence reflecting the strong influence of the Alexandrian school on the medieval Arabic philosophers' engagement with the Aristotelian curriculum.

When discussing organization, Ibn Sina's focus is predominantly onflow and coherence at the entire document level. He states:

قيل في التعليم الأول: إنه يجب الكلام الخطابي مفصلا أي ذا مصاريع و تكون التفاصيل ليس كل واحد منها يتم بنفسه بل يجب أن يكون كل واحد منها مشوقا إلى المصراع الذي يليه الذي إنما يتم به المعنى. و هذا مثل ما قال الفصيح من العرب: إياك وما يسبق إلى النفس إنكاره و إن كان عندك اعتذاره فليس كل من يسمعه نكرا بقدر ما يوسعه عذرا. فإن كل مصراع من مصراعي هذا الكلام يحتاج إلى الفقه حتى يتم . (226)

It has been mentioned in the *First Learning* [Aristotle's *Rhetoric*] that rhetorical discourse should be detailed; this means it should include sections. A detailed section should not stand alone but should lead to the following section that completes the meaning. This is similar to what the eloquent among the Arabs say, "Avoid saying what the soul [of the audience] would deny, even if you have a justification [for it] / Not all who deny it will have the open mind to accept the justification." Each hemistich needs the following one to be fully understood (Baddar 40).

The last two passages acknowledge Porphyry and Aristotle. This is a testimony to the dialogic engagement between the Arabic rhetorical, on the one hand, and the Greek and Neo-Platonic traditions, on the other. Indeed, Arabic thinkers who came before Ibn Sina, such as al-Farabi, and others who came after him, such as Ibn Rushd, have written commentaries on Aristotle's rhetoric. Ibn Sina is sure to remind us, however, that not everything said by Aristotle, Porphyry, and other Alexandrian and Syriac commentators on Aristotle for that matter should be accepted without questioning, for they wrote in a different language, to different audiences, at different time periods.[14] He says,

و أقول: إن العادات توجب في النبرات و دلائلها أمورا لا تضبط و كذلك في تلفيق الكلام و تصريفه و تسجيعه وغير ذلك. ثم لليونانيين في هذا الباب أحوال لم نحصلها و لم نقف عليها و ما نراها ينتفع بها اليوم . و العرب أحكام أخرى في جعل النثر قريبا من النظم . (224–25)

I say, habit and customs mandate issues that cannot be fully mastered in creating speech, conjugating it, presenting it as rhymed prose, and so forth. It is worth noting that the Greeks in this category used cases that we did not learn, or stop at, and we do not believe they are beneficial today. Arabs have different rules to make prose closer to poetic composition (Baddar 39).

---

14. The Arabic philosophers received translations of Greek texts as well as commentaries written centuries after the closing of the school of Athens in centers such as Alexandria, Syria, and Iraq.

Awareness of context as well as rhetorical tradition variations among languages and cultures dictate what Ibn Sina promotes as a theory of style that is both adequate, not only for Arabic discourse, but for rhetorical theory at large where awareness of context and audience are key and where cultural intricacies should be at the heart of studying the art in the twenty-first century in the words of a tenth-century philosopher.

As the most prominent medieval philosopher, Ibn Sina shaped the Islamic philosophical tradition that came after him. In fact, some of the major philosophical debates among generations of Arabic philosophers have centered around Ibn Sina. Mainstream Muslim thinkers, such as al-Ghazali, vehemently attacked Ibn Sina's reliance on Aristotelian logic in his The *Incoherence of the Philosophers*, while Ibn Rushd, a faithful Aristotelian thinker, responded to al-Ghazali in defense of Ibn Sina in *The Incoherence of the Incoherence*. Ibn Sina's work was instrumental in shaping Western thinking and his influence on Christian and Jewish thinkers such as Thomas Aquinas and Maimonides is well-known. In fact, his influence lasted until scholasticism in the nineteenth century where, similar to the medieval Arabic philosophical tradition, questions of faith and philosophy were discussed hand-in-hand.

The medieval Arabic rhetorical tradition is rich in both branches of rhetoric, *fann al-khataba* and *'ilm al-balagha*. Ibn Sina is not the only medieval Arabic thinker who discussed rhetoric elaborately. Translations of medieval Arabic treatises and publications analyzing these documents is, therefore, instrumental in expanding the field of cultural and comparative rhetorics in the twenty-first century. I hope this article encourages scholars of cultural and comparative rhetorics as well as historians of rhetoric to read medieval Arabic thinkers' work on rhetoric if only to understand the developments these thinkers introduced to the Aristotelian and Neo-Platonic theories of rhetoric in the medieval Arabic-speaking world.

Works Cited

Baddar, Maha. "Ibn Sina on Style: Article Four from his Book on Rhetoric." *Global Rhetorical Traditions*. Edited by Hui Wu and Tarez Samra Graban. Parlor Press, 2022, 66–97.

Gutas, Dimitri. *Greek Thought, Arabic Culture: The Graeco-Arabic Translation Movement in Baghdad and Early 'Abbāsid Society (2nd-4th/8th-10th Centuries)*. Routledge, 1998.

—. *Avicenna and the Aristotelian Tradition: Introduction to Reading Avicenna's Philosophical Works, Including an Inventory of Avicenna's Authentic Works*. Brill, 2014.

Ibn Sina, Abu Ali Al Husayn. *Al-Shifa': Rhetorica,* edited by Muhammad Selim Salim. Al-Amireyya, 1954.

McGinnis, Jon. *Avicenna*. Oxford UP, 2010.

17 Rhetorical Possibilities of Spectral Listening

Leah Senatro

Abstract

Today, digital mourning texts circulate not only the dead's written words, but also their multimodal representations, creating a digital, spectral sensorium for mourners. This essay draws from recent work on rhetoric as an act of listening and circulation studies to imagine a rhetoric of spectral listening within digital multimodal grief communities. After using Galen to establish a link between the hand and rhetoric, I develop a concept of re-memberance and discuss rhetoric's ability to re-compose the decomposing body. Finally, I close-read texts from a digital multimodal mourning community to argue that rhetoric complicates the temporal limits of the body, which creates a diffused *kairos*, as well as challenges what type of being can be moved. This re-composition of the decomposed body creates a digital sensorium where in which the living and the dead brush up against each other and a rhetoric of spectral listening can help us interpret such spaces.

Rhetorical Possibilities of Spectral Listening

In Galen's second century medical anatomy text, *On the Usefulness of Parts of the Body*, he works to demonstrate the way that each part of the human body is optimal and perfectly designed for its function, and how the body, as a sum of those parts, makes an ideal instrument for the soul. Galen begins with a discussion of the hand. Marveling at the hand's function, he writes, "Even now, thanks to writings set down by the hand it is yet possible for you to hold converse with Plato, Aristotle, and the other Ancients" (Galen 69). Consequently, even now we are able to hold converse with Galen today. Galen couples the hand with the word and memory, as it is the hands of Aristotle and Plato that give Galen access to their work.

In this paper, I use Galen to establish a link between the hand and writing to open a conversation about the rhetorical possibility of spectral listening as well as discuss a diffused kairotic moment within contemporary digital mourning practices. First, I establish a concept of re-memberance and discuss rhetoric's ability to recompose the decomposing body. Second, I analyze a specific contemporary multimodal grief community to showcase the ways that circulating multimodal representations of the dead re-member the body of the dead. This re-membered body opens the possibility for spectral listening within a digital sensorium where both the living and the dead brush up against each other, always enabled by rhetoric and its circulation.

Re-Membering the Spectral Body

Why start with Galen to talk about the hand's relationship to rhetoric? Especially when Aristotle describes the hand as "an instrument of instruments"—which Galen cites directly—to draw a parallel between the intellect, and when Quintilian writes of the importance of gesture for the orator? I begin with Galen because he is interested in the body, first, and the written word second. Yes, the written word is an example of what makes the human body so exceptional and therefore of best service to the soul, but it is made possible *first* by the hand and the embodied being. To illustrate this point, Galen introduces the hand not by describing the extremity or outlining its appearance, but by describing what he refers to as its extensions—buildings, structures, weapons, and tools—and most notably, the written word itself, which situates the body within its environment. This establishes a direct relationship not only between rhetoric and the hand, but with memorialization as Galen marvels at his ability to converse with the dead. Notably, within the "anatomy" of Galen's text itself, his thesis is situated in "the hand"—or at least in the chapter titled "the hand." Such a move is an articulation of the rhetorical context as a fundamentally embodied one.

I am interested in the possibility of rhetoric's ability not only to remember the words of those that are dead, as Galen remembers the work of Hippocrates and we now remember the work of Galen, but also of rhetoric's potential to re-member the dead, in the limb sense of the word member, by recomposing the body that has decomposed. The re-membered dead body functions like a phantom created by those that are actively remembering. By analyzing a particular multimodal grief community, I explore the possibility of a spectral listening made evident through the mourning processes in digital grief practices today. First, I want to make a point about the hand's relationship to the greater body. I don't reference the hand or its connection to rhetoric to create some amputated abstract, but rather to name it as a nexus point of touch and to emphasize the embodied nature of being-moved by rhetorical address. For Galen, the part is not divisible from the whole and, to fulfill the needs of the soul, every body part—hand included—must work in concert with every other part. So, if we imagine Galen "shaking spectral hands" with Hippocrates and Aristotle through the writing that they left behind, Galen's entire body is part of that exchange and, therefore, re-membering would necessitate an entire spectral body.

This spectral body, made possible by rhetoric, exists in rhetorical contexts, making rhetorical capabilities—like listening—possible. Daniel M. Gross offers a "history of rhetoric as the art of listening" in his 2020 book, *Being-Moved*. Gross explores different rhetorical ecologies—including the historical disciplinary structure of the sciences, sacred rhetoric, and the writing classroom—to offer a genealogy of rhetoric that privileges the listening ear, rather than the speaking mouth, as the foremost organ of the rhetor. Gross creates a "critical ecology of the senses where (sensory) experience is purposive, emerging from a historically situated being-world nexus" (15) to interrogate how we "configure our listening differently depending on the public space we occupy" (27). In what follows, I explore the public space of digital grief as a "critical ecology of the senses" to investigate the rhetorical phenomena of spectral listening (Gross 15). I imagine mourning as rhetorical listening and as a type of response in which re-membering is an embodied process enabled by circulation in digital environments and such remembrance "moves" the living as we are able to "listen" to the dead.

A Multimodal Crypt: The Sensorium of Networked Mourning

In their introduction to a 2014 special issue of *Rhetoric Society Quarterly*, Diane Davis and Michelle Ballif work to challenge the assumption that the rhetor is a rhetor because of their humanity. The pair work to situate "the human rhetor" as "indelibly networked in its relations to place, space, matter, and especially to technology and various media" (Davis and Ballif 348). While Ballif, Davis, and others open up these networks to the possibility of a "post-human," I am interested in the role that the post-living, particularly the post-living bodies, play in such networks to create a "critical ecology of the senses" maintained by listening (Gross 15). Mourning networks can include both digital and analog texts—think everything from tombstones, epigraphs, and obituaries, to Facebook memorial posts and Instagram accounts. These digital and analog networks, or "ecologies of the senses," develop a haptic environment, much like the one Galen creates when describing the function of the hand by the world that the hand has shaped. Just as the tombstone is carved by the hand and the corpse is buried by it, digital environments are similarly constructed by the hand. From digital, we have the "digitalis"—meaning finger—which, as Cecilia Lindhe points out, functions as a nexus for bodily connection to the virtual, but still sensorial, mode.

Such a nexus is evident in the way we listen to and create mourning texts in digital multimodal environments. Digital multimodal mourning texts have developed alongside changing cultural practices around mourning. As, over centuries, graves have moved from the church to the church yard, to within the city, and then outside the city, and now, with the proliferation of cremation, not to any location at all, social media has become a multimodal crypt. Increased popularity of cremation, proliferation of more secular funeral rituals, and digital environments offer new genres of thanotographic texts—and avenues for how those texts are circulated rhetorically. Kathleen Blake Yancey argues that the shift in mourning practices away from cemeteries has fundamentally changed the way grief circulates. Instead of mourners circulating *to* the text representing the bodies that once were, the texts are brought to the mourners in what Yancey defines as "untethered circulation," or a circulation that is not linked to a physical space or time—in this case, the grave. Whereas a grave represents the present body as dead and the past body as living, such cyber-sepulchers create a "past present" with representations of the dead that create a clearer association not to the life lost, but to a life as if it is currently being lived.

We can see such practices evidenced in a particular digital mourning community grieving the sudden and tragic loss of Ashley Corrado, a 25-year-old dancer and functional medicine and fitness coach who passed away in a car accident on January 1, 2021.[15] Ashley's digital memorials make a great example to analyze for two reasons. First, her body was cremated, and no central physical headstone or burial site exists for mourners to circulate to, rendering an example of Yancey's "untethered" circulation. Second, there is a lot of content. Ashley had a pretty robust—and frequently updated—social media presence across multiple platforms. She also had an immense impact

---

15. I am thankful to the Corrado family, particularly Kristin Corrado, for encouraging this research and granting permission to use aspects of her daughter's grief community for the following analysis. Kristin Corrado granted written permission to reproduce visuals from this grief community here.

on her loved ones and there are hundreds of multimodal posts across platforms actively circulating, offering plenty of material to analyze and emphasizing the embodied listening of the mourner through the sensorially rich, and, one might say, "living" quality of her memorial.

First, I would like to analyze some posts from a Facebook group titled, "In Loving Memory of Ashley Corrado." Posts combine photos and videos of Ashley dancing with her friends, working as a fitness trainer, and living as a young child with photos of her memorial service and written reflections on her life's impact. Scrolling through, we are asked to implicate our own bodies to read the texts with our finger, or "digitalis," as we click and scroll through the digital compositions. The grieving space becomes a multimodal sensorium for the embodied mourner who, by responding to and therefore recirculating such posts, re-members Ashley as a spectral body.

In the same special issue that Davis and Ballif question the primacy of the human as a rhetorical being, Michelle Ballif draws on Derrida's work to explore the rhetorical consequences of the dead other which is "always already the very condition of possibility for address" and the work of mourning always "haunts the possibility of address" (456). Ballif imagines the writer as the living dead—because death is always a possibility for the human—who has an ethical responsibility to respond to the dead as other that, though invisible and unknowable, is always already watching, or, we might say, waiting for response. Ballif illustrates the spectral imperative for rhetorical address, writing, "signification is possible (as iterable) only *because of death*. Death *is* the condition of address" as the writer is always anticipating their future death (459). Additionally, Ballif explains that, to mourn successfully, you must adopt the dead as the self, thereby becoming the dead and always being responsible and response-able to that dead.

Ballif speculates, that "if we knock at the crypt, perhaps the other will respond" (462). What happens when you knock on the door of social media? Ballif argues that language is haunted by the living dead, and this ghost is one we must simultaneously respond to, but also be necessarily blind to since we cannot see or know the death as a presence. So, if the writer must necessarily become the living dead, rhetoric in digital mourning communities create the dead living, or, at the very least, the dead listening. Rhetorically circulated texts of spectral bodies create sensory-rich contexts that enable listening, response, and the ability to be moved by a once-living rhetor.

Multimodal representations re-body the absent body of the dead to create a rhetorical situation that mediates the past death of the other and future death of the self. While Galen re-membered the bodies of those ancient to him to engage with their writing that they "set down by the hand," multimodal grief communities emphasize how re-membering generates response and rhetorical listening through "purposive" sensorial experience that "moves" the living and the dead in the same rhetorical space (Gross 15). To mourn, we cannot be completely blind to the ghost. We must not only acknowledge, but also respond to that presence that is illuminated in multimodal grief texts where we interact haptically by scrolling, but also auditorially and visually with videos and audio recordings that recompose a body that should not be there, but is.

Diffuse Kairos

This re-composition similarly challenges a chronological temporality with what Yancey calls the "past-present." The life-like qualities of the multimodal posts reference a context of time and space—the time that Ashley was alive and the space of her body—that no longer exists, but is continually present. Such a continual "presence" is the haunting that Ballif argues haunts all rhetoric. Such a haunt is present across platforms. Mourners have continued to tag Ashley's Instagram handle in events that have temporally occurred since her death. Tags on posts from friends' birthday parties she would have attended and places she loved to visit emphasize Ashley's presence, not her absence, and are a definitive address to the dead that invites the spectral presence of Ashley's rhetorical attention. She is invited to listen, to participate, in the rhetorical moment.

Additionally, the mourners are always listening to her as they are re-membering her. To enter this grief community that was fastened by the hands of the living, one must necessarily listen to the texts that were fastened by the once-living. Because of the assemblage nature of the multimodal memorials, mourners often collect posts and photos that were originally made by Ashley herself—that were fastened by her hand—and refasten them into a text that showcases her life as lived. A great example is a video montage originally created by Ashley's friend with the photos that other mourners posted to the group. The video opens with a short clip of orange and white balloons released into the sky during her memorial service, which is depicted in this frame here. Afterwards, a slideshow of photos plays that includes photos that were originally posted to Ashley's Instagram and then screenshotted by the video creator. In Figure 1, there are two screenshotted photographs of Ashley smiling, one at the beach with her birth and death date over it and the other with her smiling and wearing a beanie hat, as well as a screenshot of a caption she wrote for Instagram. First, the composer had to be response-able, to listen to, Ashley's original compositions. Only after such listening could the creator then respond with this video collage. Ashley is re-membered by the untethered, re-circulation of such texts into a rhetorical spectral representation of her body, which we then interact with sensorially. However, the screenshots of Ashley's original posts cast an uncanny ghostliness on the video and a reminder that grief is the reason these texts are circulating again.

Figure 1. Four screenshots from a memorial video posted on February 3, 2021 in the Facebook Group titled, "In Loving Memory of Ashley Corrado." Permission to reproduce was granted by Kristin Corrado in 2022.

This layered quality of sharing and re-sharing incorporates the dead body into our own bodies, always navigated via the hand, or the "digitalis," so that spectral listening is listening to the person that has passed away as much as it is listening to our future dead selves. Because, as Ballif articulates we are the living dead. Such an incorporation—I mean this word literally as something is brought into our bodies, our corpses—also diffuses *kairos*. In the video montage, Ashley's living kairotic moment from when she originally posted the photos haunts the new kairotic moment of the memorial. As mourners—as listeners—we are asked to become ghosts ourselves and, at the very least, peek into that kairos of the past. Additionally, we invite the kairotic context of decomposition into the present kairos by tagging the dead in our Instagram posts. Additionally, these multiple kairoses diffuse across platforms and beyond the memorial group, always bleeding out as memorial is posted to individual accounts and memory.

Digital environments illuminate the spectral we listen to and the spectral that listens to us. Writing is always both memorializing and mourning. With every post, every word, every touch, our compositions reveal as much about our deaths as they do our lives. If we attune our ears to listen to the ghosts, the dead can touch us, move us. To return to Galen's quote that I opened with, adding emphasis: "Even *now*, thanks to writings set down by the hand it is yet possible for you to hold *converse* with Plato, Aristotle, and the other Ancients." Even now. *Present* tense. *Even now*, we can still be touched by, and be moved by, the dead.

Works Cited

Ballif, Michelle. "Regarding the Dead." *Philosophy and Rhetoric*, vol. 47, no. 4, 2014, pp. 455–71.

Davis, Diane, and Michelle Ballif. "Guest Editors' Introduction: Pushing the Limits of the Anthropos." Philosophy and Rhetoric, vol. 47, no. 4, 2014, pp. 346–53.

Galen. *On the Usefulness of the Parts of the Body*. Translated by Margaret Tallmadge May, Cornell UP, 1968.

Gross, Daniel M. *Being-Moved: Rhetoric as the Art of Listening*. U of California P, 2020.

Lindhé, Cecilia. "A Virtual Sense Is Born in the Fingertips: Towards a Digital Ekphrasis." *Digital Humanities Quarterly*, vol. 7, no. 1, 2013.

Yancey, Kathleen Blake. "Tombstones, QR Codes, and the Circulation of Past Present Texts." *Circulation, Writing, and Rhetoric*, edited by Laurie E. Gries and Collin Gifford Brooke, Utah State UP, 2018, pp. 61–82.

18 Festschrift in Honor of RSA Founder Janice Lauer Rice—What Janice Lauer Rice Taught Us about Rhetoric (and Life): A Tribute

Richard Leo Enos, Janet M. Atwill, Jennifer L. Bay, Thomas J. Rickert, David Blakesley, and Richard E. Young

Janice Lauer Rice and Richard Leo Enos at the 2005 RSA Conference. Used with permission by Edward Schiappa. Photo credit to Lauren Murray.

Introduction

Richard Leo Enos

Our dearly departed colleague, Janice Lauer Rice, was a founder of The Rhetoric Society of America. The beginning of RSA came at a time when many educators in America had no real knowledge of Rhetoric as a discipline, its long and distinguished history, and the impact that Rhetoric made to education. As a founder of RSA and career-long contributor to our discipline, Janice helped to re-educate America on the value of Rhetoric. Those who think that RSA started as a "Good Old Boys Club" do not know our history and they minimize not only Janice's contributions but all the other women who shaped our discipline. Janice was a pioneer in the study of heuristics in Rhetoric and a strong proponent of multi-modality research procedures.

Janice created the Summer Research Institute in Rhetoric, which lasted for several years, and educated teachers when there were few doctoral programs in Rhetoric and Composition. Janice helped to establish at Purdue one of the strongest doctoral programs in Rhetoric and Composition in America. Janice was universally respected by colleagues throughout the discipline as a paradigm for the teacher-scholar model. In fact, so powerful was her impact that Janice has a book series named after her with Parlor Press: The Lauer Series in Rhetoric and Composition.

Janice was a "graceful" colleague. By that I mean she was full of grace. Perhaps this was because the grounding of her deep faith complemented her civility and humility. Some may not know that Janice was once a member of the Sisters of the Immaculate Heart of Mary (IHM), a Roman Catholic religious teaching order for women. Janice's many qualities were recognized and appreciated. In fact, there is hardly an award that Janice did not win in our field but she won the greatest of all awards . . . she won our hearts. There were about twenty-thirty rhetoricians in the generation that preceded my own who changed higher education in America. We may quibble over who ought to be on that august list but we would all agree that one person who is on that list is Janice Lauer Rice.

Honoring Janice Lauer Rice

Janet M. Atwill

I met Janice in the mid-1980s when she came to a community college where I was teaching to deliver a lecture and workshop on her first textbook. We talked about the textbook and the PhD program at Purdue. Then I asked her for advice on a state-based National Endowment for the Humanities

(NEH) grant I was writing at the time. The theme was women artists in the Midwest, and I needed suggestions for conference speakers. She recommended the playwright Megan Terry, celebrated for her iconoclastic, activist work in theater that included the first rock musical, *Viet Rock*, which confronted attitudes on the Vietnam War.

In her essay and 2014 interview in *Rhetoric Review*, Janice described rhetoric and composition's propensity to challenge boundaries, in this context the boundaries between disciplines. Janice challenged boundaries in her life and encouraged her students to do the same. Boundary-crossing was implicit in her theory of invention and her own pedagogy. I will always remember a comment she made on one of my papers in grad school: "Don't tell me something I already know. Show me something I don't." I think she was the most true intellectual I've ever known. We are indebted to her for helping to invent the discipline that created a space for our diverse paths of inquiry. Many of her friends and students are indebted to her for being a part of inventing our lives.

Jennifer L. Bay and Thomas J. Rickert

Dr. Janice Lauer (1932–2021), Reece McGee Distinguished Professor Emerita of Rhetoric and Composition, Purdue University. Photograph by the authors.

It is our honor to provide a memorial resolution for Janice Marie Lauer, Reece McGee Distinguished Professor Emerita at Purdue University, who died on April 7, 2021.

This is one of our favorite photos of Janice Lauer. Seated at a wedding, she is obviously captivated by the off-camera speaker. Janice had a way of sitting in rapt attention to a speaker, carefully listening and taking in all that was being said. She delighted in rhetoric in every way, as we see here, and as many of us got to know firsthand.

In 1980, Professor Lauer founded Purdue's internationally respected graduate program in Rhetoric and Composition, one of the first in the United States. She built and directed that program for twenty-three years. Her influence across the field is unmatched. Her scholarly work on invention and heuristics, on disciplinarity, and on empirical research methods in composition are widely known. Her institutional work with the Consortium of Doctoral Programs was lesser known but also of importance. Janice was strong in her commitment to service. She mentored students and colleagues with rigor, respect, and love. It would be an understatement to say that many of us would not be here without her work and vision. Perhaps we take Rhetoric and Composition graduate programs for granted now, but they were less assured in 1980. Janice envisioned that we could have seminars and courses on rhetoric, first through her work via the NEH, and then through becoming established in an English department. She envisioned that we could have dissertations that focused on rhetoric—not literature or linguistics—as a basic framework for studying language and life. We all recognize her scholarly work on rhetorical invention, but what is clear is that her work on it ran deep—she lived invention.

When she retired in 2003, Purdue's Rhetoric and Composition program had over two hundred doctoral graduates, over a quarter of whose dissertations she had directed. Even after she retired, she stayed active in the field for a long time. As recently as two years ago, she approved a request to have her book on invention translated into Russian.

During her career, she received numerous awards and recognitions, including the Conference on College Composition and Communication's Exemplar Award, which is the highest award in our field; the Rhetoric Society of America's Distinguished Service Award; Purdue's College of Liberal Arts' Excellence in Education Award; the Hopwood Award from The University of Michigan; and an honorary doctorate from St. Edward's University in Austin, Texas.

Janice was deeply supportive of our coming to Purdue in 2001. She had already initiated her retirement, but she stayed in continual contact with us. She would regularly invite us to dinner at her house, where we would visit and discuss the graduate program, our dappled discipline, and issues of the day. Afterwards, we would settle down for a discussion of rhetorical theory over a nice bottle of Pinot Noir.

After retirement, Jenny saw her regularly for daily mass at St. Thomas Aquinas Catholic Church. Her work in the church was a continuation of her love of rhetoric and service. Or perhaps this was just a re-beginning. She reinvigorated the Aquinas Educational Foundation at St. Tom's, finding fresh ways to combine her rhetorical knowledge and spiritual commitment, and helping to bring in esteemed Catholic intellectuals who spoke to the Church's rich spiritual and rhetorical traditions.

We'd like to close with Thomas's first real encounter with Janice. It was during his on-campus interview at Purdue, way back in 2001:

> I was a typical academic newbie, on fire with ideas and not much else. Janice of course had seen it all before. We had an hour to ourselves on the first day of the visit, and we got along immediately, talking about our mentors—she knew my mentor, Victor Vitanza, very well—and many other things. She never once mentioned the job. I was far from being assured of being hired, but she treated me like a colleague-to-be anyway. The next day, I was scheduled to give a teaching demonstration. I was tasked with running a TA's peer critique day. Janice and the search committee observed from the back of the room as I in my suit went from desk to desk trying to help students with papers I had never seen before. The students were great, but Janice, it became clear, was not happy with this use of my time. Upon wrapping up the demonstration, as we were exiting, Janice mumbled to me in sympathy, "Well, that wasn't very rhetorical." Janice never missed a beat!

She will be deeply missed by all, but her impact on Purdue, the field of Rhetoric and Composition, and the larger community will continue to be felt for decades to come.

JANICE LAUER'S RHETORICAL LEGACIES

David Blakesley

Janice Lauer's legacy lives for all of us who study and teach rhetoric and composition. The quality, integrity, and scope of her scholarly work speaks for itself. All those fortunate enough to have been her student or colleague feel her influence and inspiration. Her legacy endures in other ways that run deep, like an underground river or a heartbeat.

Here's one of those ways. In 1997 and just a few years after the sudden death of her friend and colleague James Berlin, Janice guided his last book, *Rhetorics, Poetics, and Cultures: Refiguring College English Studies,* to publication with the National Council of Teachers of English (NCTE). The following year, *Rhetorics, Poetics, and Cultures* won the Conference on College Composition and Communication (CCCC) Outstanding Book Award. Despite its success, NCTE let it go out of print in 2002, which, as you can imagine, disappointed Janice tremendously, as well as many others in the field who recognized its importance.

I was Janice's fairly new colleague at Purdue and had only a few months earlier founded Parlor Press. Janice spied an opportunity. She asked me about the possibility of republishing *Rhetorics, Poetics, and Cultures*. We wrote NCTE to ask if they would give us permission to bring the book back. We received a resounding "no" and that was the end of it. Janice was especially frustrated, mostly because it felt like an insult to her friend. We commiserated but moved on.

However, Janice was persistent, as we all know. Her persistence rubbed off. It was by then February, 2003, just a month before the CCCC meeting in New York City and Janice's retirement party. Sandra Berlin, Jim's widow, lived around the corner from me in West Lafayette, Indiana, so I hatched a plan to surprise Janice. I asked Sandy to ask NCTE to return the copyright to her. They complied. Sandy and I negotiated a new contract. Over the next couple of weeks, I scanned the original book, did the layout, created a new index, and secured the rights to include tribute essays about Jim published in *JAC: A Journal of Composition Theory*. We had a few copies of the book printed in time for the retirement party. Janice didn't know any of this, of course. Pat Sullivan and Catherine Hobbs agreed to be the editors of a new Lauer Series in Rhetoric and Composition.

At the retirement party, when it was my turn to say a few words, I made the announcement that Parlor Press was launching a new book series in Janice's honor, the Lauer Series. That brought a big smile and hugs all around. Just before the moment faded, I said, "But hold on a minute! We have another announcement. Here's the first book in the series!" I showed her the shiny new edition of *Rhetorics, Poetics, and Cultures*. Janice was always known for being unflappable but this one got her.

Rhetorics, Poetics, and Cultures has gone on to sell about 2,000 more copies. The Lauer Series is now in its twentieth year, with more than thirty titles. Janice's legacy beats on every time the current editors, Jennifer Bay and Thomas Rickert, and I discuss a new submission. It had better give rhetoric its due; that's for sure.

Richard E. Young

I suppose I knew Janice as well as any of us did. I first met her in 1965 at the CCCC. Pete Becker and I were waiting in a restaurant for a table when two nuns offered us theirs, one of whom was Janice, who said 'I bet you birds are glad to see us." We were, though we had never seen them before. Subsequently, I served on her doctoral committee at The University of Michigan when the New Rhetoric was just getting under way; traveled abroad with her; hiked together in the Southwest; lectured in her summer conferences at Detroit and Purdue; and encouraged her when she was pondering a move to Purdue, a move that has had a large effect on the discipline. Anyway, I knew her well. Each of us has known people who made our lives better, richer—Janice was one of those people for me. It is gratifying that her achievements will be remembered even by those who never knew her.

ACKNOWLEDGMENTS

We wish to thank all those who participated on the panel, all who attended in person as well as through mediated communication, the many RSA program officials who supported this panel honoring Janice, and David Beard and Elizabethada Wright who edited the 2022 RSA Conference Proceedings and who encouraged us to submit our panel proceedings for this volume.

Contributors

Janet M. Atwill is a Professor of English at the University of Tennessee (Knoxville). She earned her PhD at Purdue University. She co-edited *Perspectives on Rhetorical Invention* with Janice Lauer Rice and remained a life-long colleague.

Maha Baddar is a lecturer at Pima Community College. Her research interests include the medieval Arabic Translation Movement and the Arabic commentary tradition on Aristotle's *Rhetoric*. She has written about theories of medieval Arabic rhetoric by al-Kindi, al-Farabi, and Ibn Sina. She has also published on the Medieval Arabic Translation Movement and topics related to slavery during the Middle Ages in the Islamic world.

Jennifer L. Bay was fortunate to be a friend and colleague of Janice Lauer at Purdue University, visiting and sharing holy communion with her until her passing. She is a Professor of English at Purdue University.

David Blakesley was a friend and colleague of Janice Lauer's at Purdue. He's currently the Campbell Chair in Technical Communication at Clemson University and the publisher behind Parlor Press.

Daniel A. Cryer is Associate Professor of English at Johnson County Community College in Overland Park, Kansas. His work focuses on the intersection of materiality and rhetoric and has appeared in *Rhetoric Society Quarterly, Rhetorica, English Studies*, and *the New Mexico Historical Review*.

Richard Leo Enos is an Emeritus Piper Professor for the State of Texas and the Quondam Holder of the Lillian Radford Chair of Rhetoric and Composition at Texas Christian University. He is a Past President of the Rhetoric Society of America. He has co-authored research with Janice Lauer Rice and was a life-long colleague.

keondra bills freemyn is an archivist and memory worker focused on Black cultural production and social movements. She is founder of the independent digital humanities and archival discovery initiative, Black Women Writers Project, and is the inaugural coordinator of the grassroots archival consortium Project STAND at the University of Maryland. keondra is a Society of American Archivists Digital Archives Specialist and holds a Graduate Certificate in Museum Studies from Harvard University. She is an alumna of Fordham University (BS), Columbia University (MPA), and University of Maryland (MLIS).

Wallace S. Golding (he/him/his) is a doctoral candidate in the Department of Communication at the University of Illinois Urbana-Champaign. His research investigates the rhetorical history of Black reparations debates and civil rights activism in the United States.

Aaron Hess is an Associate Professor of Rhetoric and Communication at Arizona State University, Fulbright Scholar in Norway, and member of the International Network for the study of Credibility, Ethos, and Trust (INCET). His work features the use of participatory methods in rhetoric, and examines the role of digital technology on public discourse.

Heidi E. Hamilton is a professor in and chair of the Communication and Theatre department at Emporia State University. Her work is primarily in foreign policy rhetoric, social movement persuasion, and political argumentation, including those issues involving gender.

Mohammed Sakip Iddrisu is a multiple award-winning PhD candidate in the Writing, Rhetorics, and Literacies program at Arizona State University. In his research, he employs transnational rhetorical and decolonial theories to explore rhetorics and literate social practices of resistance, healing, and belonging among minoritized Indigenous, racial, and linguistic populations. To do these, he uses a combination of methods such as qualitative interviews, on-the-ground participant observations, and public discourses across digital spaces to collect and produce data for analysis. His research has been published in *Teaching/Writing: The Journal of Writing Teacher Education*, *Community Literacy Journal* and *Reflections*. He has presented at conferences including the Rhetoric Society of America conference, Conference on College Composition and Communication, and the Conference on Community Writing.

Kathryn Lambrecht is an Assistant Professor of Technical Communication at Arizona State University. Her research draws on risk communication, the rhetoric of science, corpus analysis, and data visualization to strengthen communication between experts and public audiences.

Amy J. Lueck is Associate Professor of Rhetoric and Composition at Santa Clara University, where her research and teaching focus on histories of rhetorical instruction and practice, women's rhetorics, feminist historiography, and public memory. She is the author of *A Shared History: Writing in the High School, College, and University, 1856–1886* (SIU Press 2020). Her recent research builds on this work by attending to the conceptual boundaries and metaphors shaping history and remembrance at various sites, from universities and the tribal homelands on which they are built to historic attractions like the Winchester Mystery House.

Jason Michálek is a PhD candidate at Indiana University. His research interests have been historically broad with a BA in English language & literature and linguistics from Grand Valley State University, and an MA in American Studies from The George Washington University. His dissertation project takes up a local controversy concerning transient residents without residence as a foundation for troubling rhetorics of belonging and alienation.

Abandoning his career as a professor, **Keith D. Miller** levitated to become an independent scholar. His publications include *Voice of Deliverance: The Language of Martin Luther King, Jr., and Its Sources*; *Martin Luther King's Biblical Epic: His Great, Final Speech*; and an essay on Malcolm X that appeared in *College Composition and Communication*. He assisted Rene Billups Baker in writing her memoir, *My Life with Charles Billups and Martin Luther King: Trauma and the Civil Rights Movement*. Recently interviewed on KPFK, Los Angeles, and on Roland Martin Unfiltered, he has almost finished writing a book about Malcolm X. His website is drkeithdmiller.com.

Thomas J. Rickert is Professor of English at Purdue University, where he directs the graduate program in Rhetoric and Composition, a program founded by Janice Lauer in the 1980s. His research interests include the prehistory and histories and theories of rhetoric, critical theory, composition, and cultural studies. Janice helped hire Thomas as an Assistant Professor at Purdue in 2001.

Patricia Roberts-Miller, Professor Emeritus, Department of Rhetoric and Writing, University of Texas at Austin, former Director of the University Writing Center, is a scholar of train wrecks in public deliberation, the author of various books including *Rhetoric and Demagoguery* (SIUP 2019), *Speaking of Race* (The Experiment 2021), and *Fanatical Schemes* (U of Alabama 2009). Her current project is tentatively called *Deliberating War*, and concerns the vexed relationship of deliberation, persuasion, and war.

Leah Senatro is a PhD Candidate in the English Department at the University of California, Irvine where she is also completing an emphasis in the Medical Humanities. She is currently serving as the Campus Writing and Communication Fellow at UCI.

Andrew Lee Sigerson is a professor of English at Universidad Austral de Chile–Valdivia, where he teaches composition, translation, and literature courses, among others. He is also a PhD candidate at Old Dominion University, focusing his research on how today's EFL students in developing nations such as Chile acquire and begin to compose in English in both formal and informal educational environments and the interplay between these spheres in their development as multilingual writers.

Ryan Skinnell is an Associate Professor of Rhetoric and Writing in the Department of English at San José State University. He is the author, editor, or co-editor of six books, and has published more than one hundred essays, articles, and reviews in academic and popular press outlets related to rhetoric, politics, and higher education. He is also a founding member of The Write to Vote Project, a 2020–2021 Op-Ed Project Public Voices Fellow, and a Faculty Expert in Political Speech, Politics, and Rhetoric at San José State University. He is currently writing a book about Adolf Hitler's rhetoric.

Jeffrey St. Onge is an Associate Professor of Communication and Media Studies at Ohio Northern University. His research focuses on rhetoric and media, with a particular interest in how rhetorical criticism can be used to shape political culture toward more productive ends. His work has appeared in *Rhetoric and Public Affairs*, *Rhetoric Society Quarterly*, and *Rhetoric Review*, among other venues. This essay appeared at the 2022 Rhetoric Society of America conference with the title "Up-tempo Discourse: A Case for Better Conceptualizing Speed in Rhetoric and Public Culture."

M. Elizabeth Weiser is an Arts & Sciences Distinguished Professor in the Department of English at The Ohio State University. A two-term member of the executive board of the Kenneth Burke Society, Weiser is now the only American on the executive board of the International Committee for Museology (ICOFOM), the world's largest network of museum studies scholars, and is the managing editor of the *ICOFOM Study Series*.

Richard E. Young is an Emeritus Professor of Rhetoric, former Head of the Department of English at Carnegie Mellow University, and a founding member of the Rhetoric Society of America. His research emphasis is rhetorical invention. While at The University of Michigan, he served on Janice Lauer's dissertation committee. He was a life-long friend.

Index

9/11, xi, 50, 122

Abrams, Stacy, 54
activism, 26, 28, 29
ad bellum purificandum, 54, 56
Adotey, Edem, 18, 23
Africa, 14, 44, 54, 83, 113
Alcatraz, 4, 11
al-Farabi, 155, 165
al-Ghazali, 166
al-Shifa', 155–157, 159, 166
Alim, H. Samy, 15, 23
Amin, Forough, 110, 117
American Weekly, 6–7, 12
Anderson, Benedict, 92, 97
anti-Blackness, 35
Anzaldúa, Gloria, 92, 94, 97
Aquinas Educational Foundation, 179
Aquinas, Thomas, 166, 179
Arabic language, 156
Arabic rhetorical tradition, 157, 166
Arbery, Ahmaud, 28
arbitrary nature of signs, 150
archival profession, 26
archival research, 41, 46
archivists, 26, 28
Aristotle, 79, 149, 155, 159, 161, 165, 168–169, 174; *Organon*, 155; *Poetics*, 154–155
armed citizenship, 98–99, 103, 106
assassination, xiii, 44, 45
Atwill, Janet M., xv, 175–176
Austin, Lloyd, 106, 111, 113–114, 117, 178

authorship, 40, 41, 46, 138
Autobiography of Malcolm X, The, xiii, 40–42, 44–47

Baddar, Maha, xv, 154, 157–166
Baker-Bell, April, 14–15, 23
Balko, Radley, 100, 106
Ballif, Michelle, 169, 171–174
Bay, Jennifer L., xv, 6, 9, 106, 175, 177, 180
Beard, David, x, 181
Becker, Pete, 181
belonging, 17–18, 20, 63, 93, 96
Bergland, Renee, 9, 11
Berlin, James, 51, 130, 148–150, 152, 179–180; *Rhetorics, Poetics, and Cultures*, 179–180
Berry, Dorothy, 27, 29
Berthoff, Ann, xiv, xv, 142–147, 149–152; *The Making of Meaning*, 152
Bible, The, 101, 102
Biden administration, 109–113, 116
Biden, Joseph R., xiv, 75, 77, 108–118, 120, 126–127, 129
Birch, John, 120
BitChute, 76–77
Black Lives Matter, xii, 126
Black students, 13–15
Black women, 27, 28
Black Women Writers Project (BWWP), xiii, 25–28, 183
Blackness, 15, 32, 33, 38
Blakesley, David, x, xv, 175, 179
Blinken, Antony, 111, 113–117

Bloomington Homeless Coalition (BHC), 93–96
bodies, 4, 69, 94, 169–171, 173
Bollinger, Ty and Charlene, 75
border crossing, 94
borders, 29, 96, 113–114
British colonialism, 14, 19
Bruyneel, Kevin, 5, 11
Bunch III, Lonnie, 50
Burke, Kenneth, 48, 54, 56, 119
Bush, George and Laura, 120

Canon of Medicine (Ibn Sina), 155
capitalism, 3, 8, 67
care ethics, 99, 102
care work, 98–99, 101
Center for Countering Digital Hate (CCDH), 72, 79
Centers for Disease Control and Prevention (CDC), 61–65, 69–72, 76
Central America, 113
change, ix–x, xii, xiii–xv, 17, 26, 49, 50, 81, 88, 99, 108–111, 113–117, 123, 142, 146, 149, 152
character, 71, 73, 78, 99, 146, 148, 151
Charland, Maurice, 55–56
Chicago, 38, 63, 65, 67, 70
Child, Lydia Maria, 38, 46, 47
China, People's Republic of, 14
Christensen, Loren W.: *On Combat*, 100–101, 103, 105, 106
Christianity, 36, 124
Christians, 102, 120–121, 125, 128–129, 137, 153, 166
Christmas, xiv, 119–121, 124, 125, 129, 131
chronotopes, 55
citizenship, 14, 18–20, 23, 82
civic culture, 8
civil rights, xii, 45, 127
civil rights movement, xii
Civil War, 48, 51–53, 56, 57
climate change, 110–111, 113

climate crisis, xiv, 108, 110, 112, 118
Cold War, xii, 128–129
Collins, Randall, 41, 47, 100, 105–106
colonial logic, xiii, 13–15, 21
colonial logics of domination, 13–14
colonialism, xii, xv, 5, 8–10, 16, 21, 49
coloniality, xiii, 5–6, 10–11, 19, 21
community, xiv, 16, 22, 26–29, 50–51, 62, 66–70, 73, 91–97, 110, 121, 139, 167–170, 172, 176, 179
comparative rhetoric, 155, 166
Conference on College Composition and Communication (CCCC), 178, 180–181
conocimiento, 92, 94–96
Consortium of Doctoral Programs, 178
conspiracy theories, xi, 87, 138–139
constellations, 26, 27
Constitutional rights, xi
constitutive rhetoric, 48, 55
conventional wisdom, 81, 84, 86–88
Corrado, Ashley, 170–173
Coulter, Ann, 120, 126, 128
COVID-19, xi–xiii, xv, 25, 27, 29, 61–64, 66–75, 77–81, 84, 89
credibility, 73, 76–78, 99, 128
The Crisis, 30, 32, 36–38
critical description, xiii, 30, 32–34, 36, 37
critical race theory, xiii, 56
Crummel, Alexander, 52

Dake, Mawuli, 17–18, 20, 22–23
Davis, D. Diane, 169
deception, 71, 160–162
decolonization, 17, 20–21, 23, 94
deliberation, 84, 88, 93, 121–124
demagoguery, 104, 121, 126
Democrats, 120
Derrida, Jacques, 171
de-scripting, 30, 32–33
dialogue, xii, 16, 21–22, 145, 156

digital archives, 25
digital mourning, 167–168, 170–171
Dinauer, Leslie, ix
disciplinarity, 178
discourse, 154, 159, 161–164
disinformation, xiv, 71, 72, 74–79, 82, 84
Disinformation Dozen, 71–75, 77–79
domesticity, 3, 5–6, 10
Doxtader, Eric, 54–56

editing, xiii
ekphrasis, 30
emancipation, 53
empirical research methods, 178
empowerment, 72, 146
enargeia, 30, 139
Enos, Richard Leo, xv, 175–176
entangled remembrance, xii, 3. 5–6, 10–11
epistemic space, 14
epistemological decolonization, 14, 16–17, 21–23
epistemological value, 21
ethics, xiv, 99, 102, 106, 155
ethos, xiv, 19–20, 71–78, 98, 99, 102
Ewe (language), 14, 17–18, 20, 24
Exemplar Award (CCCC), 178
expertise, 71, 73, 75–76
extermination, 119, 121, 124, 126; political, 119, 124

Facebook, 9, 12, 16–20, 22–23, 76, 79, 83, 95, 128, 170–173
Fauci, Anthony, 72, 85
feminism, xiv, 5, 101, 108–112, 115, 118
Ferguson, Herman, 47
Finnegan, Cara, 31, 38
First Amendment, 124
Fisher, Murray, xiii, 42–44, 47, 51–52, 56
Fiske, A.T., 105, 106
flag, 48, 84–85, 87, 125
Floyd, George, xi, 28

Folbre, Nancy, 101, 106
Foucault, Michel, 65, 70, 87, 89
Fox News, 87, 117, 120, 127, 129–131
Freeman, Elizabeth, 35
freemyn, keondra bills, xiii, 25
Freire, Paulo, xiv, 142–152; *Pedagogy of the Oppressed*, 152
Front Line COVID-10 Critical Care Alliance (FLCCC), 74–75, 77–78
Fryer, Lucy, 34

Ga (people and language), 20
Gagaridis, Alessandro, 110, 117
Galbraith, John Kenneth, 86, 89
Galen, xv, 167–171, 173, 174
Garvey, Marcus, 45, 152
Gates, Bill, 76
gender, 3–6, 10, 27, 49, 62, 109, 118, 126, 159
Ghana, xiii, 13–14, 16, 18–20, 22, 23
Gibbs, Anna, 86, 89
Gibson, John, 120, 124–125, 128; *The War on Christmas*, xiv, 119, 124, 127–130
Gingrich, Newt, 126, 128
Global South, 116, 142, 145
Goebbels, Joseph, 138–140
Golding, Wallace, xiii, 30
Goliath, 102
graduate programs, 178
Grassley, Chuck, 120, 128
Great Britain, 123
Greene, Marjorie Taylor, 127
Greenwood Rising Center, 49–50, 56
Gross, Daniel M., 169, 172, 174
Grossman, Dave, 98–106; *On Combat*, 99–100, 106; *On Killing*, 99–100, 105–106; *On Spiritual Combat*, 102, 106
gun culture, 98–100, 106

Haines, Avril, 111, 113–114, 116–117
Haley, Alex, 40–45, 47
Hallenbeck, Sarah, 55–56
Hamer, Fannie Lou, 45

hashtags, 27
haunt, 73, 172; haunted house, 3, 5–6; haunting, 8, 10, 172
Hauser, Gerard, ix, 16, 24, 30, 38
health, 29, 61–75, 78, 83, 115, 126
hegemony, 18, 20, 22, 36, 53
Hess, Aaron, xiv, 71, 74, 77, 79
heuristics, 176, 178
Hippocrates, 168–169
historiography, 5
Hitler, Adolph, xiv, 54, 56, 123, 128, 135–140
Hobbs, Catherine, 180
homelessness, 91–93, 96
Hopi, 4
Houck, Davis, 31, 38
housing crisis, xiv
Hussein, Saddam, 122, 155

Ibn Rushd, 155, 165166
Ibn Sina, xv, 154–166
Ibn Sina (Avicenna), 155–156, 166
Iddrisu, Mohammed Sakip, xiii, 13
identity, xiv, 3, 6, 8–9, 32, 36, 40–41, 44, 46, 49, 56, 66, 98–99, 103–105, 123, 125, 139
ideology, 87
Ignoffo, Mary Jo, 8, 11
Incidents in the Life of a Slave Girl (Jacobs), 46–47
Indian, 6, 9. 11
injustice, 13–15, 17–23, 49, 51, 55z
Instagram, 27, 78, 170, 172–173
intercultural forums, 16
intercultural knowledge-building, 16
invention, 14, 82, 85, 139, 177, 178
Iraq, 122, 165
Islam, 44
Ivermectin, 75–77

JAC: A Journal of Composition Theory, 39, 180
Jack, Jordynn, 24, 31, 38, 122, 129
Jacobs, Harriet, 46–47
Jarvis, Malcolm, 41, 47

justice: linguistic, 13, 15, 16, 21, 23; social, 28

Kafui, 17
kairos, 167, 173
kairotic moment, xii, 168, 173
Kennedy Jr, Robert F., 72, 99
King Jr, Martin Luther, xii, 45–46, 185
Kyle, Chris, 99

Lambrecht, Kathryn, xiii, 61, 63, 70
land, 3, 5–6, 9–10, 20, 53, 102
language education, 151
Lauer Rice, Janice, x, xv, 175–180
Lauer Series in Rhetoric and Composition, 176, 180
Legacy Museum, 49, 55–57
Lindhe, Cecilia, 170
linguistic: hegemony, xiii, 13, 15, 20, 23; injustice, xiii, 13–14, 16–17, 19,–23; justice, 13, 15–16, 21, 23; minorities, 14, 16, 19–20, 23; pluralism, 18, 20
linguistic literacy, 15–16, 20, 142–147, 149, 151–152, 154, 161
linguistic minority, 14, 16, 19–20, 23
Little, Earl and Louise, 43
Los Angeles, 64, 66, 70
Lost Cause, 52–53
love, 26, 98, 100–102, 106, 178–179
Lueck, Amy, xii, 3
lynching, xiii, 30, 34–37, 49, 55

Maimonides, 166
Malcolm X, xiii, 40–47
Mamdani, Mahmoud, 14, 17, 21–22, 24
Marable , Manning, 41, 47
marginalized communities, 27, 49
Martin, Trayvon, 54
mass shootings, xi, 87
McClellan, Judge, 43
McCormick, Kenneth, 42, 45, 47
McGee, Michael, 55–56, 177

McKerrow, Raymie, 31, 38
Mecca, 41, 44, 46
medical professionals, 71
Mein Kampf (Hitler), 135–136, 138, 140
memorials, 170, 172
memory, 3, 5–6, 50, 52–53, 162–163, 168, 173
Mercola, Joseph, 72, 75–78
metaphor, 35, 102, 139, 156, 159–161
methodology, xiii, 32, 46
Michálek, Jason, xiv, 91
Milbourne, Chelsea, 55–56
Miller, Carolyn, 55
Miller, Keith, xiii, 41
minorities, 14, 19, 23
misinformation, xv, 26, 71, 76, 82–85, 87, 89–90
Monroe, Richard Irby, 34, 95
Mother Emanuel A.M.E. Church, 51, 56
mourners, 167, 170, 172–173
museums, xiii, 48–51, 53, 55, 56
Musk, Elon, 76

NAACP, 30, 34
Nation of Islam (NOI), 41, 42
national belonging, 13–15, 20, 22–23
National Council of Teachers of English (NCTE), 180
National Democratic Congress (NDC), 18
national guilt, 6, 8
National Museum of African History and Culture (NMAHC), 50, 53, 56
National Museum of American History (NMAH), 48–49, 57
National Rifle Association (NRA), 99
Native Americans, 9–10
Native ghosts, 8, 9
Native peoples, 8
Nazis, 42, 51, 126, 138–139
Nazism, 135, 137
negotiation, 121
neoliberalism, xiii, 61–62, 70

New Patriotic Party, (NPP), 17–18, 20
New Rhetoric, 38, 181
New York City, 4, 24, 28, 44, 47, 63, 65, 67–68, 70, 83, 87, 89, 118, 128–129, 131, 180
Newsmax, 126, 131

Obama, Barack, 15, 23, 110, 129
Odysee, 76–77
oral discourse, 162
O'Reilly, Bill, 120, 125, 130
Organon, 155

Pan-Africanism, 45
pandemic, ix, xi–xiv, 25–27, 29, 61–69, 71–73, 76, 78, 81–83, 85, 88
Parlor Press, x, 166, 176, 180
partisanship, 26
Payne, Les, 41
Payne, Tamara, 41, 47
Pearl Harbor, 122
pedagogy, 15, 31, 142–146, 149–152, 177; critical, 142–143, 146, 151–152
Peirce, C.S., 143, 146
persuasion, 92, 96, 147, 158, 160, 162
phantasia, 30
philosophy, 45, 142–150, 155, 166 medieval, 155
philosophy of language, 142–146, 150
Plato, xiv, 142, 147–150, 153, 155, 168, 174
Playboy, 41–42, 47
poetics, xv, 154–159, 161
poetry, 26, 147, 156–160, 164
Poland, 123, 125
polarization, 49, 86
Porphyry, 155, 164–165
poverty, 95, 113
preemptive aggression, 121–122
preventive war, 119, 122
Project STAND, 28–29
propaganda, 82, 85
protection, 70, 98, 101, 105, 109, 114–115

Protocols of the Elders of Zion, 137, 139–140
psychology, 98, 100, 155
public health communication, 64
public intellectuals, 17, 21
public memory, 3, 5, 11
public rhetorics, 16–17
Pulitzer Prize, 41
Purdue University, 176–181
purification of war, 54
Putin, Vladimir, 54

Quintilian, 148, 153, 168

race, xii, 4–6, 10, 40, 50, 55, 62, 123
racial: abstraction, xiii, 30, 32–34, 36–37
radicalization, 113
reading, xiv, 4, 27, 29, 52, 65–66, 74, 135–138, 140, 152, 156, 159, 162
reconciliation, 5, 48, 50–55
religion, 120, 124–125, 128, 130
remembrance, xiii, 3–6, 10, 11, 169
representation, 6, 9, 106, 150
Republican Party, 127, 130
revision, 159, 163
rhetoric, x,–xiv, 13, 18, 26, 30–31, 33, 44, 48, 51, 55, 81–82, 86, 94, 108–109, 111,–113, 115–116, 119, 121, 123, 126–127, 138, 146–150, 154,–160, 162, 163, 165–169, 171–172, 177–180
Rhetoric Society of America (RSA), ix–x, xii, 32, 50, 57, 175–176, 178, 181
Rhetorica (Ibn Sina), 89, 155, 166
rhetorical criticism, 30–31, 37, 73; invention, 86, 178; situation, xii, 71, 121, 159–160, 163, 171; theory, xv, 155, 159, 166, 178
Rice, Jenny, 139–140
Rickert, Thomas J., xv, 175, 177, 180
Roberts-Miller, Patricia, xiv, 104, 107, 119, 122, 126, 130
Roof, Dylann, 51

Roots (Haley), xv, 42, 47, 128, 131, 142
Ryback, Timothy, 136, 140

San Fransico Chronicle, 3, 11–12, 130
San Jose, xii, 4–5, 8–9, 12, 186
Saussure, Ferdinand de, 150
Schomberg Center for Research in Black Culture, 28, 42–44, 46–47
Second Amendment, xi
self-defense, 99, 104, 121–124
semiotics, 143, 144, 146, 150
Senatro, Leah, xv, 167
sensus communis, 86
Sharpe, Christina, 32, 38, 140
sheepdog ethos, 98–99, 101–102, 104–105
Sigerson, Andrew L., xiv, 142
Sisters of the Immaculate Heart of Mary, 176
Skinnell, Ryan, xiv, 119, 135, 137, 141
slavery, 40, 43–44, 46, 52–53
Smitherman, Geneva, 15, 19, 23–24
Smithsonian Institution, 49–50, 57
social media, 14, 21–22, 27, 71–74, 76–78, 82–83, 85, 95, 170–171
social scripts, 30, 32–35, 37
social-epistemic rhetoric, 149
Socrates, 148, 152
spectral body, 169, 171; listening, 167–169, 173
spiritualism, 3, 5
St. Edward's University, 178
St. Onge, Jeffrey, xiv, 81
St. Thomas Aquinas Catholic Church, 179
Starbucks, 119–120, 127, 129–130
Stevenson, Bryan, 55, 57
stranger-relationality, 21, 23
Sturken, Marita, 10, 12
style, xv, 73, 154–159, 161, 163; theories of, 154, 156–159, 161–166
Substack, 76–77, 79
Sullivan, Pat, 180

Summer Research Institute in Rhetoric (Purdue), 176
systemic racism, 49

Tallahatchie River, 49
Tapper, Ben, 72
Taylor, Breonna, 28, 127
Tell, Dave, ix, 32, 38
Tenpenny, Sherri, 75
Terry, Megan, 177
The Crisis, 30, 32, 35–38
Tibetan minority languages, 14
Till, Emmett, 38, 49, 57
Togolese, 17–20
totalitarianism, 54
Tronto, Joan, 99, 101–105, 107
True, Jacqui, 89, 111–112, 117–118, 136
Trump, Donald, 54, 76, 84, 89, 110, 116–117, 119–120, 126, 128, 130
Twi (language), 14, 15, 18–20, 22
Twitter, 74, 76–77, 79, 83, 128

United Nations Security Council Resolutions (UNSCR), 109, 111, 118
University of Michigan, 178, 181
up-tempo discourse, 81–82, 88
Uvalde, Texas, 87, 90

Vietnam War, xii, 12, 177
violence, 3, 5, 8, 26, 30, 32–33, 35–36, 49, 87, 99–106, 111, 113, 118
Virilio, Paul, 84–86, 89
visual grammar, 31
Vitanza, Victor J., 179
von Clausewitz, Carl, 123, 128; *On War*, 128

Waco Horror, xiii, 32, 34–36, 38
war: preemptive, 121; preventive, 119, 122
war on Christians, xiii, 130
War on Christmas, 119, 121, 124–126
Warnick, Barbara, 73, 80; Rhetoric Online; Persuasion and Politics on the World Wide Web, 73, 80
Washington, Jesse, xiii, 30, 32, 34–38, 47, 48, 50, 52–53, 56–57, 106, 117–118, 124, 128–129
Weapons of Mass Destruction, 122
Weiser, M. Elizabeth, xiii, 48, 50, 57
White Mainstream English, 15
white privilege, 8
white supremacy, xiii, 15, 30, 32–36, 51
whiteness, 15, 32–34, 36–37, 42
Wilson, Kirt, ix, 74, 80
Winchester Mystery House, xii, 3, 5, 8–9, 12
Winchester, Sarah, xii, 3–12
Women, Peace, and Security (WPS), 108–109
World Health Organization (WHO), 22, 72, 76
Wright, Elizabethada A., x–xi, 181
writing instruction, 148–149, 151
writing studies, 13

Yancey, Kathleen Blake, 170, 172, 174
Yellin, Jean Fagan, 46–47
Young, Richard E., xii, xv, 73, 79, 140, 175, 181
Yousef, Odette, 87, 90
YouTube, 57, 76–77, 79, 83, 131

Zoom, xii, 77, 92–93

About the Editors

Elizabethada A. Wright is Professor of English at University of Minnesota Duluth, and teaches in the Department of English, Linguistics, and Writing Studies and is a member of the faculty at the University of Minnesota Twin Cities' Literacy and Rhetorical Studies Program. With Christina R. Pinkston, she co-edited *Catholic Women's Rhetoric: Ethos, the Patriarchy, and Feminist Resistance*, and she has published in *Rhetoric Society Quarterly*, *Rhetoric Review*, *College English Association Critic*, as well as in a number of other journals and books.

Photograph of Elizabethada Wright by Scott Segee. Used by permission.

David Beard teaches writing and rhetoric at the University of Minnesota Duluth, where he is a professor in the Department of English, Linguistics, and Writing Studies. He works eclectically in listening studies, in rhetorical studies, in popular culture studies, and in health humanities. He is a founding member of the Professional Wrestling Studies Association, where he has done some work on rhetoric, gender, and politics (with John Heppen, published in *Geographies of the 2020 US Presidential Election* and in *Political Landscapes of Donald Trump*). With Heather Graves, he co-edited *The Rhetoric of Oil* for Routledge; with Richard Enos, he co-edited *Advances in the History of Rhetoric: The First Six Years* for Parlor Press. He has twice served as vice president of the Canadian Society for the Study of Rhetoric and edited a special issue of *Rhetor*. With Steve Katz, Suzanne Black, and Julia Brown, he co-edits *Survive & Thrive: A Journal for Medical Humanities and Narrative as Medicine*. In 2016 he was recognized for service by the Rhetoric Society of America for the Blogora; he is happy to return to serving RSA as co-editor of this collection.

Photograph of David Beard by Russell Stewart. Used by permission.

www.ingramcontent.com/pod-product-compliance
Lightning Source LLC
Chambersburg PA
CBHW021857230426
43671CB00006B/420